IMAGES
of America

LINDSAY

On the Cover: This is one of the earliest photographs of the Lindsay Ripe Olive Company, believed to have been taken in 1919. Employees at the plant pose among boxes stamped with "Lindsay Olives—Lindsay Brands." A banner with the phrase "A Boost for Lindsay Olives" hangs above a doorway. (Courtesy of LMG.)

IMAGES
of America

LINDSAY

Sarah Troop

ARCADIA
PUBLISHING

ISBN 978-1-4671-1572-8

Published by Arcadia Publishing
Charleston, South Carolina

Printed in the United States of America

Library of Congress Control Number: 2015955955

For all general information, please contact Arcadia Publishing:
Telephone 843-853-2070
Fax 843-853-0044
E-mail sales@arcadiapublishing.com
For customer service and orders:
Toll-Free 1-888-313-2665

Visit us on the Internet at www.arcadiapublishing.com

For the people of Lindsay—past, present, and future

Contents

Acknowledgments

First and foremost, thank you to the individuals who guided, advised, inspired, supported, and contributed hours of work to this project: Pam Kimball, Gary Meling, Stephanie Lenihan, and Jann McGuire. This book could not exist without all of you, and it is as much a result of your work as it is my own. In addition, I want to extend my heartfelt thanks to members of the Lindsay Cultural Arts Council. It has been such a joy and a privilege working for you and helping to preserve Lindsay's history. I am forever grateful for the opportunity.

Much gratitude goes to those who contributed family photographs and history to this volume, including Donna Coday (DC), Bill Clark (BC), George Hostetter (GH), Peter Neely (PN), Sandy Woodward, Ida Fitton (IF), Lindsay's Sacred Heart Roman Catholic Church (LSHRCC), Pam Kimball (PK), and Stephanie Lenihan, as well as Janice Bedwell Moore (JBM), who week after week brought more and more of her incredible family archives, and Gary Meling (GM), whose personal collection fills many of the pages herein and who helped fill in many gaps in my research. Deep appreciation goes to photographer DeLea Davis for her beautiful work. Most of the other photographs in this book are from the collection of the Lindsay Museum and Gallery (LMG) and that of the Special Collections Research Center, California State University, Fresno (CSUF). Special appreciation to the wonderful staff there, especially to Adam Wallace, library services specialist, and Tammy Lau, head of special collections, for their work and assistance.

I would be remiss if I did not recognize the historians whose work dedicated to the preservation of Lindsay's history has led the way: Kathleen Edwards Small, Annie R. Mitchell, Harold Schutt, Joe Doctor, and Ford Chatters.

Heartfelt gratitude to my wonderful editors at Arcadia, Ginny Rasmussen and Stacia Bannerman, for their talents, wisdom, and encouragement.

Special thanks to Bruno Huerta for his unyielding support, advice, and confidence, from help with research to dozens of hours spent in libraries, museums, and special collections, scanning a plethora of photographs. You are the best. Additional thanks to Lily Dale, who provided her own brand of "assistance."

On a personal note, I thank my grandmother Lillian Chavez, as well as Chase and Koren Stevens, who are the heart of everything I do.

INTRODUCTION

A distinctive foothill ridge gives way to the snowcapped Sierra Nevada east of Lindsay. The city itself is surrounded by fragrant citrus groves. To the west lies all the fertile San Joaquin Valley. It is an especially attractive location.

Few lived here before the 20th century. Native Americans had no permanent village, though rock paintings offer evidence of visits. Explorers and mountain men utilized the Indian trails favoring our higher and drier eastside route up the Valley, and later the Butterfield Stage Coach would stop at a local watering hole. The first permanent settlers in the Lindsay area ran cattle and dry farmed grain.

Early farmers and ranchers included the Berry Brothers. George Stockton Berry revolutionized wheat harvesting with his invention of the first self-propelled combine harvester in 1886. It was powered by steam from a straw-fired boiler. He later served in the state legislature.

Julius Orton is credited with planting the first orange trees in the District, in the 1880s. His land was adjacent to the earlier Keeley ranch, southwest of current Lindsay. Tree crops could do well but had to be irrigated with water diverted from elsewhere or hand pumped from wells. John Jolly Cairns invented a way to mechanically pump ground water for irrigating his crops in 1892, the first in the nation to do so. This made possible successful commercial agriculture and set the stage for the district's economic development. Mt. Whitney Power and Electric Company, a precursor to Southern California Edison, was established in Lindsay in 1899 to power Lindsay well pumps.

The Southern Pacific Railroad came in 1888 and brought a wealthy potential investor, Captain Arthur J. Hutchinson, of Bermuda, and his wife, Sadie Lindsay Patton Hutchinson (a relative of General Patton). They bought land and in conjunction with others organized the Lindsay Land Company, named after Sadie. As manager, Hutchinson laid out the townsite and marketed the area for citrus during California's "second gold rush," i.e. oranges. Sadie is said to have planted the first orange tree in Lindsay proper and recorded that "everything grew and flourished marvelously". Rail excursions brought prospective land buyers on a regular basis. Many acres of citrus and olives were planted. The community expanded steadily, with churches, schools, and businesses of every kind. Numerous clubs and fraternal organizations thrived.

The Lindsay Board of Trade, later Lindsay Chamber of Commerce, was organized in 1908. They led the incorporation effort. Dissent over boundaries and size of the town delayed action for two years, but on February 26, 1910, an election was held, and incorporation was approved. With a population of 1,500, the Town of Lindsay was officially recognized. Also that year, Lindsay High School had its first graduate: Ronald Shoemaker. The first yearbook, *The Comet*, was produced, named after that year's sensational Haley's Comet.

Lindsay soon became Central California's citrus center. In 1918, Lindsay gained notoriety for shipping more citrus than any other district in California. By the 1920s, many thousands of railcar loads of citrus were being shipped to market per year, handled by 16 large packinghouses. Responding to the annual threat of freeze damage, the use of wind machines for frost protection was pioneered in Lindsay and patented by the Towt family. Lindsay continues to be the center of the Central Valley orange belt today.

Olives rivaled oranges from early on as an important part of the Lindsay economy. Lindsay Ripe Olive Company formed in 1916 as a cooperative, with a small group of growers. Olive cultivation and processing grew from there. In 1961, acquisitions made the cooperative, now named Lindsay Olive Growers, the world's largest processor of ripe olives. The facility featured a gift shop and tours for visitors and local schoolchildren. The Lindsay label was known and respected worldwide. Many patents were given to the professional staff for innovative machinery and methods in olive processing.

The Great Depression of the 1930s brought challenges and changes. Local citizens came together to create economy opportunity by building a downtown hotel: the Mt. Whitney. It was the first and only "air-cooled" facility in the San Joaquin Valley at that time. The chamber organized the first Orange Blossom Festival in 1932, to raise spirits and promote the orange industry. This important event continues to be held every year during the month of April. Lindsay's iconic and beautiful city hall was built in 1936, funded in part by the Works Progress Administration, as was a similarly styled library. These three buildings are Lindsay landmarks today. Many Dust Bowl refugees migrated to Lindsay and found work in the fields, groves, and packinghouses.

Lindsay residents made big sacrifices during the World War II. One example was Edwin J. O'Hara, a merchant marine, who holds the distinction of being the only American to sink a German surface vessel during World War II, losing his life in the process. A significant Japanese population in Lindsay, including local businessmen and farmers, was relocated to concentration camps. Lindsay Japanese Americans, such as Hiyoshi Imoto, volunteered for combat out of the camps and served in the famous 442nd Regimental Combat Team or 522nd Field Artillery Battalion. Through the federal Bracero Program with Mexico, immigrant workers of Mexican heritage and their families began arriving in increasing numbers, filling vacancies in the agricultural workforce and contributing to the ever evolving culture of Lindsay.

The postwar decades (1950–1980s) were a time of economic stability and almost idyllic small-town charm. Activities of the vibrant, thriving community were captured in the local weekly paper since 1901, the *Lindsay Gazette*. Pomegranates joined citrus and olives as a major export in the 1960s. The development of the 32 lb. box by the Slayman Fruit Company led to their becoming the largest packer and shipper of pomegranates in the nation. In 1982, citizens of the community united to purchase and restore the old vaudeville theater for performances under the Lindsay Community Theater banner. The growing school district, with an increasing percentage of students speaking Spanish as their first language, was in the forefront of embracing bilingual education.

However, difficult times followed. A devastating freeze in the winter of 1990–1991 destroyed 90 percent of the citrus crop, put thousands out of work, and negatively impacted all businesses, closing many. General Cable, the only significant nonagricultural employer, closed. In 1992, the olive plant and the City of Lindsay lost a multimillion dollar lawsuit concerning brine pond leakage and contamination, and Lindsay Olive Growers closed. Reeling from such massive economic losses, the city held a mock funeral, burying a "casket of the past" in City Park filled with frozen oranges, cable wire, and olive cans. Having hit bottom, it was time to focus on creating a new future. That determined spirit was rewarded in 1995 when Lindsay was the only unanimous choice for the title of All-American City.

Inspired by a history of innovation and vision, Lindsay embarked on an ambitious effort to upgrade, expand, and reinvent its assets. Allowing the past to inform the future, a vision collated around creating public spaces with a health and wellness emphasis. This effort involved many community partnerships and effective grant writing. A mural program brought beauty and historical memory to a blighted downtown. The old train depot property was transformed into the Sweet Brier Plaza, which hosts a Friday Night Market, drawing thousands. An abandoned packinghouse became the McDermont Fieldhouse, a state-of-the-art 172,000-square-foot regional sports, recreation, and events center.

Additionally, when the Lindsay hospital closed in 2000, the city and hospital district partnered to create the Lindsay Wellness Center on site. The attached City Park was revamped to promote greater outdoor enjoyment and activity. Improvements downtown encouraged pedestrian traffic and business growth, and joint-use gymnasiums and sports fields were built in partnership with Lindsay Unified School District. Tulare County partnered to build a new downtown library. The Lindsay Cultural Arts Council opened the Lindsay Museum and Gallery in the historic library building just in time for the Centennial Year celebration in 2010.

Strained by rapid change and financially exhausting initiatives, the city of Lindsay is nonetheless poised for greater future growth, with new assets and improved opportunities, in this City of Innovation.

—Pam Kimball, Lindsay city councilwoman and third-generation Lindsay resident

One

The Pioneering Era

Pres. Ronald Reagan once said, "Lindsay has been blessed with pioneers of foresight and courage." President Reagan was accurate in his description of Lindsay's pioneers. They were adventurous, resourceful, hardworking, creative, and tenacious. Several notable persons passed through the area prior to its development, including explorer Jedediah Smith with a group of trappers that likely passed through Lindsay along what is now Highway 65. Not long after him came another explorer of note, John C. Freemont, guided by famed American frontiersman Kit Carson in 1844. This trail eventually became part of the Los Angeles–Stockton Road used by the Butterfield Overland Stage Route. Early settlers and wheat farmers like John Tuohy, the Berry brothers, John J. Cairns, Elias Jacob, and the Ortons gave way to the era of travel and the coming citrus boom. With the arrival of the Southern Pacific Railway came the Hutchinson family and the advent of Lindsay itself. These pioneers would experience a rapidly changing world full of life-altering innovations like trains, electricity, and automobiles. It was a time in history that was both exciting and difficult, but those who made Lindsay their new home rose up to meet the era with courage, hope, and ingenuity.

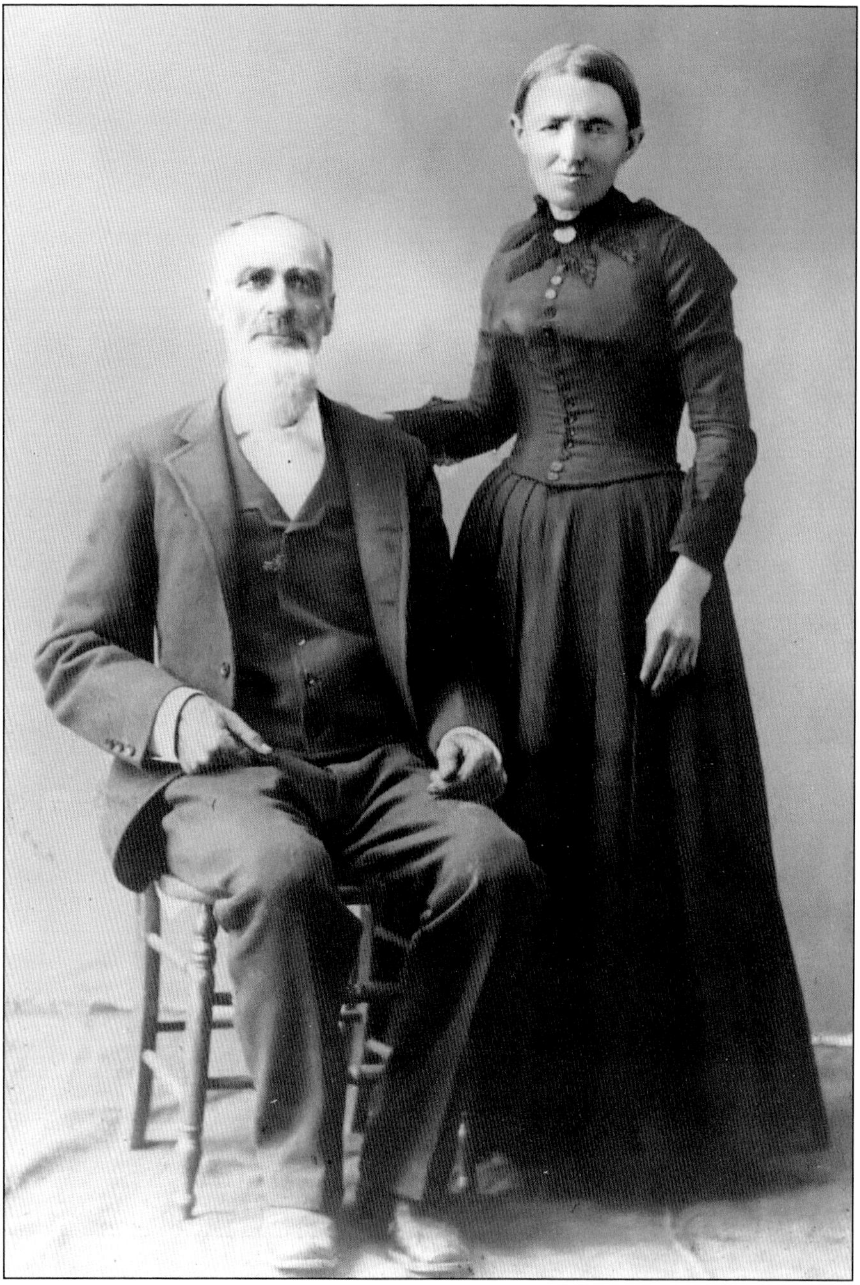

Julius Orton was a teamster in the US Army during the Mexican-American War. He then worked as a guard for pack trains on their way to the heart of California's Gold Rush—Hangtown, now known as Placerville. Alas, Orton struck no gold himself and moved on to the town of Soquel, where he was able to build up his own herd of cattle. In 1859, Julius and his wife, Lucretia, pictured here, and their two daughters began a 200-mile journey entirely on foot to drive their cattle south, finally settling near the Tule River at the most southwestern edge of what would become Lindsay. The family worked together to raise cattle and grow various crops. According to some accounts, Julius might have planted the first citrus trees in Lindsay; however, there are several others who also made this claim. (LMG.)

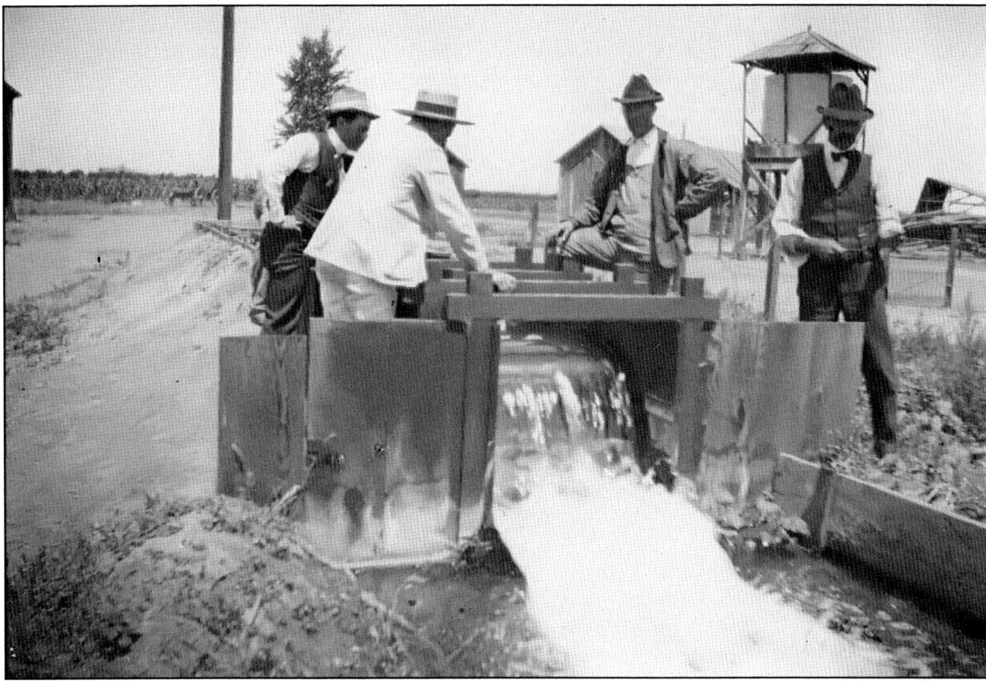

John Jolly Cairns arrived in Lindsay in the 1880s, and as one of the town's first pioneers, his contributions were not only numerous, but also significant. In a single year, he planted over 22,000 acres of wheat. Cairns became a pioneer of Lindsay's famed olive industry when he planted the first commercial olive trees, which are still standing and marked with a historical marker. At the end of the century, he would help revolutionize irrigation. (CSUF.)

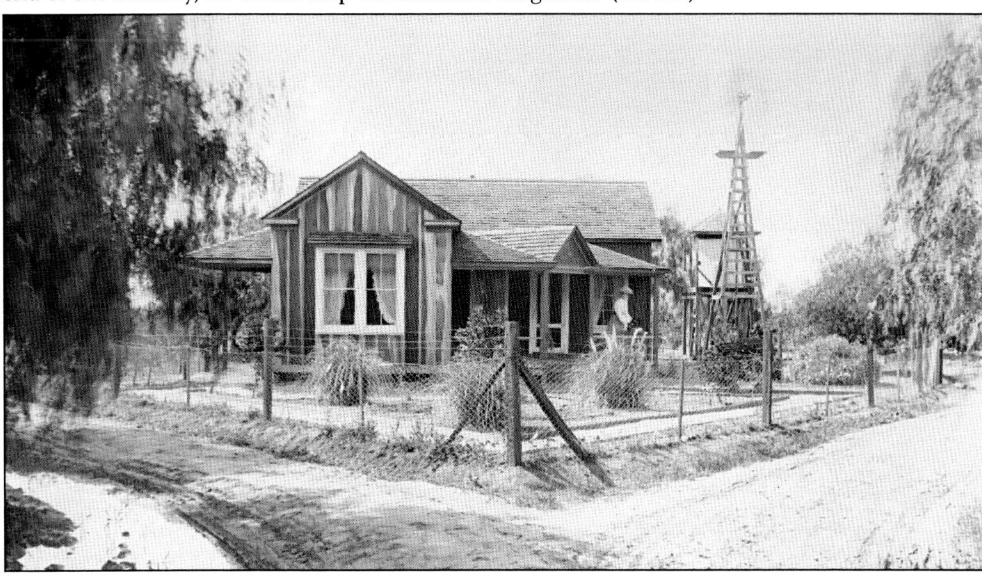

Here is a postcard view of Lindsay pioneer Basil Prior's property. Prior arrived in Lindsay in 1893 and became the superintendent of the Lindsay Water Development Company and, later, a city trustee. He purchased 20 acres and grew citrus and olives bordered by 67 palm trees, which he planted himself in 1894. Prior kept detailed journals for many years, recording everything from the weather to personal information to current events in Lindsay. (CSUF.)

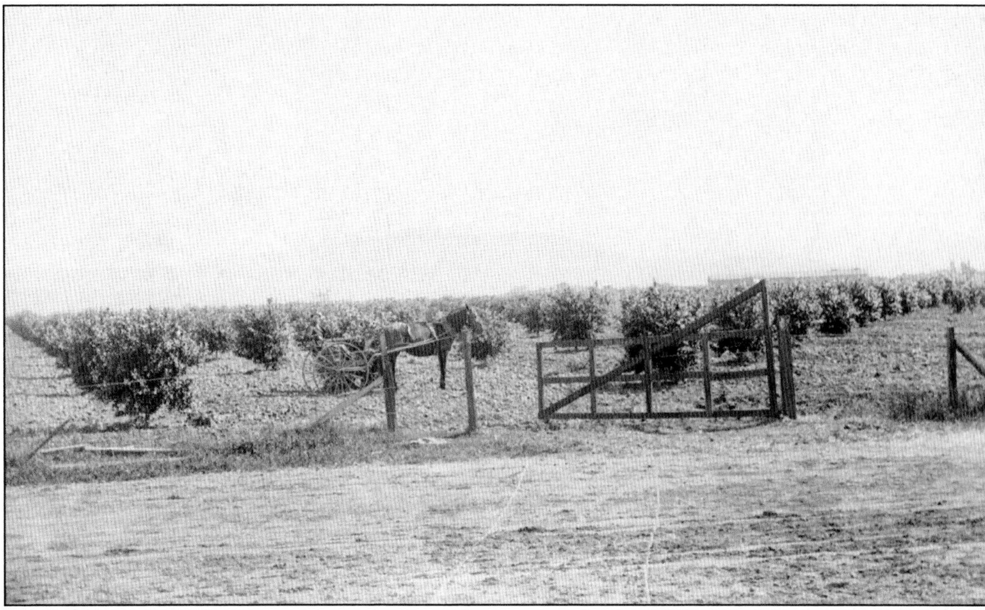

This image includes the following handwritten caption on the back: "Home of Basil and Dorthea Prior, 1896 on old Palmer Ranch. Since owned by Mrs. Cairns." Dorthea Prior arrived in Lindsay from England in November 1896. Basil Prior wrote about this photograph in his diary on April 20, 1896: "The photos that Porter took of the Palmer house arrived today. Paid him $1.00 for them." (CSUF.)

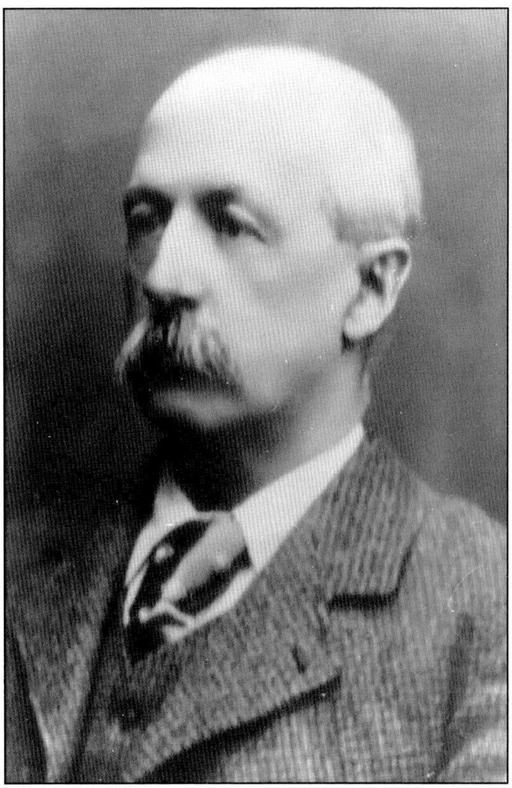

In 1888, Capt. Arthur J. Hutchinson headed a group of Los Angeles investors to form the Lindsay Land Company, named after his wife's family. Hutchinson's initial idea was to irrigate the land with water from the Kaweah River. However, once J.J. Cairns had demonstrated success with his well, Hutchinson adapted the method and sold "40 acres of land together with engine, pump and well for $4,000." (CSUF.)

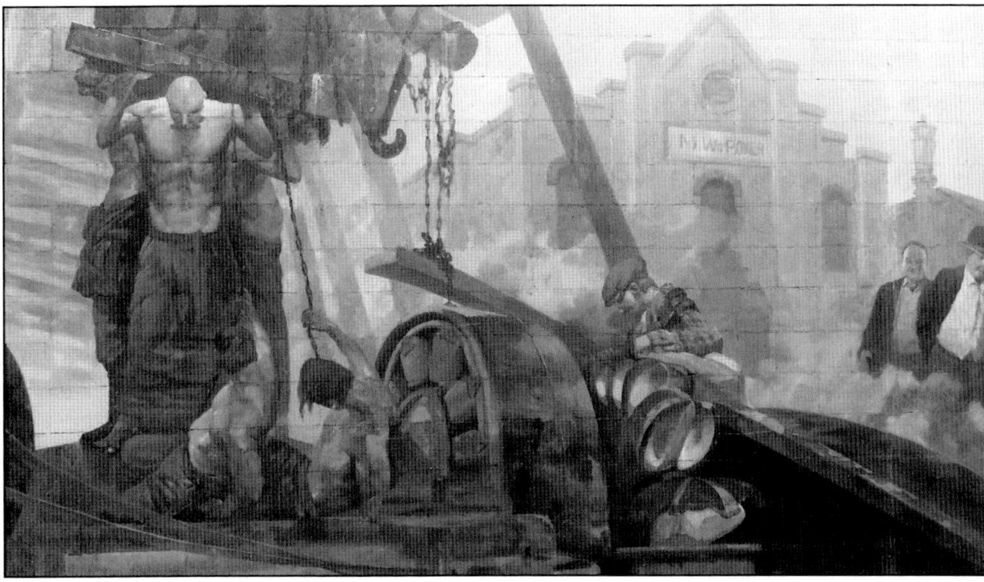

J.J. Cairns had the largest hand in developing a method of using electric motors and a steam pump to draw water from wells, revolutionizing modern irrigation in 1899. The Mount Whitney Power Company was established in June 1899 and later acquired, along with a few other power companies, by Southern California Electric. The event is commemorated in a mural by Wei Luan. (Photograph by DeLea Davis.)

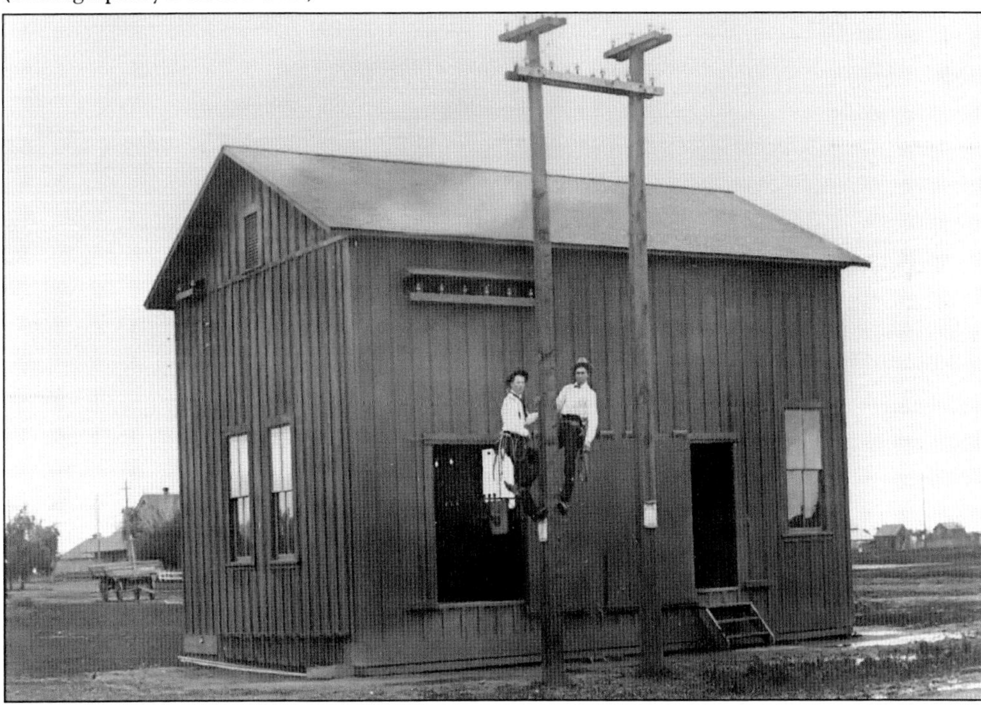

Unidentified linemen pose in front of the first substation built in 1899. It was through this historic building that power flowed for the first large-scale irrigation pumping project in the United States, headed up by William Hammond, John Hays Hammond, A.G. Wishon, and Ben Maddox. (CSUF.)

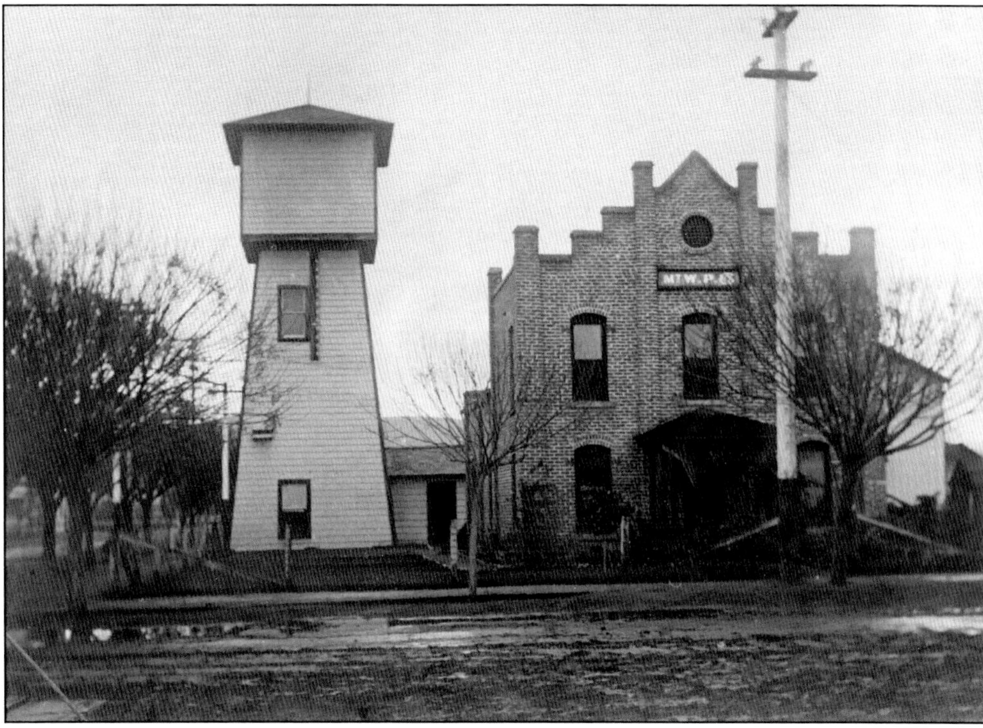

The new Mount Whitney Power Company's substation is pictured in 1905 after it had been reconstructed in more permanent brick. The irrigation pump industry took off from here. An early builder was C.F. Flagg, who worked with Jack Stansfield. Stansfield later opened the prominent supply outfit Stansfield & McKnight. (CSUF.)

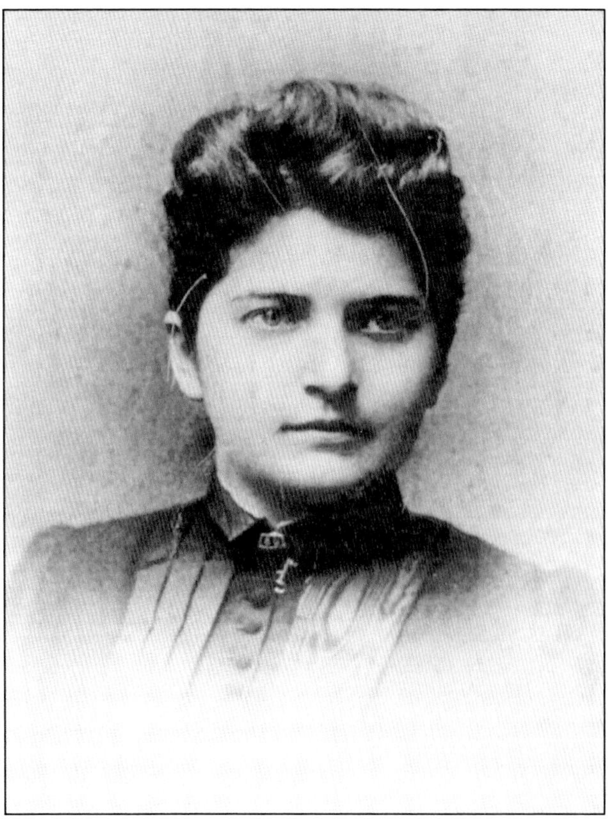

Sarah "Sadie" Lindsay Patton Hutchinson, Lindsay's namesake, planted the first commercially successful orange trees. Although some had tried their hand at growing citrus in the era, the Hutchinsons set out to make it a viable business enterprise to appeal to land buyers. It was incredibly successful—however, not without great struggle. (LMG.)

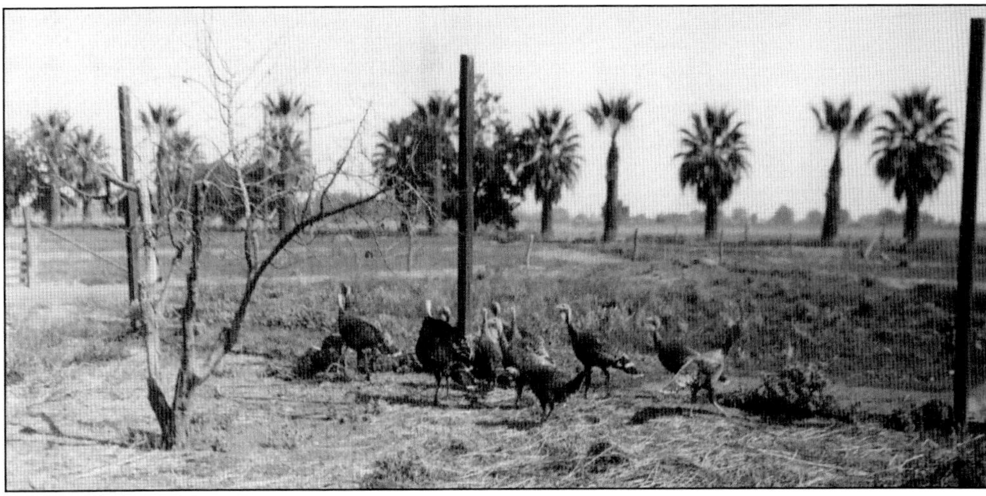

In her memoirs, Sadie Hutchinson recalls the struggle to keep those first orange trees alive after locusts—or "hoppers," as she called them—had besieged them. One of the steps taken to save the plantings was to purchase every turkey they could find to eat the hoppers. The turkeys were quickly sated and instead resorted to "giving the insects rides on their backs." (CSUF.)

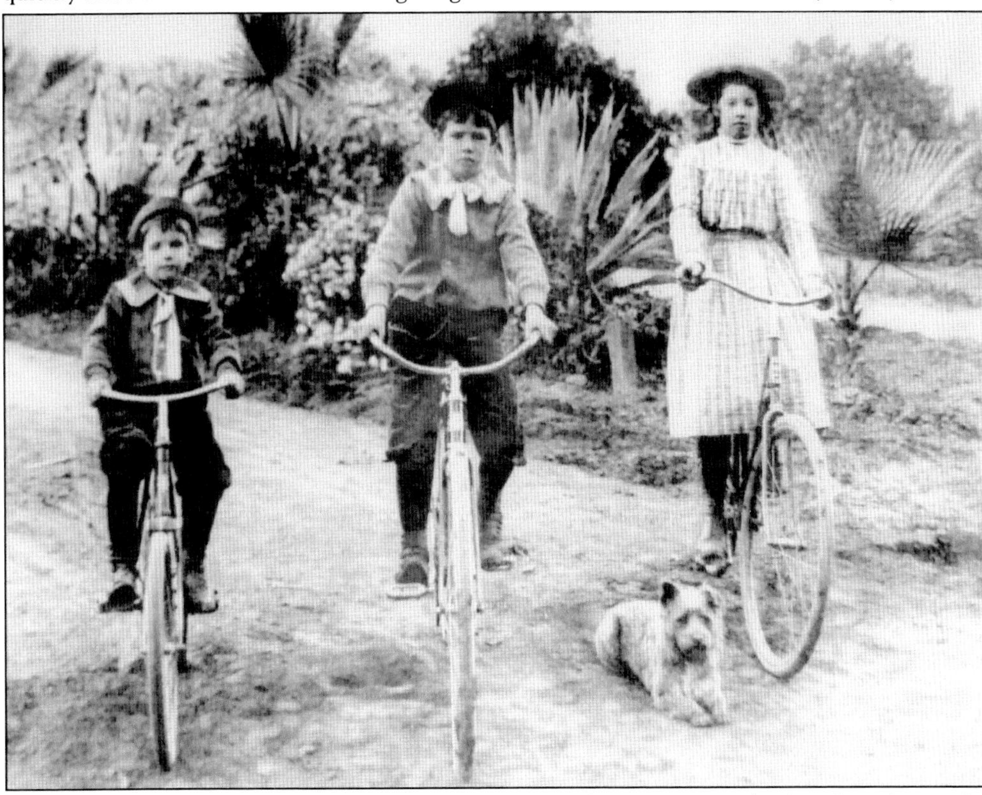

From left to right, William, Arthur Sr., and Mary Hutchinson sit astride their bicycles on the palm tree–lined driveway of the Hutchinson home. In her memoirs, Sadie Hutchinson addresses the decision to leave Lindsay was due to her desire to have the children grow up in a town where their social status was unknown. She did not want her children to be given special treatment or favors and learn to navigate the world according to their own merits. (LMG.)

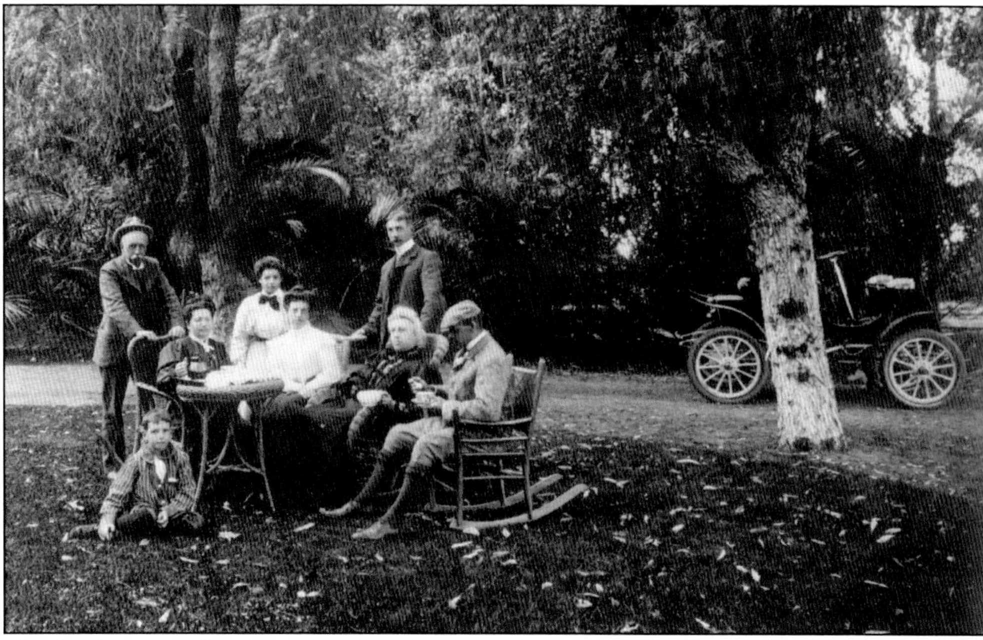

This lovely scene of Lindsay's founding family was captured in 1906, just prior to their departure to San Francisco. The family selected an unfortunate date to leave: April 18, 1906, the day of the devastating San Francisco earthquake. From left to right are William Hutchinson (seated in front), Capt. Arthur J. Hutchinson, Sadie Lindsay Patton Hutchinson, Mary Hutchinson, a Miss Warrings, Lawrence White, Augusta Hutchinson, and Spens Black. (LMG.)

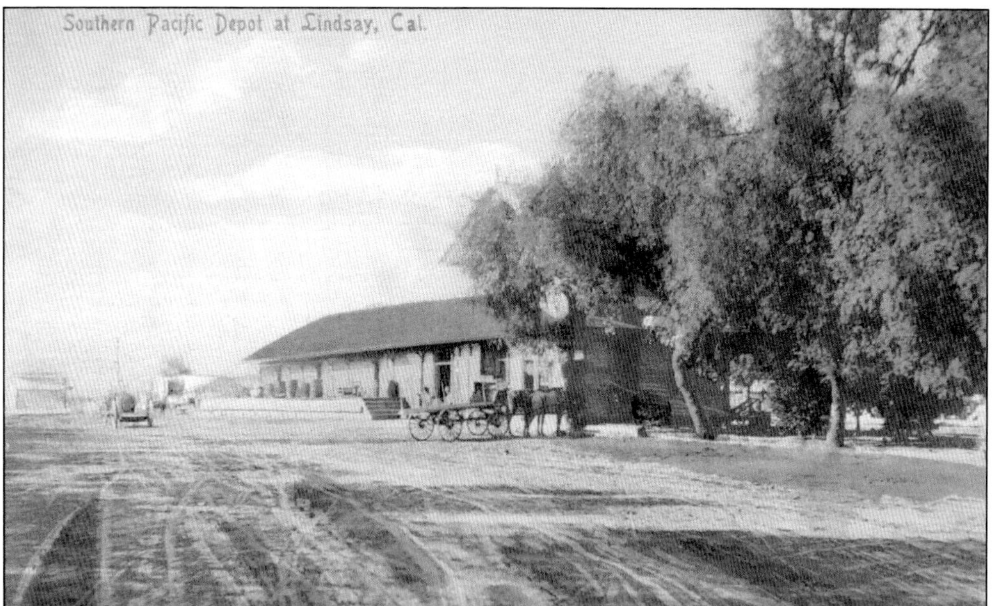

From 1888 to 1889, tracks for the Stockton & Tulare Railroad were laid here in Lindsay, providing easy accessibility to ports and the rest of the United Sates, thereby opening the developing town of Lindsay to the world. In 1896, John Jolly Cairns shipped the first railroad car of oranges to San Francisco from Lindsay. (LMG.)

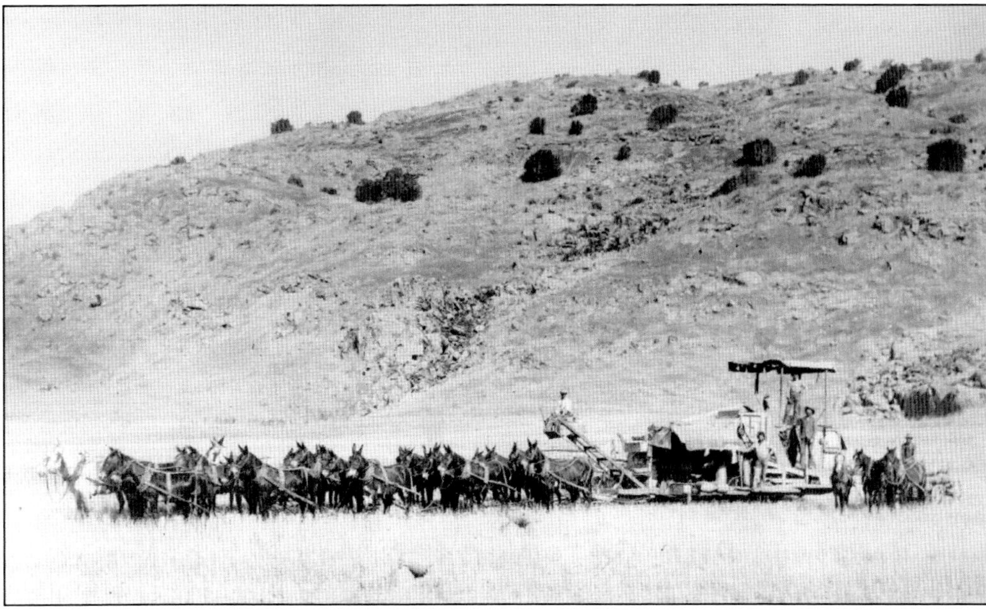

Shown working their land with a team of horses are, from left to right, John, Ralph, L.C., Bill Keeley, and unidentified. It was typical for entire families, children too, to spend the majority of their time pitching in where needed. (CSUF.)

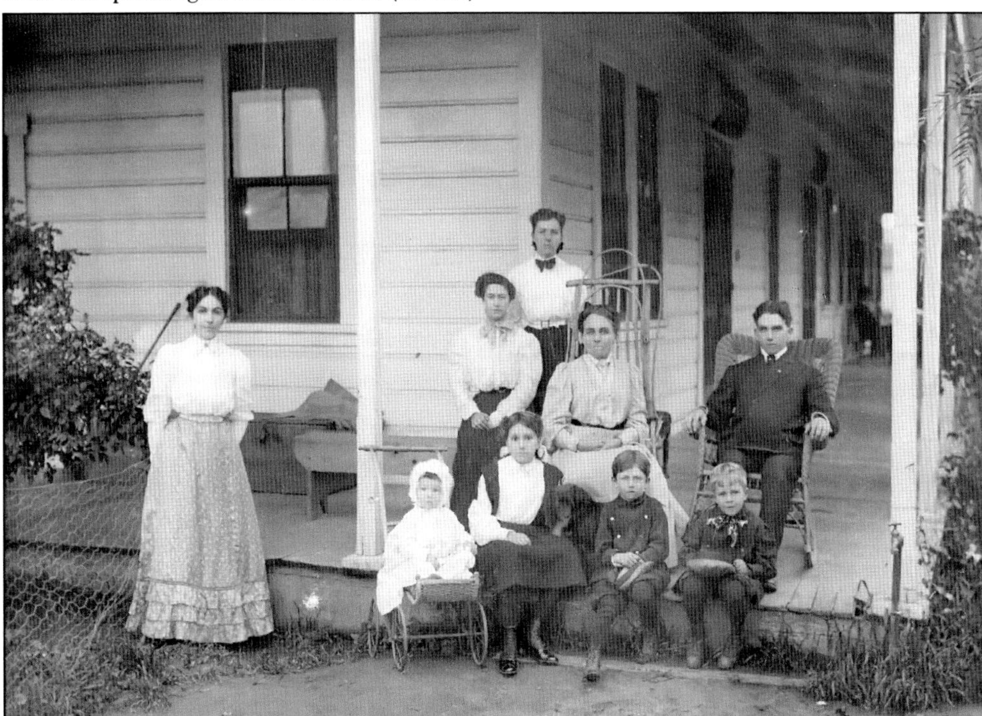

The Lindsay Hotel, pictured here in 1904, located on the corner of Sweetbriar and Samoa Streets, featured 14 rooms, a dining room, kitchen, and parlor. Guests could enjoy ample porch seating, as seen here. Pictured are various members of the Adams-Cox families. To the left stands the hotel proprietress, a Mrs. Adams. The hotel burned down in 1908. (LMG.)

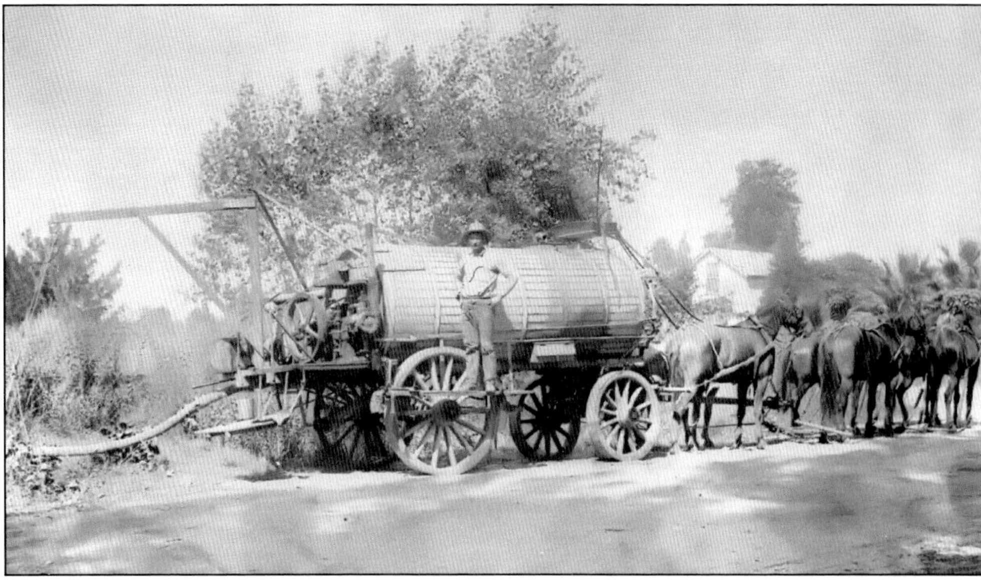

Lindsay's most prominent club got its start in 1904 as the Arbor Club. Lindsay's pioneer women, including Sadie Lindsay Patton Hutchinson, Margaret Hostetter, and two women only known by the last names of Cairns and Berry, organized the group to plant trees along Lindsay's newly created streets. By 1910, the women had planted 1,018 trees. Water for the trees had to be hauled in large wooden barrels pulled by a team of horses. (LMG.)

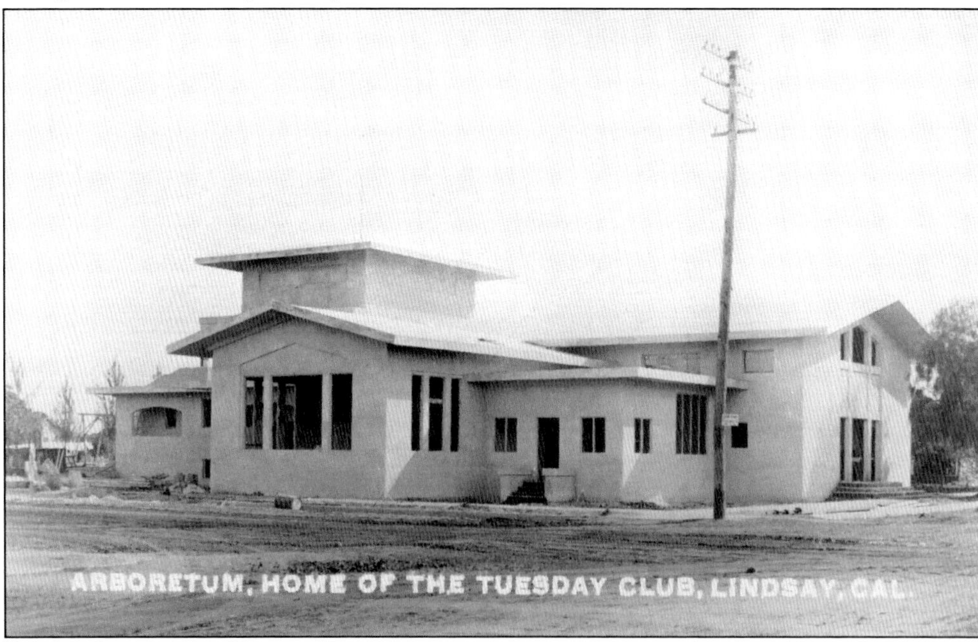

According to a 1916 publication, the Tuesday Club was considered the "leading local enterprise," with 115 members strong. In 1913, they constructed Lindsay's first community building, the Lindsay Arboretum, later renamed the Tuesday Club, which still stands today. This building became the heart of early community life, playing host to all town meetings and social gatherings. To this day, many Lindsay residents comment on how their grandparents met or fell in love at a dance at the Arboretum. (LMG.)

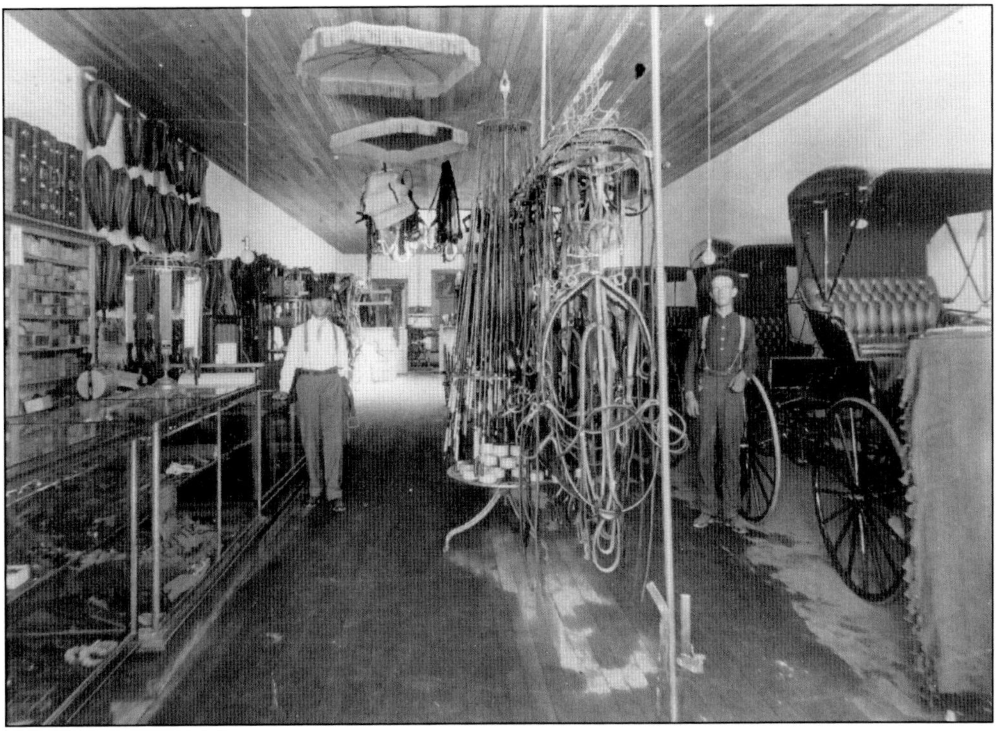

This buggy and harness store was located on Main Street during Lindsay's pioneering era. It was finally forced to close its doors, as have many other businesses throughout time, with the advent of the automobile. (LMG.)

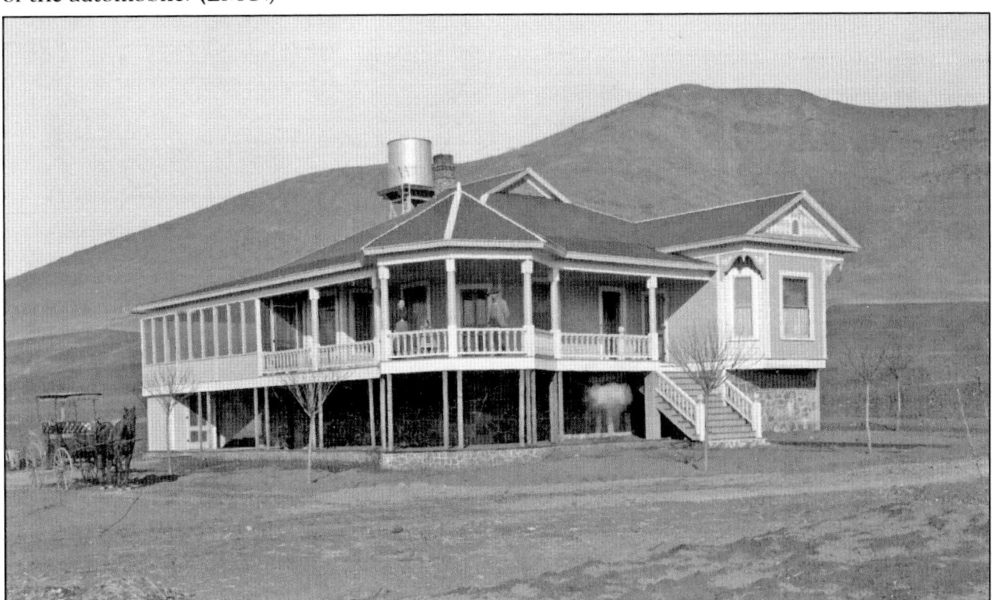

An early ranch house is pictured in 1900. The hill behind it is now the site of the Lindsay "L." Upon closer inspection, people can be seen standing on the second-floor balcony, along with a horse-drawn buggy parked out front. On the back of the photograph is the following note: "Lindsay place before the yard was planted." (PN.)

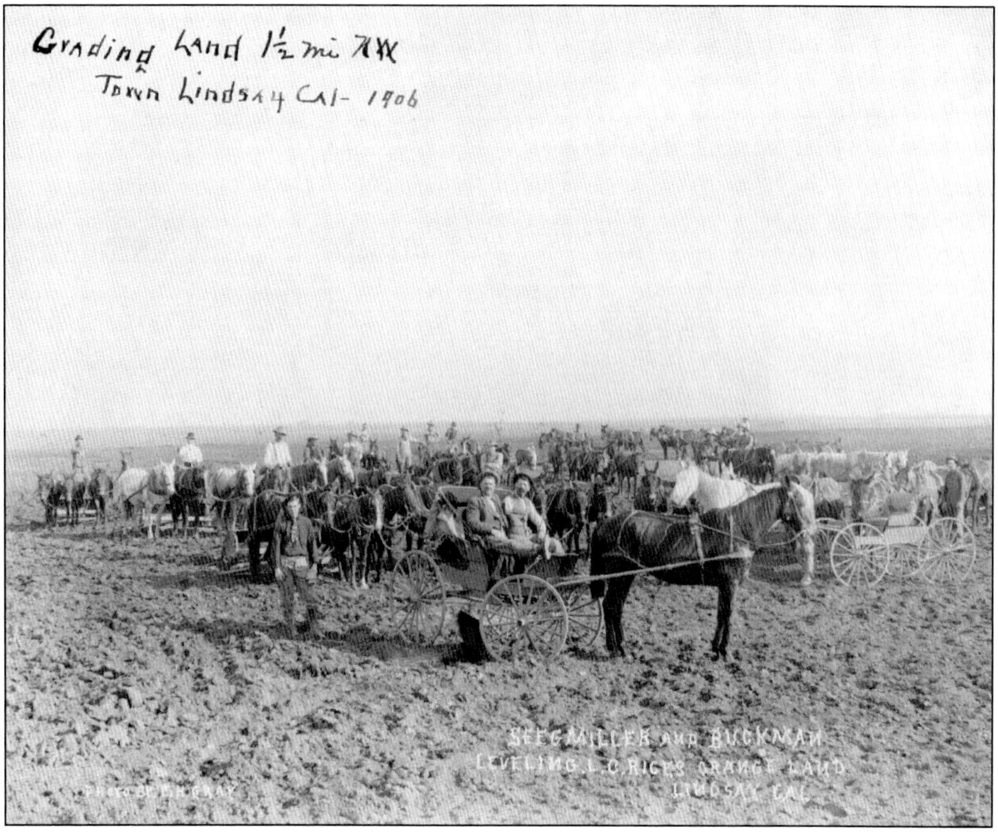

These men are seen grading land in Lindsay in 1906. Grading was an incredibly laborious process that required many hours of hard work to prepare the land for farming. The caption says, "Seeg Miller and Buckman leveling L.C. Rice's orange land, Lindsay, CA." (CSUF.)

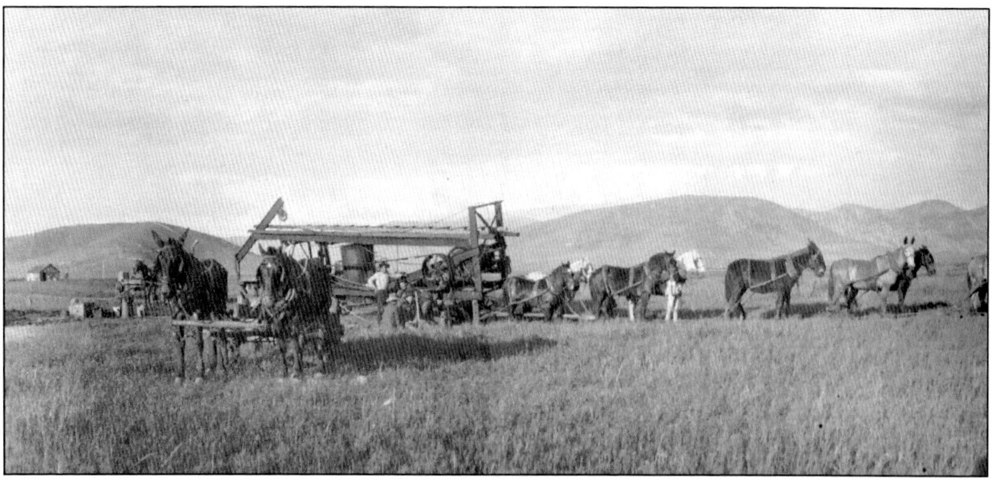

A crew prepares to drill one of the first deep irrigation wells on the W.B. Kiggens property, two miles east of Lindsay, in 1906. W.B. Kiggens, director of the First National Bank, owned an orange grove and was selected as chairman of the committee to govern the newly incorporated City of Lindsay. The *Lindsay Gazette* described Kiggens as a "forceful and brilliant speaker" and "successful business man." (LMG.)

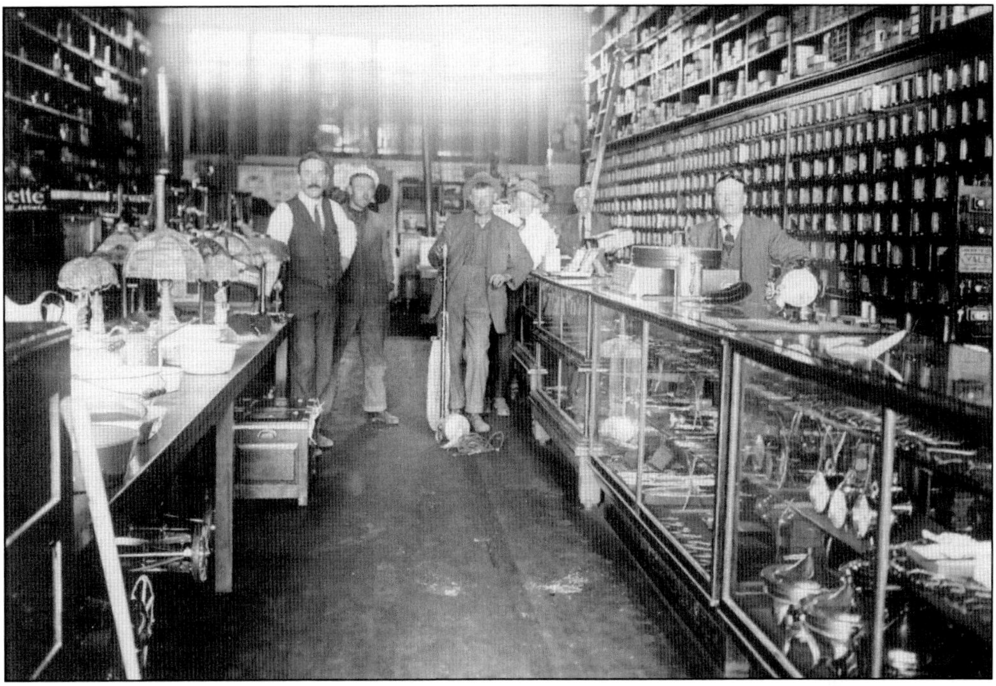

Clerks and customers gather for a picture in the Ostrander-Race Hardware Company. P.T. Ostrander arrived during the 1800s, initially buying out another store, the Mathes Hardware Company. He then partnered with W.D. Race and B.E. French to establish Ostrander-Race in 1910. French, a citrus grower, was a great asset to the business, as his practical experience enabled him to select the best stock for the many other growers in the district. (LMG.)

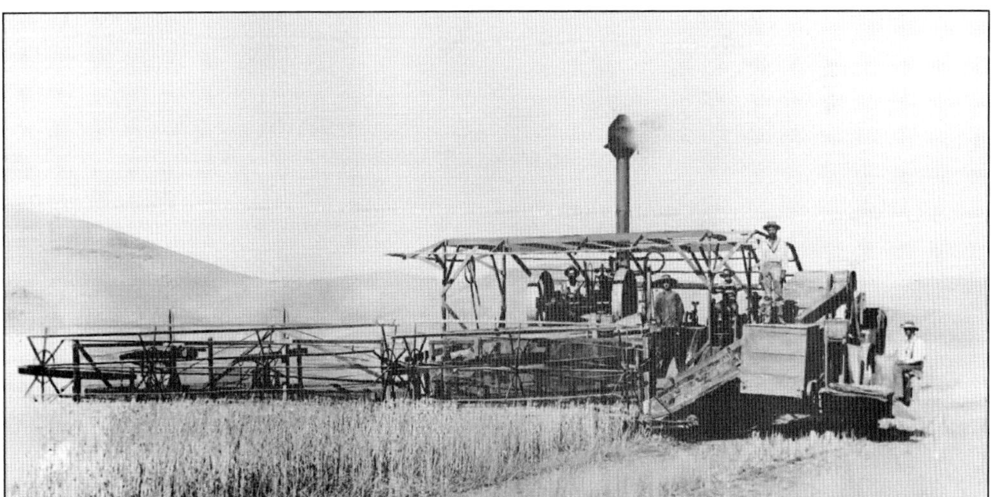

George Stockton Berry, a prominent figure in early Tulare County, purchased 2,000 acres of railroad land adjacent to what is now Lindsay in 1875. He had an extensive grain business and later sold most of his land to live on 100 acres of farmland. As a prolific inventor of mechanized farm equipment, he received a patent for the G.S. Berry Steam Harvester in 1887. (CSUF.)

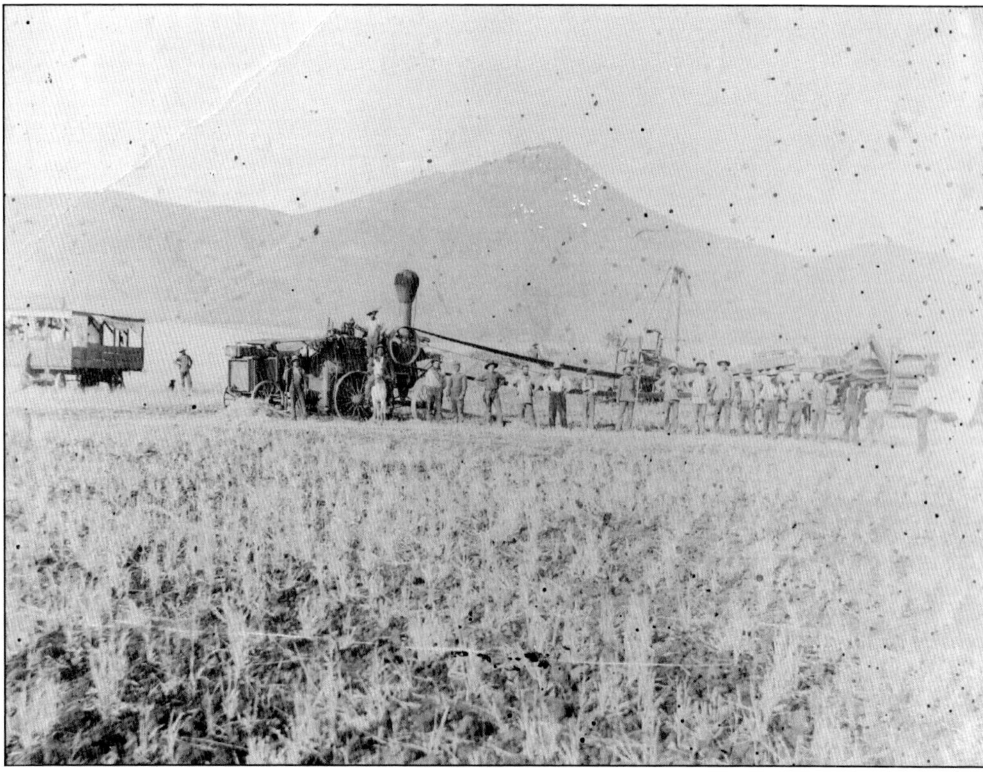

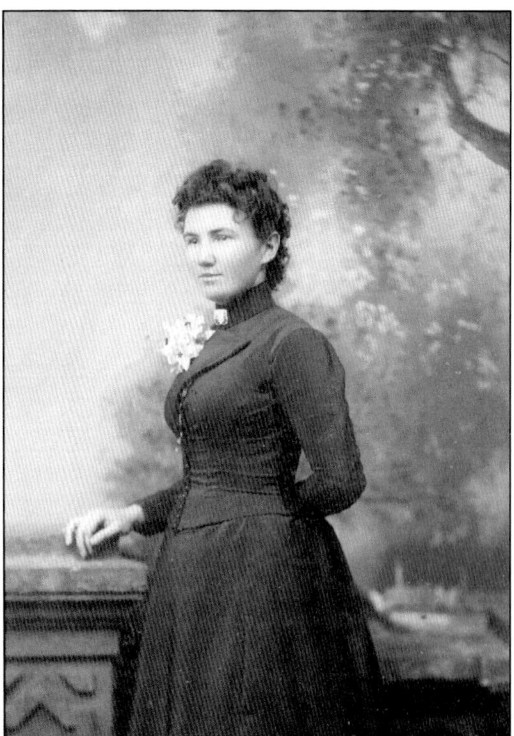

In 1887, George Stockton Berry invented the first self-propelled combine for the harvesting of grain crops. Said to be "fueled by the land," it was powered by a straw-burning steam boiler. The equipment traveled forward for plowing and in reverse for harvesting with a traction engine and power turning, using differential gears instead of conventional wheel clutches. In 1888, it was equipped with a 40-foot header and utilized nighttime lighting. It harvested over 100 acres per day. (CSUF.)

Dr. Jennie Krepps, sister of Dr. Bond, also became a physician in the late 1800s. She resided in San Francisco but spent a great deal of time in Lindsay. After the devastating San Francisco earthquake of 1906, Dr. Krepps and her family lost their home and had to live in Golden Gate Park. There, she tended the wounded and cooked food for other homeless families on her Bunsen burners. (LMG.)

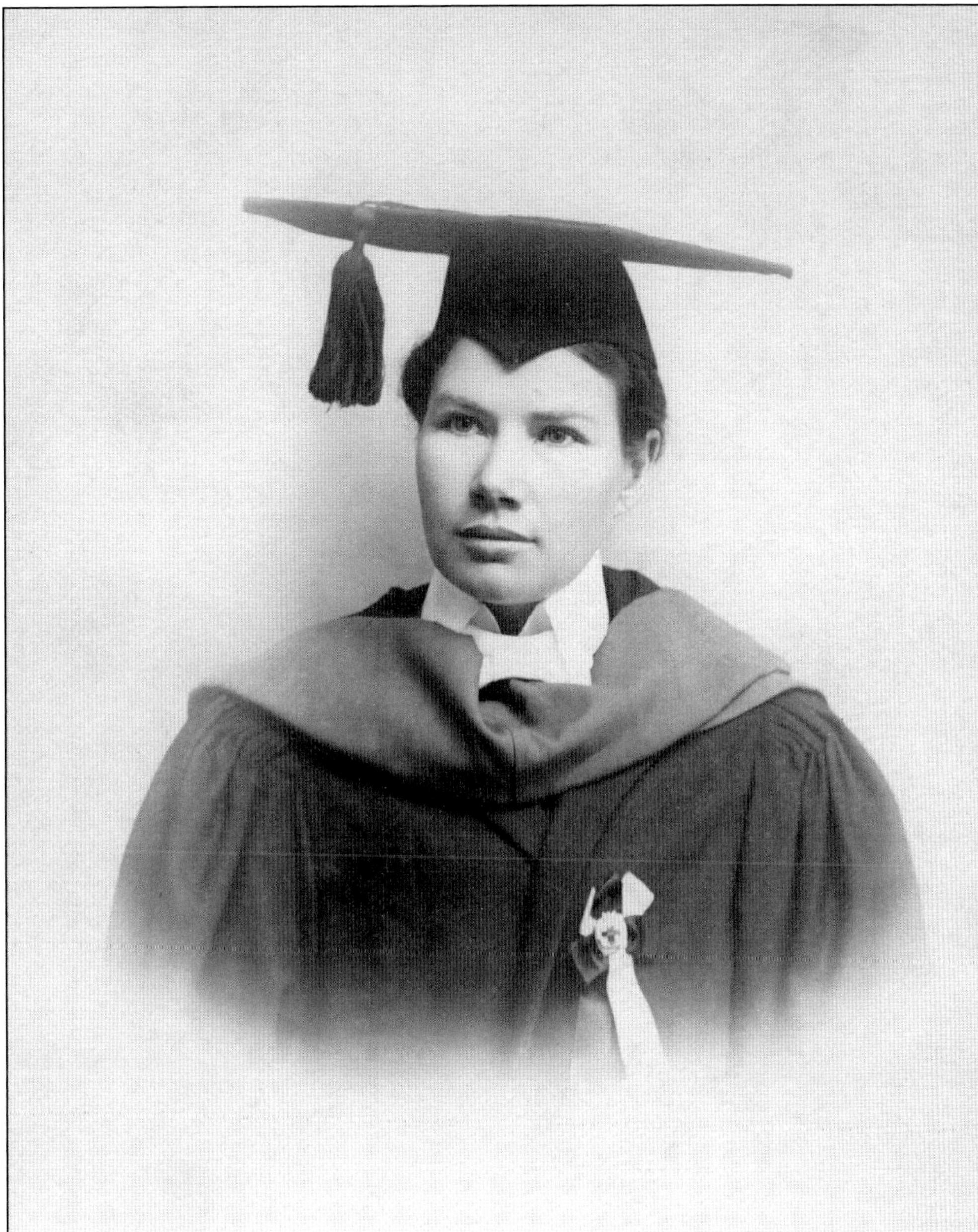

Dr. Annie L. Bond graduated from Eclectic Medical School in San Francisco in 1884 as the only female in her class. Women had only just entered the field and faced many obstacles, beginning with their education. Harassment at school or even from their own families was common, as was being blocked from attending important surgical demonstrations in anatomical theaters. In 1898, she settled in Lindsay, becoming the town's first physician. A female physician was not exactly welcomed with open arms, but with tenacity and her obvious talent, she quickly gained the trust and admiration of the community. Once, a male doctor arrived in Lindsay and publicly declared his plans to "run that woman out." Instead, it was he who departed a couple of months later, and he had to sell every last piece of his medical equipment and supplies to pay his fare out of Lindsay. (LMG.)

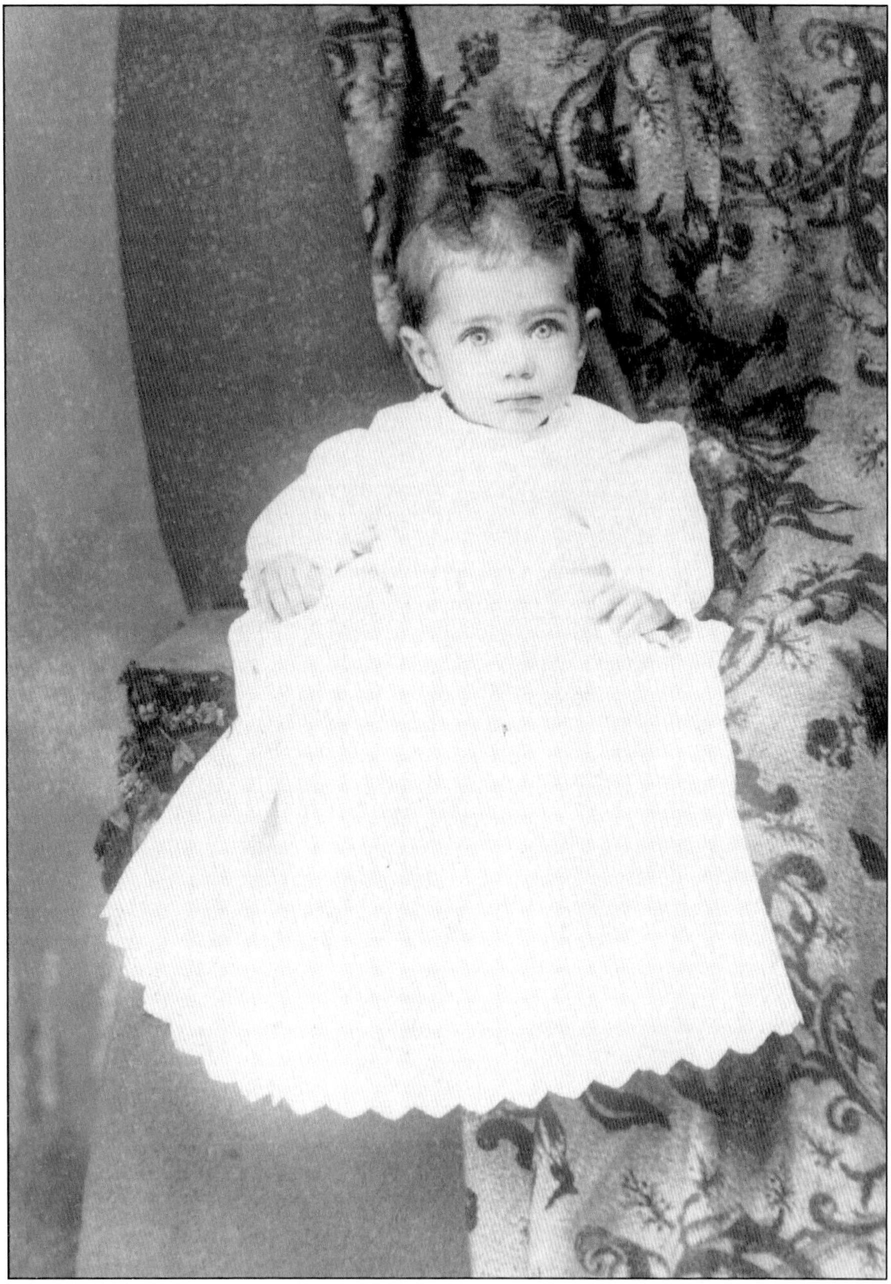

Dr. Bond's daughter Ruth played a large role in her mother's decision to become a physician when she fell seriously ill as an infant. Dr. Bond took Ruth to a nearby physician who claimed that he could do nothing to help the child, although she was near death. Such diagnoses were common in this era of limited knowledge and resources. Bond took Ruth to see another doctor, who happened to be a woman. It was this doctor who saved Ruth's life and inspired Annie Bond to enter the medical profession herself. In the Lindsay Museum and Gallery's collections, there are numerous letters from parents and children alike who tell a similar story to that of Ruth, whereby they were taken to a doctor and either misdiagnosed or "left for dead" until Dr. Bond intervened, saving lives many times over. (LMG.)

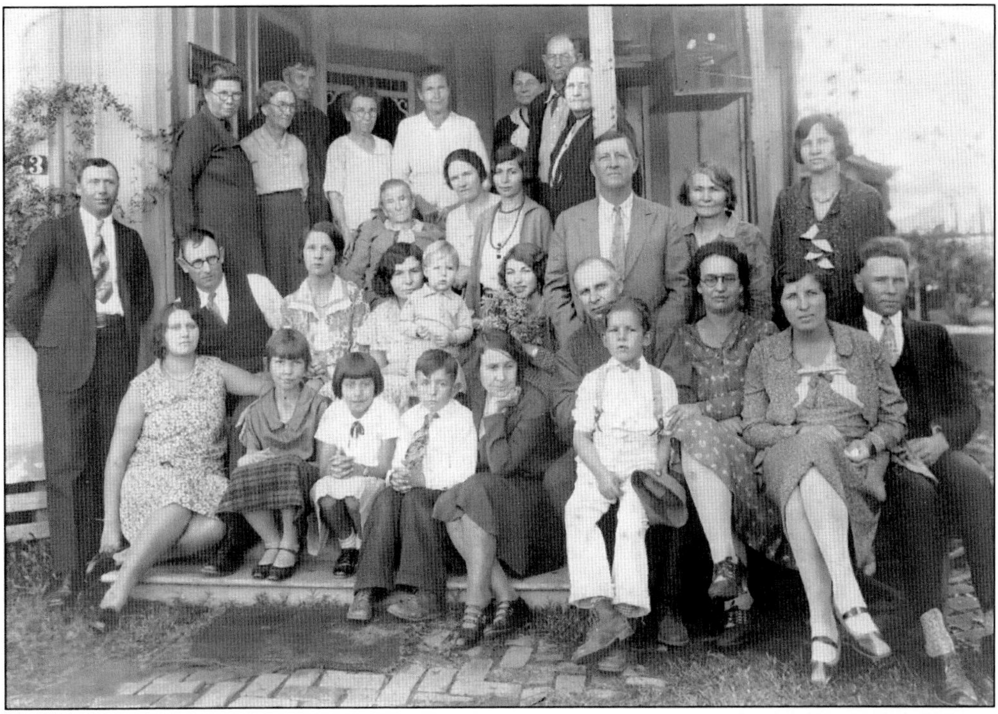

The Krepps-Bond family gathers for a photograph on the front porch of the Bond house to commemorate the 90th birthday of Malinda Scovell Krepps (third row, seated), the mother of both doctors. Dr. Annie Bond can be seen standing at far left in the top row. Just behind her head is her doctor's shingle. Dr. Jennie Krepps can also be seen standing in this row (forth from the left), just behind their mother. (LMG.)

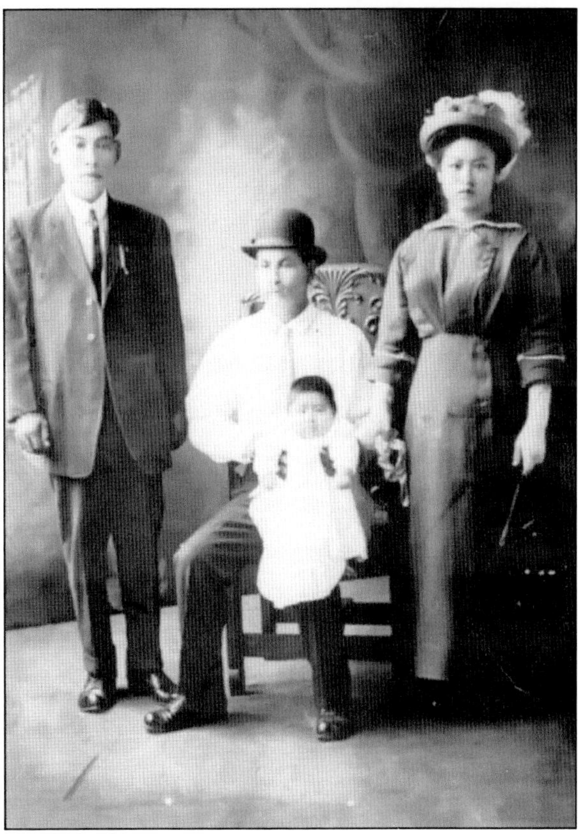

This lovely 1915 portrait of the Shimasaki pioneering family was taken in the Lindsay-Strathmore area. From left to right are Kurazo Ideta, Jisaburo Shimasaki (holding baby Tom Shimasaki), and Hatsu Shimasaki. There were many other Japanese and Japanese American families who immigrated to Lindsay during this time. (LMG.)

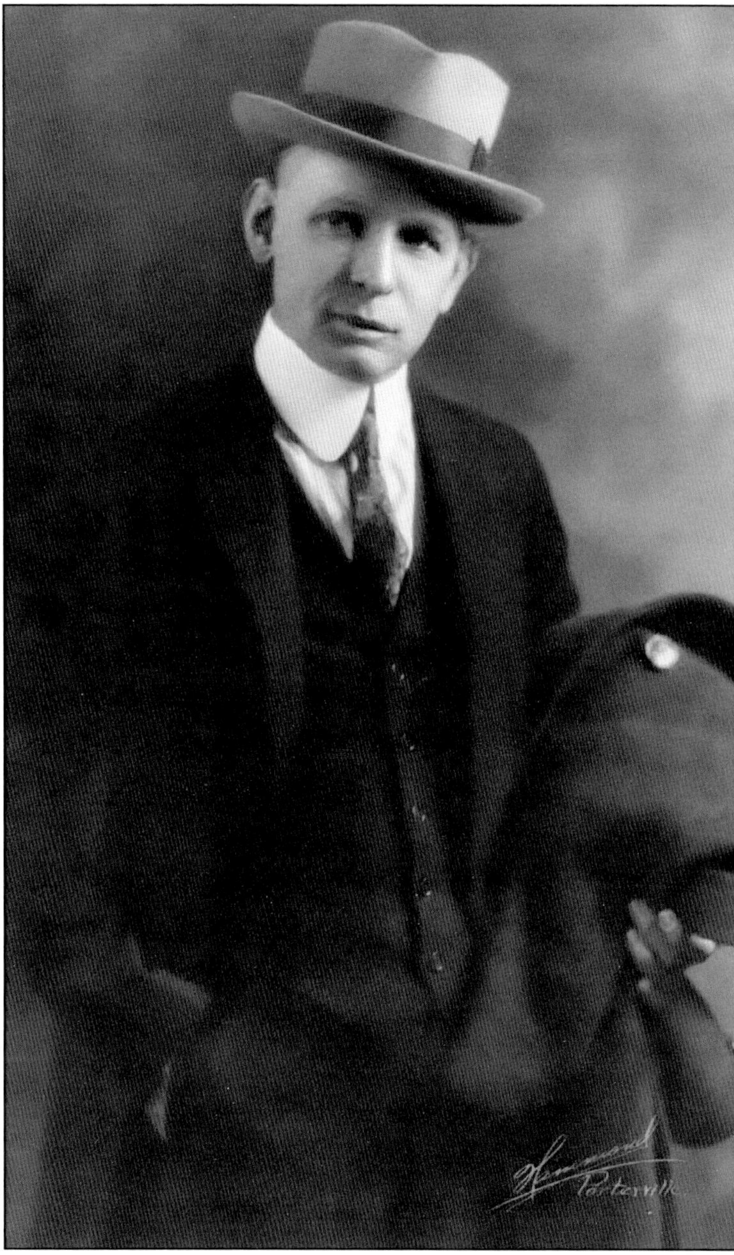

Albert Conrad Tienken and an unnamed partner established the Lindsay Drug Company in 1905. A 1910 publication described the pharmacy as follows: "There is an air of strength and reliability everywhere about the store. You are impressed with the size, variety and character of the stock and you feel absolutely safe in dealing here." As a photography enthusiast, Tienken not only filled his store with cameras and film when they first became available to the public, but he also took many photographs, some of which are featured in this book. Many of the items used in the early years of the apothecary, including ingredients to make medicines, record books or prescriptions and recipes, tools to make pills, and a show globe, are on display at the Lindsay Museum and Gallery. Tienken and his descendants are known for being involved in countless endeavors toward betterment of the town. (LMG.)

A hallmark of a successful early-20th-century pharmacy was the creation and marketing of personal remedies, most of which were quack medicines and often caused the patient more problems than they actually cured. A.C. Tienken created Phen-O-Cel, a remedy for "headaches neuralgia and pains centering on the trigeminal nerve, prepared in powder or tablet form." Phen-O-Cel was successfully marketed not only to local customers, but also to pharmacies all over the country through the 1920s. (LMG.)

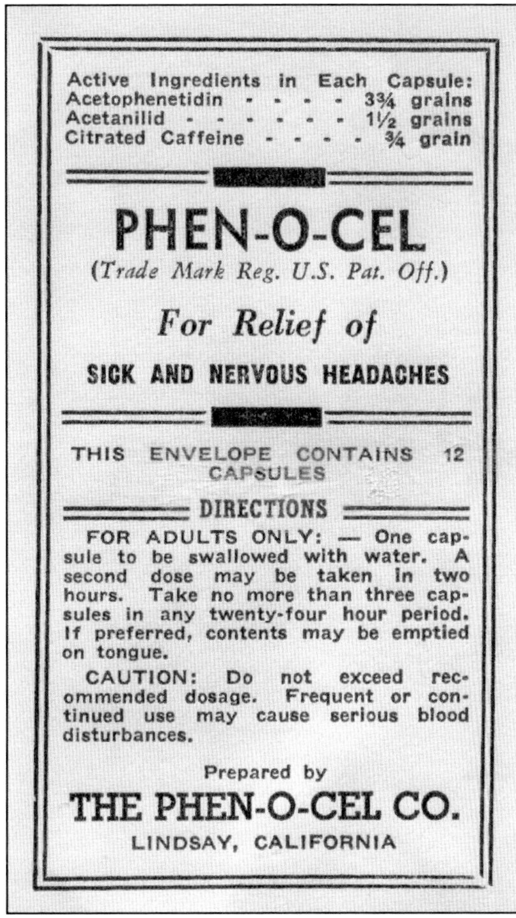

The Lindsay Talc Mill was started in 1905 after its proprietors discovered there was soapstone in Yokohl Valley. Once a mine was created, the stone was blasted and then hauled the eight miles into Lindsay using a large team of horses. At the mill, the rocks would be crushed and ground into a fine powder, then placed in sacks that held 200 pounds. (CSUF.)

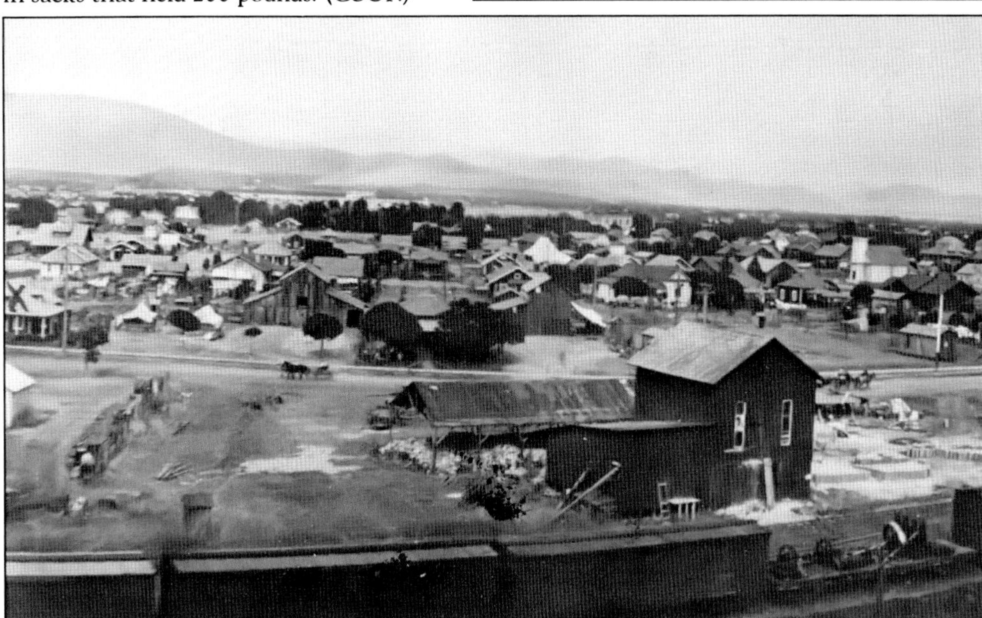

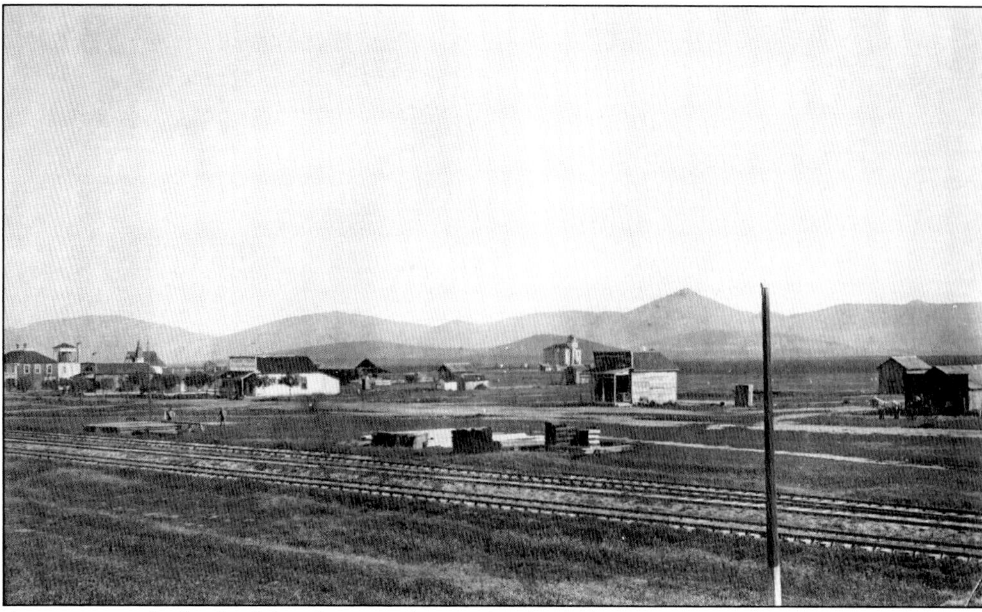

A caption on the back of the photograph provides the following description: "General view over present business section, Lindsay in the year of 1902—Watch Us Grow." This pioneer-era store might have been Ostrander-Race. The Lindsay Hotel can be seen at far left, along with the first schoolhouse at center in the distance. (CSUF.)

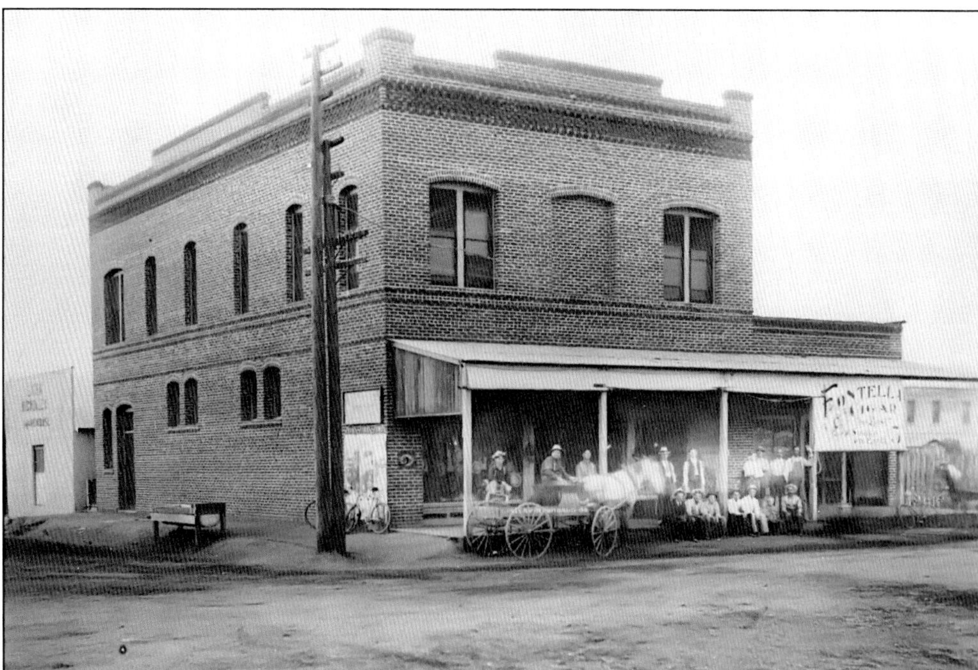

The Roachdale building stood in the heart of the Lindsay business district on the corner of Honolulu Street and Elmwood Avenue. In 1909, the building became the Lindsay Mercantile, run by Ernest L. Daniells. (LMG.)

Ernest L. Daniells got his start as a printer in Kansas. He later moved to Colorado, where he became the chief law enforcement officer during the violent and deadly Leadville miners' strike and remained in this position for 30 years. Daniells retired to the Lindsay district, where his uncle Dexter Bishop, a charter member of Lindsay's Masonic Lodge, and other family members had settled in 1898. There, Daniells did anything but actually retire. He was voted director of the Lindsay-Strathmore Irrigation District when it was being established in 1915. In the 1920s, Dexter's son Earnest "Ernie" L. Bishop, who had been working as the operator at the Booster station for the irrigation system, invented an algae wheel to eliminate the buildup of moss and debris that was clogging the flume and meters. Prior to this invention, many hours were dedicated to cleaning the debris by hand. (JMB.)

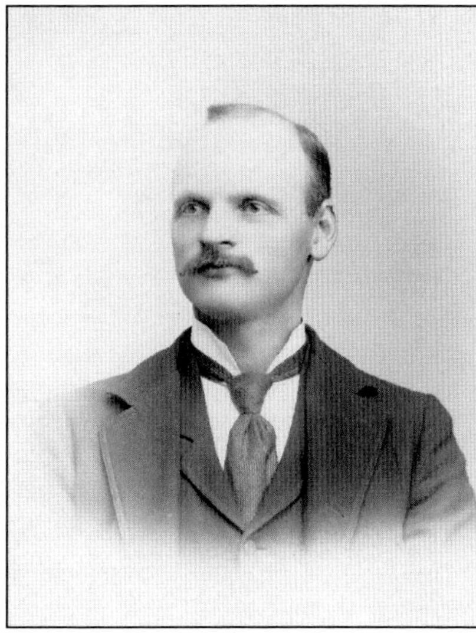

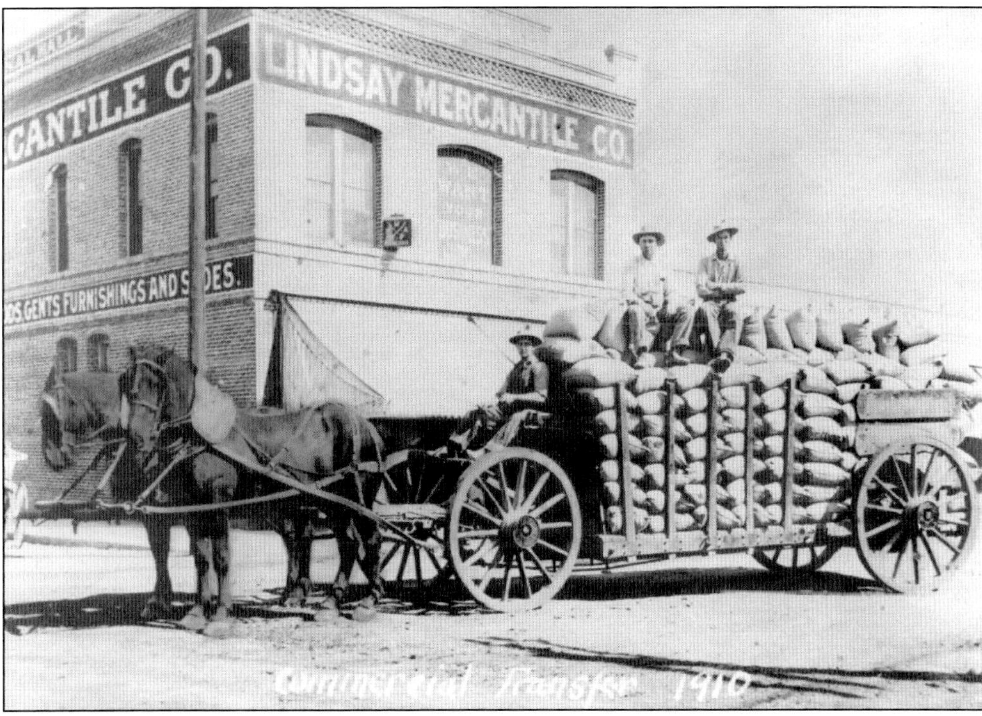

This is a 1910 photograph of a commercial transfer freight wagon. Essential to pioneer life, wagons like this were used to haul commercial goods to train stations or nearby towns. During this time, the freight companies in Lindsay were Wells Fargo Freight Company and Lindsay Commercial Transfer. Lindsay Commercial Transfer is now Young's Commercial Transfer and is still in operation in nearby Porterville, California. In business from the late 1800s, the Lindsay Mercantile Company, visible in the background, quickly became Tulare County's second-largest mercantile establishment. This pioneer-era department store was presided over by G.K. Hostetter. It carried food, clothing, farm equipment, hardware, and anything else a Lindsay pioneer might need. Purchases were recorded by hand in a large, heavy book, including the name of the buyer, the items purchased, the amount or weight, and the date of sale. (LMG.)

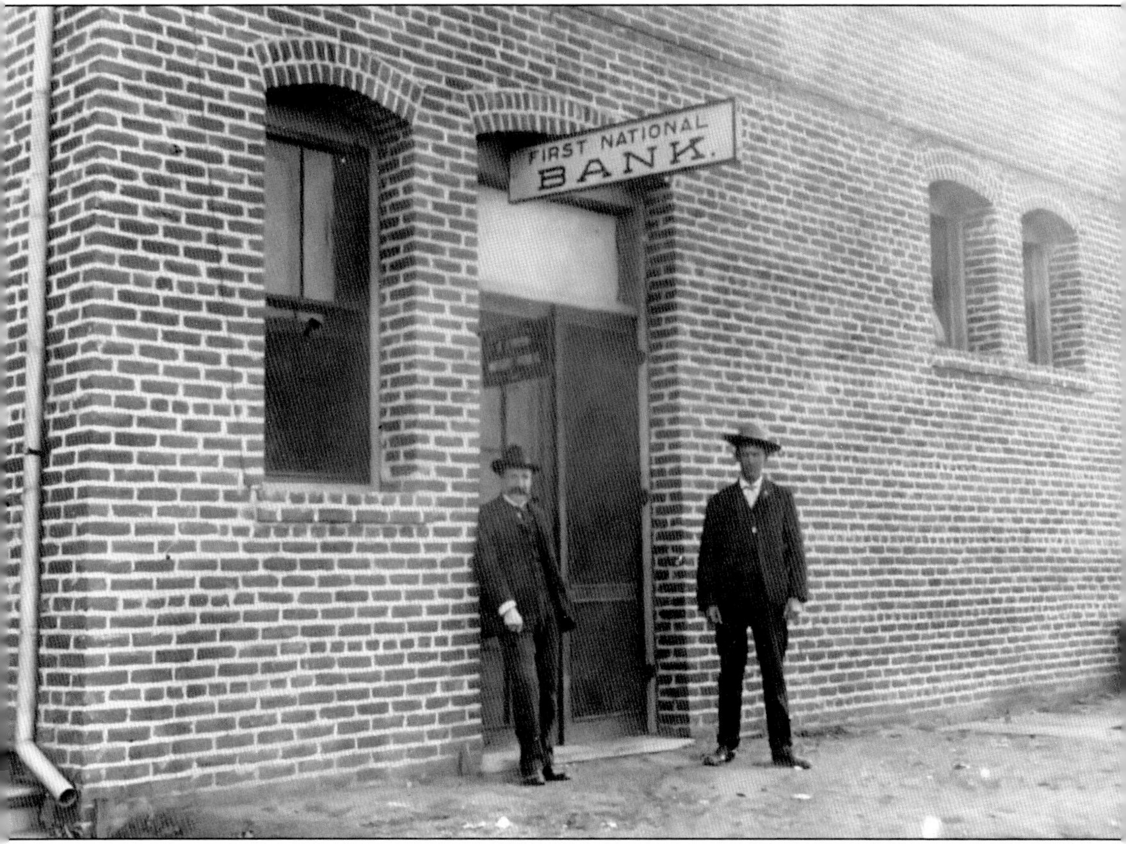

George Victor Reed (right) is pictured here in 1896 with H. Bucksbaum, who settled in Lindsay. Reed led quite an interesting life that ended in tragedy. He was appointed deputy in Tulare County by the sheriff there and was shot in the line of duty during a train robbery. In 1898, Reed ran for the office of county tax collector as a member of the Populist Party and won. He eventually moved to Lindsay, where he helped to establish the First National Bank of Lindsay and served on the Lindsay School Board. He and his wife, Jennie, fully participated in the social life of the community and were involved in many local organizations. In October 1923, residents of Lindsay were shocked to discover that Reed had committed suicide, leaving behind a note that, in part, read, "I am sorry; the work is so depressing. I cannot stand it any longer." (CSUF.)

The First National Bank of Lindsay opened its doors on November 7, 1905. By November 9, residents had deposited $31,053.41, providing a healthy start for the town's first financial institution. From left to right are (seated) G.V. Reed, bank cashier, and A.M. Hostetter, vice president; (standing) Charles B. Lyons, E.B. Varian, R.E. Wolf, and Calude Rupert. (LMG.)

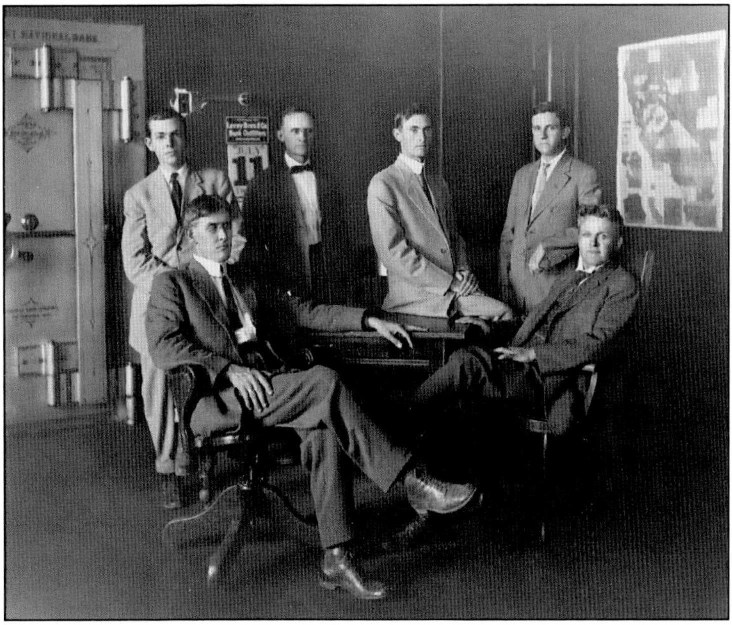

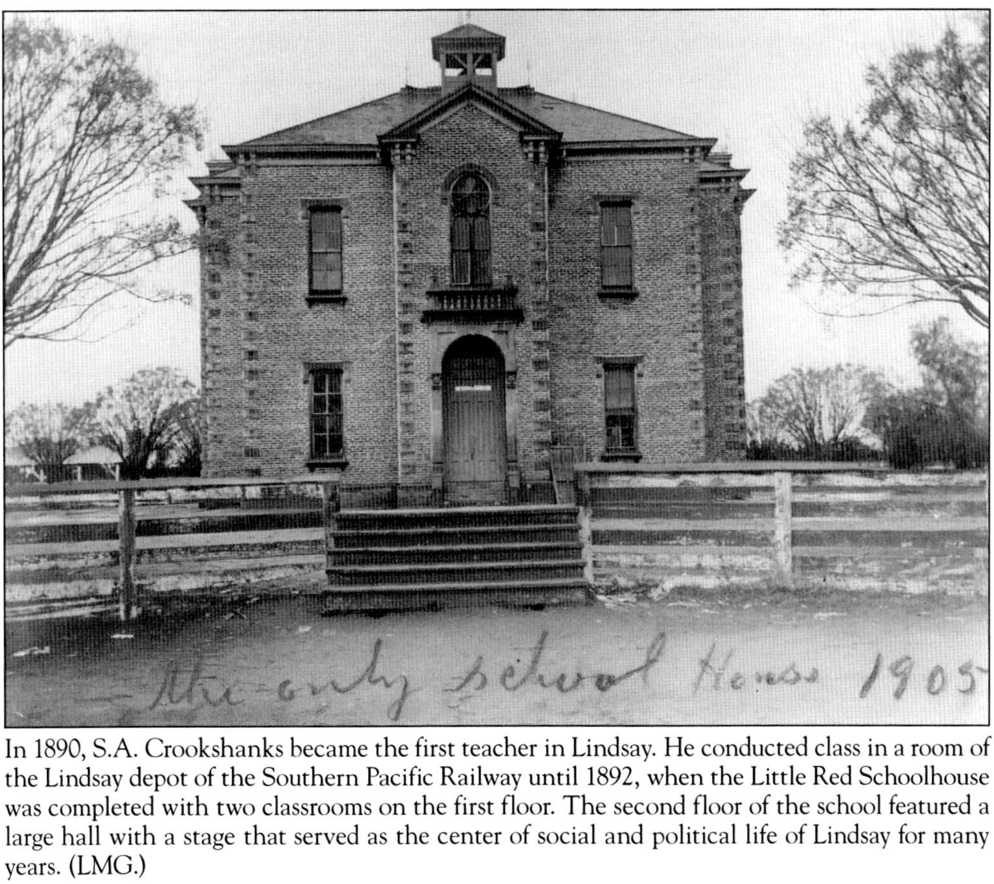

In 1890, S.A. Crookshanks became the first teacher in Lindsay. He conducted class in a room of the Lindsay depot of the Southern Pacific Railway until 1892, when the Little Red Schoolhouse was completed with two classrooms on the first floor. The second floor of the school featured a large hall with a stage that served as the center of social and political life of Lindsay for many years. (LMG.)

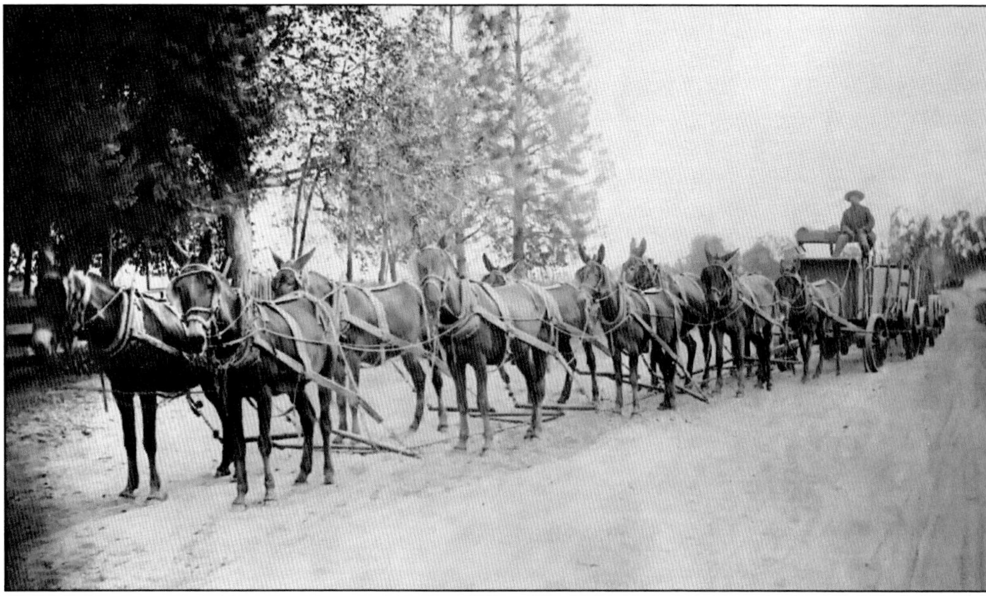

In 1891, the decision was made to build a permanent school, as the number of students had outgrown the train depot. Thus, the following year, J.J. Cairns began hauling bricks from the kilns in nearby Porterville with his team of horses. (LMG.)

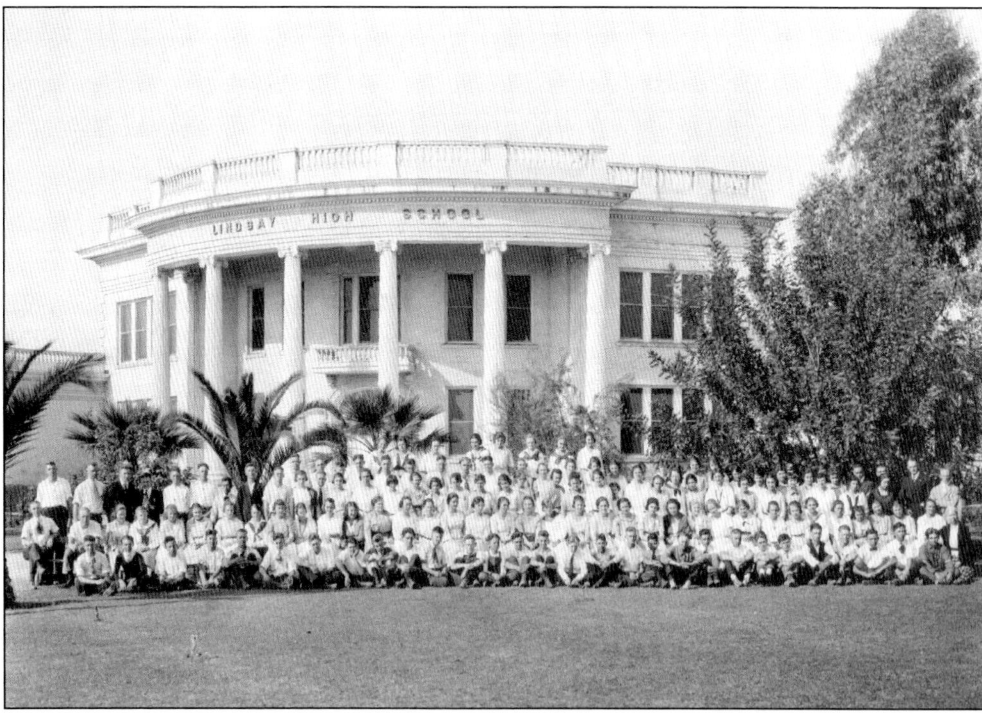

In September 1907, the Lindsay School Board set about creating the first high school, which was finally accomplished in 1909 at a cost of $30,000. Located on the northeast corner of Harvard Avenue and East Hermosa Street, this beautiful building served as the high school until 1923. The facility was then utilized as a junior high until it was demolished to make way for the Lincoln Junior High School in 1937. (LMG.)

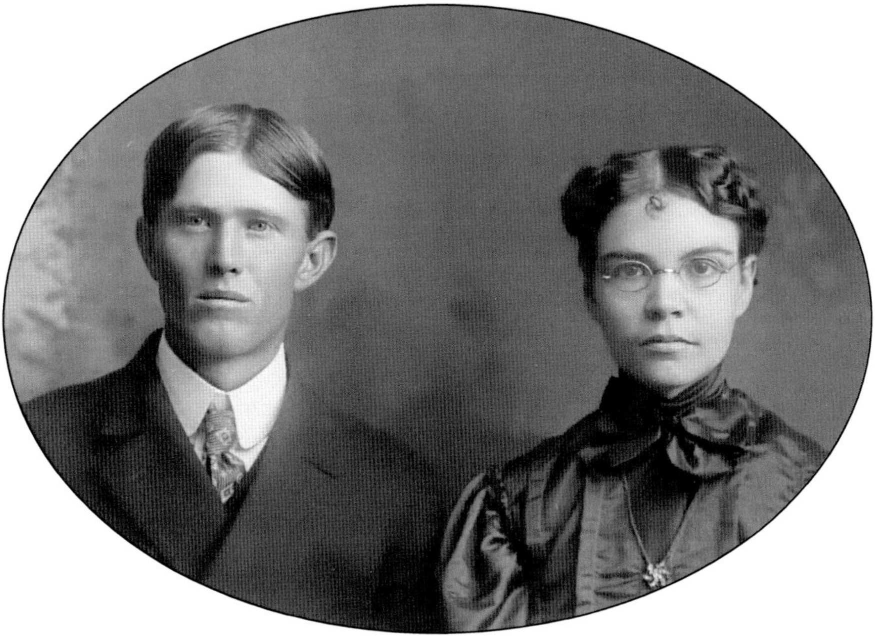

This photograph of Albert and Anita Clark was taken in November 1904. The Clarks got their start as employees of Lucky Baldwin, an immensely successful businessman and real estate mogul. Baldwin was considered one of California's greatest and most colorful pioneers. Among his exploits were becoming a dear friend of Wyatt Earp, being sued for "seduction" and shot at by several women for "breach of promise," and creating the Santa Anita Racetrack in Los Angeles. (BC.)

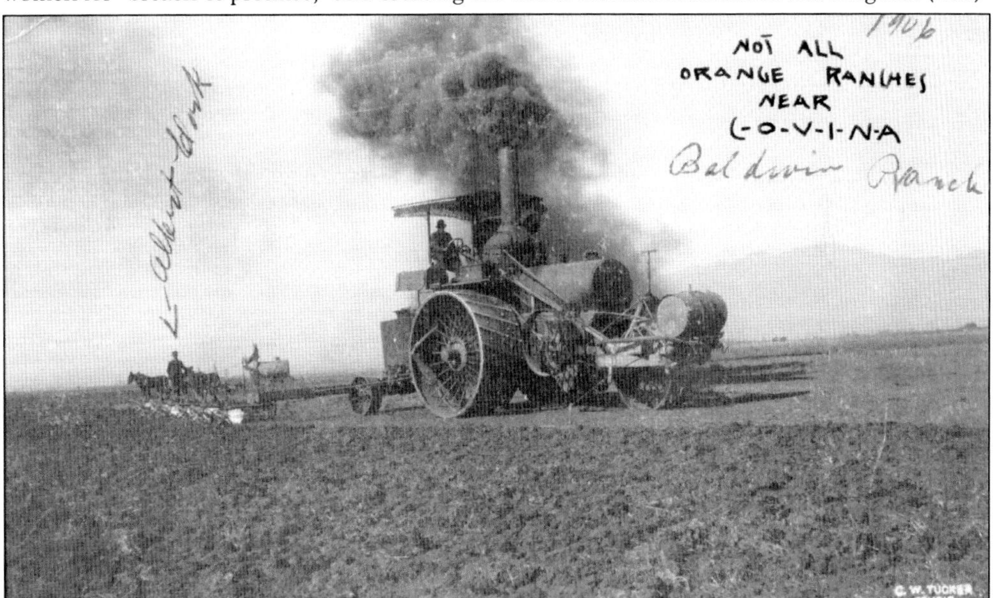

Baldwin made headlines for providing jobs to "people of color" during a time of open discrimination and racism, even paying train fare from North Carolina to California for some 70 black workers. Albert Clark can be seen here working on Baldwin Ranch. His wife, Anita, was tasked with the challenging job of cooking meals for the many workers there. Not long after this photograph was taken, the couple relocated to Lindsay, where Albert worked as a ranch manger. (BC.)

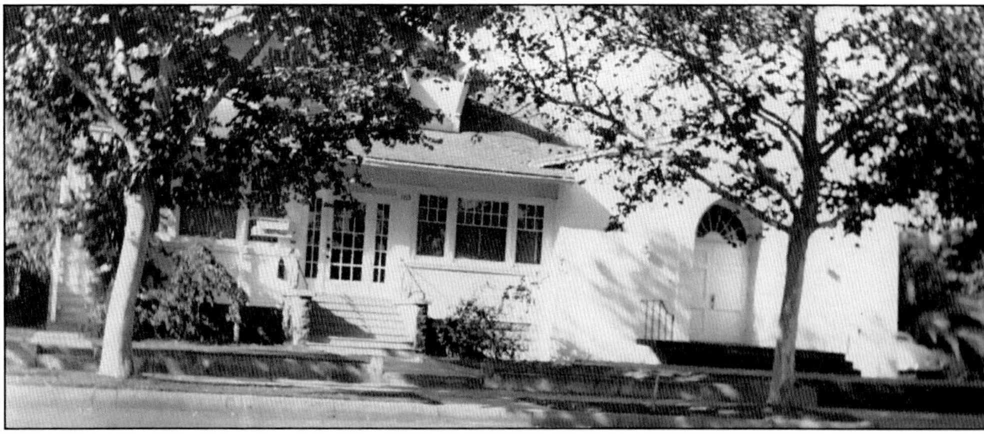

Joshua Milton Hadley was born in Nebraska in 1886. His father, Manley R. Hadley, was a scout and interpreter for famed scout, hunter, and showman William F. Cody, better known as "Buffalo Bill." Joshua Hadley moved to Lindsay, and after residing there for several years, he formed a partnership with a furniture maker and undertaker in Lindsay. This may seem like an odd combination of businesses; however, it was quite common during the pioneering era. Before Word War I, all funerals were held in the home, and families cared for their own loved ones. Since furniture makers possessed the carpentry skills to build coffins, their responsibilities logically expanded to "undertake" the practical tasks for families in mourning. In addition to making the coffin, the undertaker would transport the corpse to the church and then to the cemetery, the mourners following behind in a processional. (LMG.)

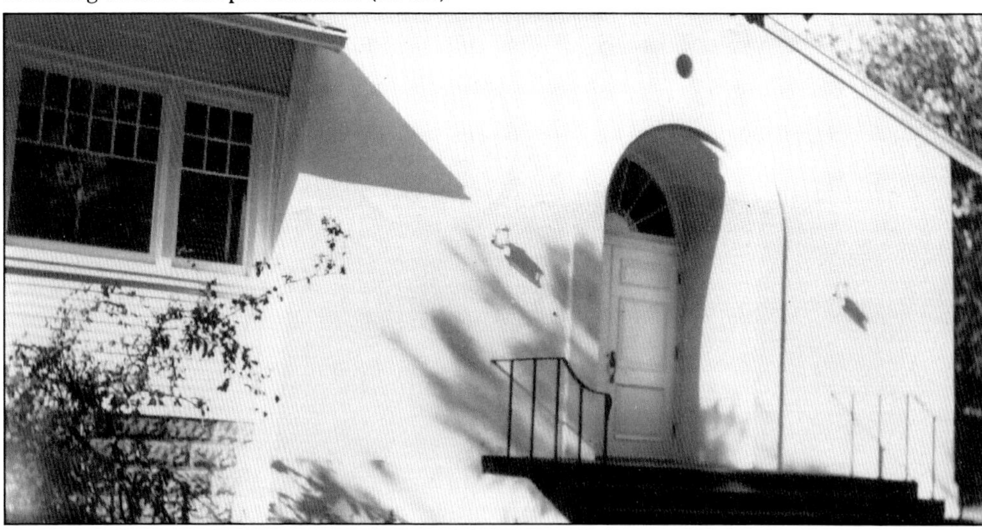

Joshua Hadley rented a hearse from Guy Webb, who worked in a livery, a place where horses and vehicles were kept and rented out. Dr. Annie Bond was also a frequent customer of Webb, as she often rented a horse and buggy to make house calls before acquiring her own. In 1909, Webb married Elizabeth Keeley, a descendant of one of Lindsay's most prominent pioneer families. In 1915, he started working full time as an undertaker with Hadley until 1919, when Hadley was elected as the very first coroner of Tulare County. His new position as county coroner necessitated relocation to Visalia, so Webb took over the business, located in the building pictured here on Mirage Avenue in 1919. To this day, this same building still houses the original business and operates as the Webb-Sanders Funeral Home, which has been serving the families of Lindsay for well over a century now. (LMG.)

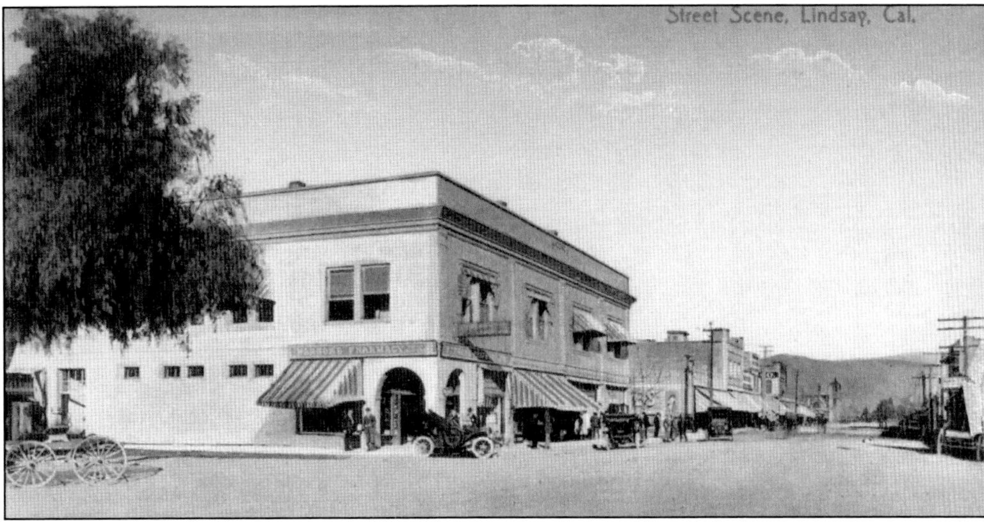

Starr Warson arrived in 1911, purchasing 80 acres of land and the Standard Drug Company. Warson promptly moved his pharmacy into the corner room of the Moore Building. In addition to his pharmacy, Warson was a director of the First National Bank, as well as that of the Lindsay-Strathmore Irrigation District. As such, he served an integral role in the efforts to find outside water sources. (GM.)

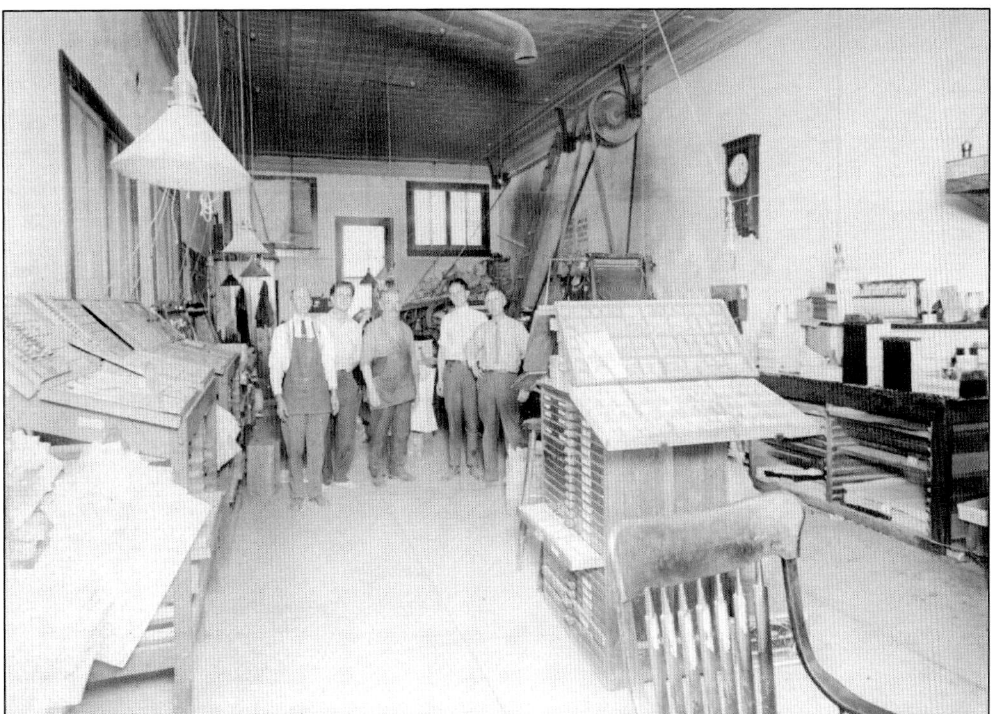
Founded by Henry Dockham in 1901, the *Lindsay Gazette* was the pioneer newspaper for the town. Dockham eventually sold it to Aaron Lloyd Evans from Wisconsin in 1907. Evans also purchased a permanent office from which he would run the paper. This 1913 photograph was taken inside the *Gazette* offices. These early newspapermen are, from left to right, Myron Hallack, Lloyd Knight, William "Billy" Roach, Ford Chatters, and Evans. (LMG.)

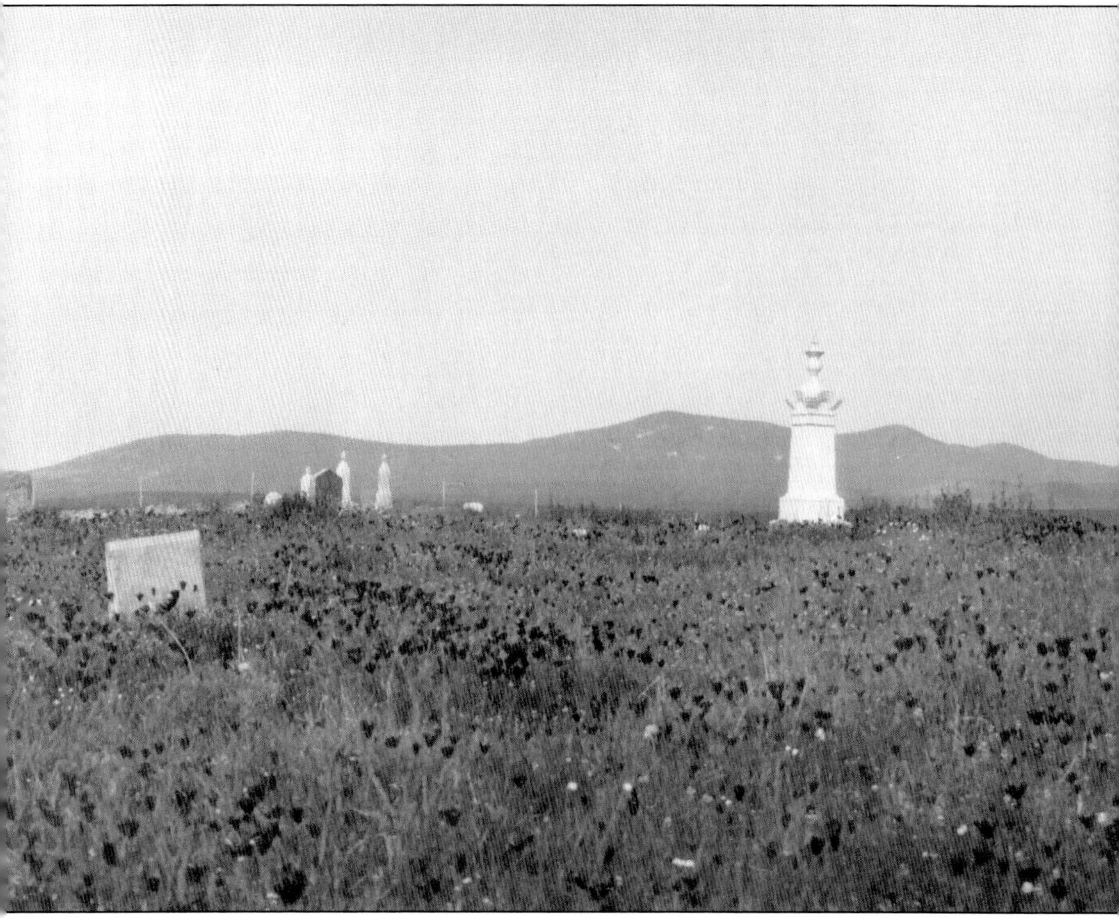

Frazier Valley Cemetery was the first community burial ground in the area. Now it is part of the Lindsay-Strathmore Cemetery District. Prompted by a devastating diphtheria epidemic that caused countless deaths in the area during the late 1870s and 1880s, James Kincaid donated land for a cemetery in 1881. When no one in the surrounding area would step forward to take responsibility for the cemetery, Kincaid's daughter took on the tasks of record keeping, grounds

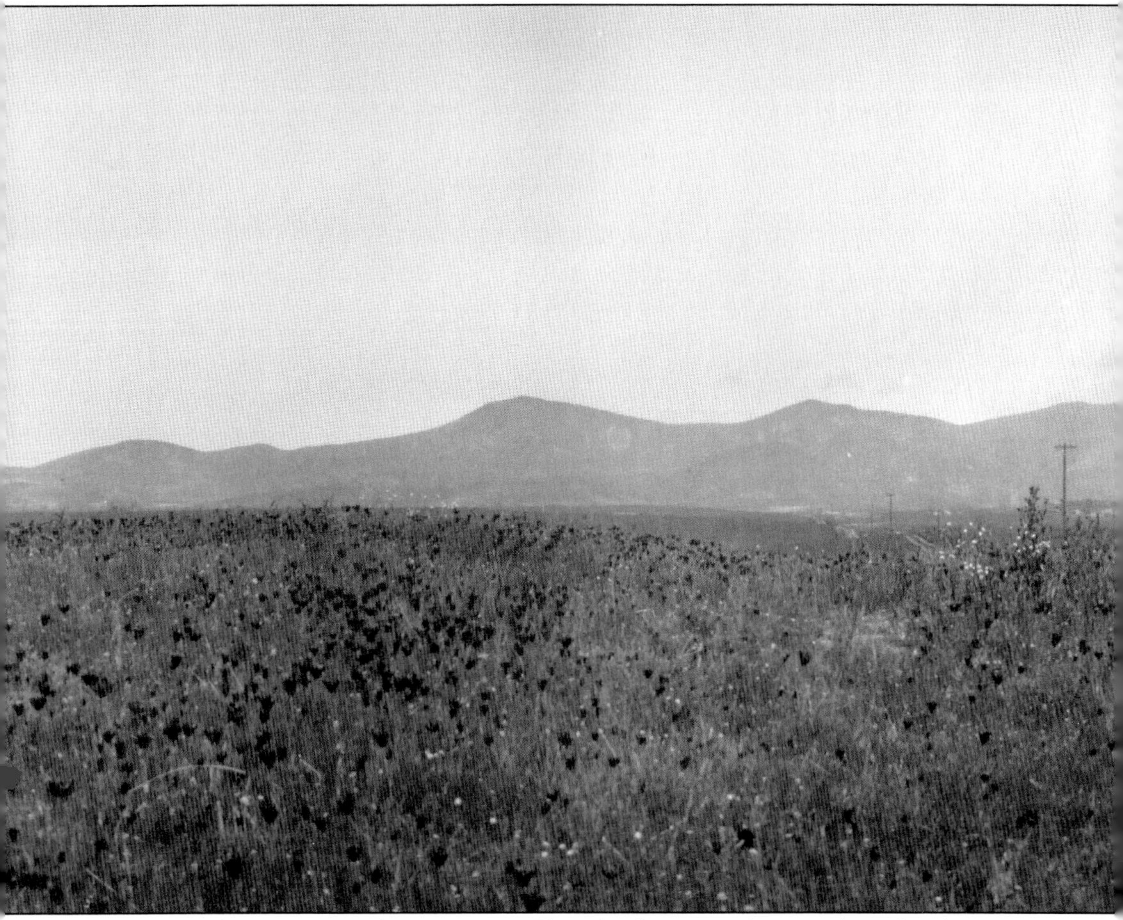

keeping, and even digging graves when necessary. The role of women taking on the tasks of caring for and burying the deceased victims of the diphtheria epidemic was not uncommon. Although established much later in 1910, the Lindsay-Strathmore or "Olive" Cemetery became the central cemetery. One account states that the cemetery was notable, as income was derived from cotton and oranges grown on the land while in use. (LMG.)

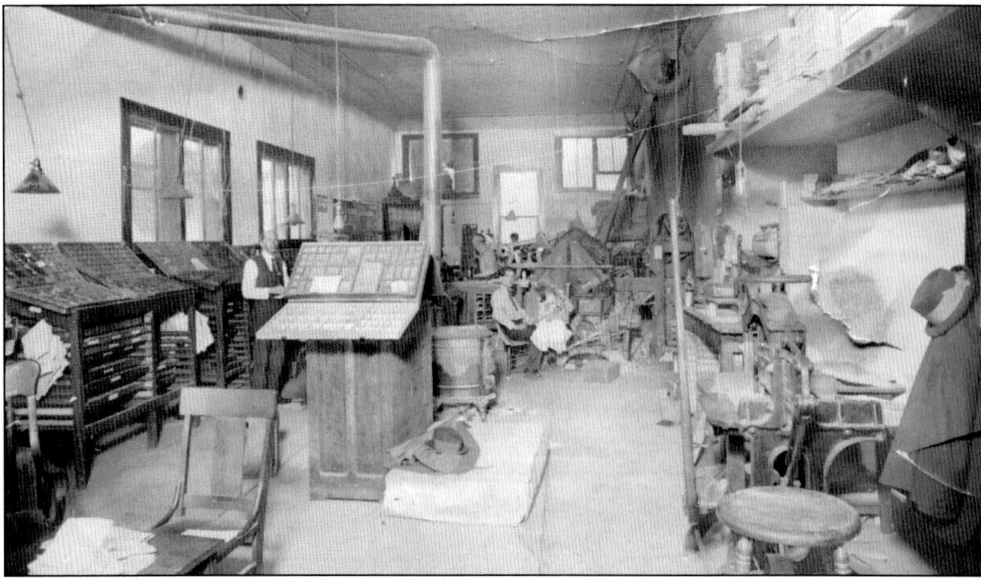

In 1914, Ford Chatters joined his uncle Myron Hallack at the *Lindsay Gazette* as a reporter and learned to work in the print shop, seen here. After serving in the Army during Word War I, he returned to Lindsay and launched into a lifetime of community service, even serving as a member of the California State Assembly. Chatters took over the paper in 1952. (LMG.)

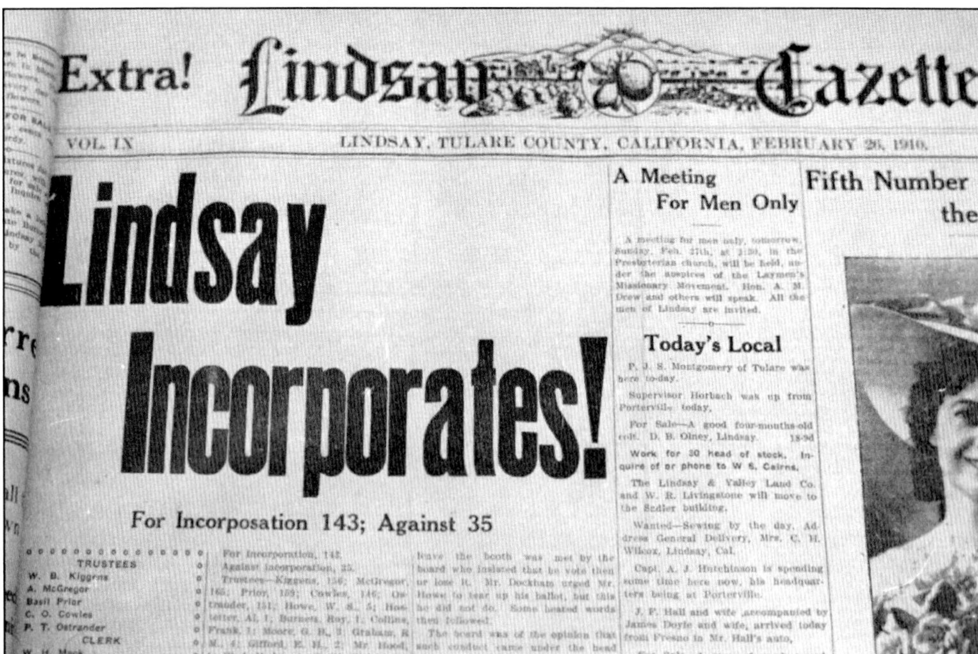

Extra! Lindsay Gazette

VOL. IX LINDSAY, TULARE COUNTY, CALIFORNIA, FEBRUARY 26, 1910.

Lindsay Incorporates!

For Incorposation 143; Against 35

TRUSTEES
W. B. Kiggens
A. McGregor
Basil Prior
C. O. Cowles
P. T. Ostrander
CLERK
W. H. Mack

For Incorporation, 143.
Against incorporation, 35.
Trustees—Kiggens, 156; McGregor, 165; Prior, 159; Cowles, 146; Ostrander, 151; Howe, W. S., 5; Hostetter, Al, 1; Burnett, Roy, 1; Collins, Frank, 1; Moore, G. B., 3; Graham, R. M., 4; Gifford, E. H., 2; Mr. Hood, 1; W. I. Hodge, 1; C. W. Wright, 1;

leave the booth was met by the board who insisted that he vote then or lose it. Mr. Dockham urged Mr. Howe to tear up his ballot, but this he did not do. Some heated words then followed.

The board was of the opinion that such conduct came under the head trying to advise a voter.

A Meeting For Men Only

A meeting for men only, tomorrow, Sunday, Feb. 27th, at 2:30, in the Presbyterian church, will be held, under the auspices of the Laymen's Missionary Movement. Hon. A. M. Drew and others will speak. All the men of Lindsay are invited.

Today's Local

P. J. S. Montgomery of Tulare was here to-day.

Supervisor Horbach was up from Porterville today.

For Sale—A good four-mouths-old colt. D. B. Olney, Lindsay. 18-9d

Work for 30 head of stock. Inquire of or phone to W S. Cairns.

The Lindsay & Valley Land Co. and W. R. Livingstone will move to the Sedler building.

Wanted—Sewing by the day. Address General Delivery, Mrs. C. H. Wilcox, Lindsay, Cal.

Capt. A. J. Hutchinson is spending some time here now, his headquarters being at Porterville.

J. F. Hall and wife, accompanied by James Doyle and wife, arrived today from Fresno in Mr. Hall's auto.

For Sale—A span of good, sound,

Fifth Number of the

"Lindsay Incorporates!" declares the *Lindsay Gazette* on February 26, 1910. Spearheaded by Earnest L. Daniells, the effort to incorporate Lindsay had begun in 1908. Over the next couple of years, many committees were formed and reformed amid disputes regarding boundaries, as well as opposition from George Stockton Berry. On February 26, 1910, an election was held with enough votes in favor of incorporation, and on February 28, Lindsay was officially named as "a city of the 6th class." (CSUF.)

Two

Lindsay's Gold Rush

The citrus rush was likely the direct result of a publicity campaign in the late 19th century, when the slogan "Oranges For Health, California For Wealth" was created. Following the Gold Rush, people were ready for another kind of "gold," and California's year-round golden sun as well as her golden fruits beckoned many a pioneer. Elaborate advertisement campaigns were launched in publications and newspapers all over the United States, depicting California as a place of unparalleled beauty and prosperity where anyone could come and "get rich." The Southern Pacific Railroad held a campaign to colonize California by offering a special one-way fare and promising "the Greatest Opportunity Ever Offered." Hundreds of thousands of people came to California seeking a better life for themselves and their families. The vast majority of those looking to make their fortune in the citrus trade in Central California came to Lindsay, the heart of the valley's gold rush. Lindsay attracted prestigious businesspeople like King C. Gillette and young, inexperienced immigrants alike. It was not long before California citrus growers began organizing themselves into cooperatives with the goal of increasing profits by pooling their risk and increasing their collective bargaining power. In 1905, the Lindsay Citrus Association was established with prominent pioneers Fred Hostetter and Basil Prior at the helm. In 1919, the California Fruit Growers Exchange was established as the main organization for all growers in California. Lindsay's R.C. Merryman of the Merryman Fruit Exchange represented Lindsay on their board of directors. This entity would later become Sunkist Growers, known the world over.

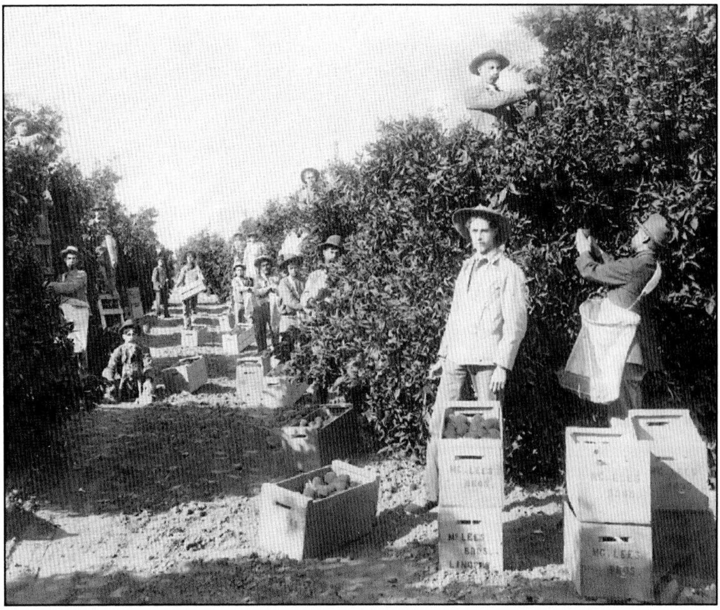

In this beautifully composed promotional photograph, workers pick oranges from the McLees' orchard, located in the western part of Lindsay, in 1905. Among Lindsay's 16 packinghouses, McLees Bros. was one of the earliest. (CSUF.)

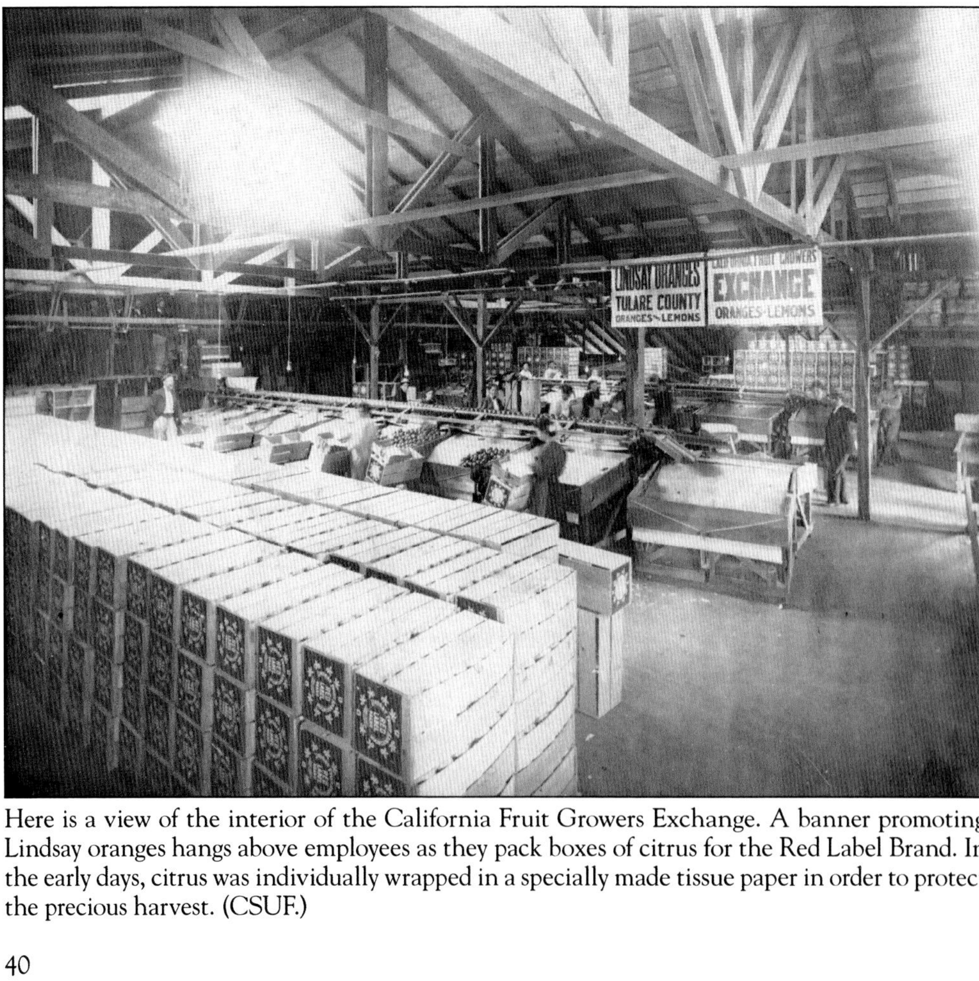

Here is a view of the interior of the California Fruit Growers Exchange. A banner promoting Lindsay oranges hangs above employees as they pack boxes of citrus for the Red Label Brand. In the early days, citrus was individually wrapped in a specially made tissue paper in order to protect the precious harvest. (CSUF.)

William Hutchinson is captured here near one of the orange tress his mother had planted. William and his siblings often played with their cousin, who would grow up to become Gen. George Patton, when he visited Lindsay. The Hutchinson children were merry pranksters who would push Patton off his bicycle. One family member mused that this is how Patton became such a competent horseman. (LMG.)

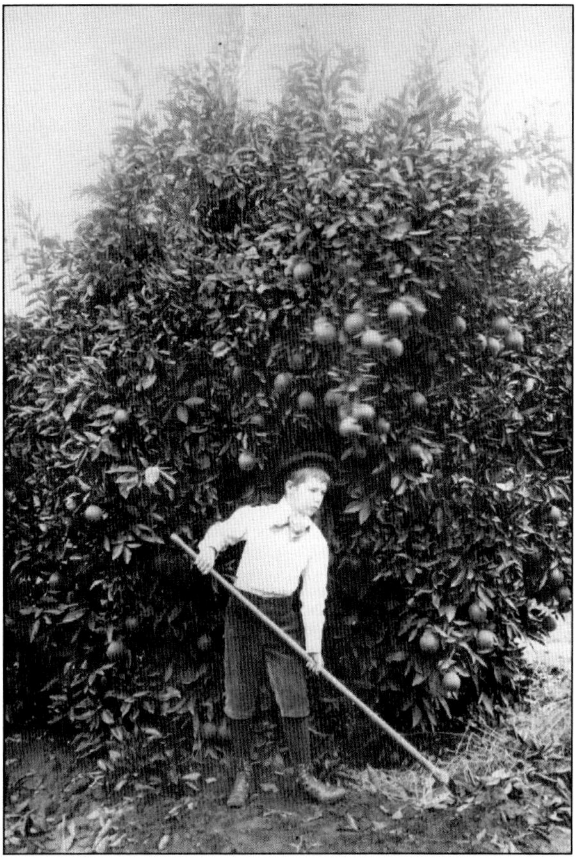

Postcards like these were often produced as a marketing tool for real estate businesses around the country. This particular card emphasizes the profitability of the land by proclaiming, "Famous 8 ½ acre 14-year-old Valencia grove; C.O. Cowles owner 108 crop paid $11,664 net to owner." Cowles sold his oranges to the Hillside Packing Company. (CSUF.)

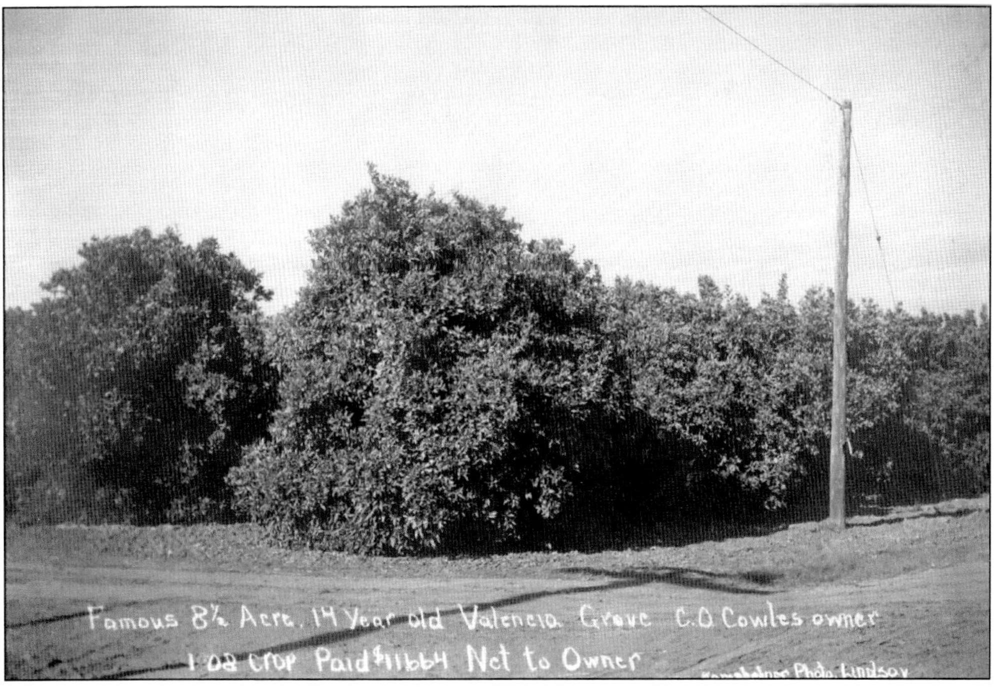

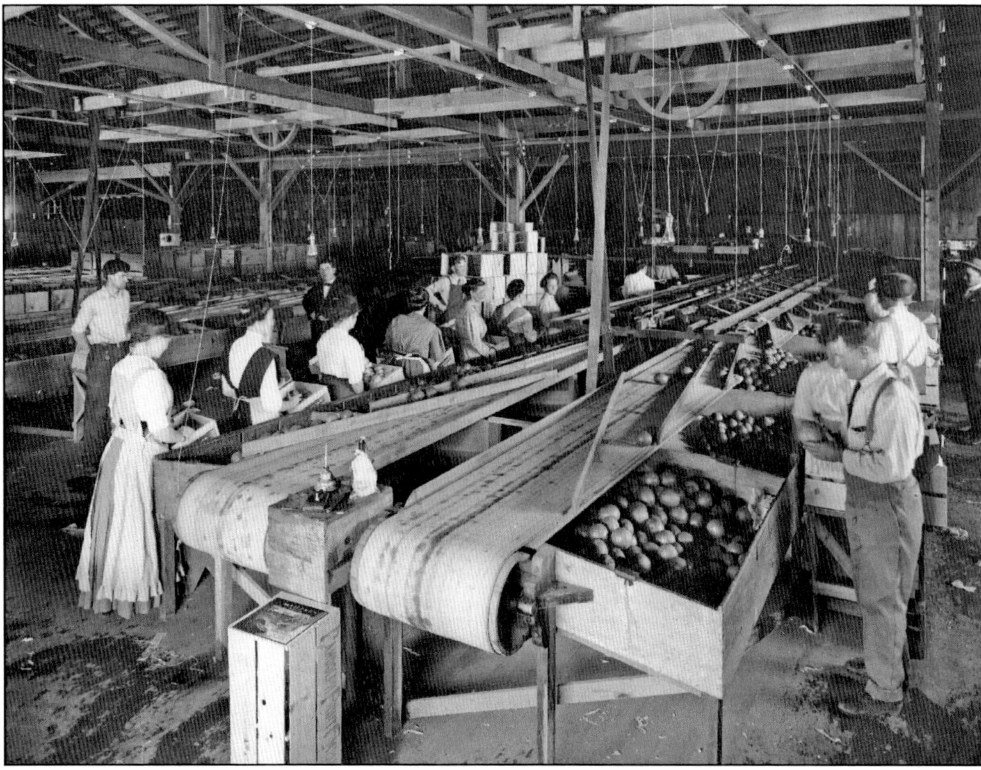

The packing area of the Randolph Fruit Company is pictured here in 1910. Packinghouse managers and possibly proprietors stand to the left, overlooking the work of the packers. A caption written on the back of the photograph reads as follows: "The mechanical sizer or grader is in the middle background. The bins of sized fruit show alongside which the packers pick out an orange, wrap it in tissue and place in a wood box which held twice as much as the modern carton." (CSUF.)

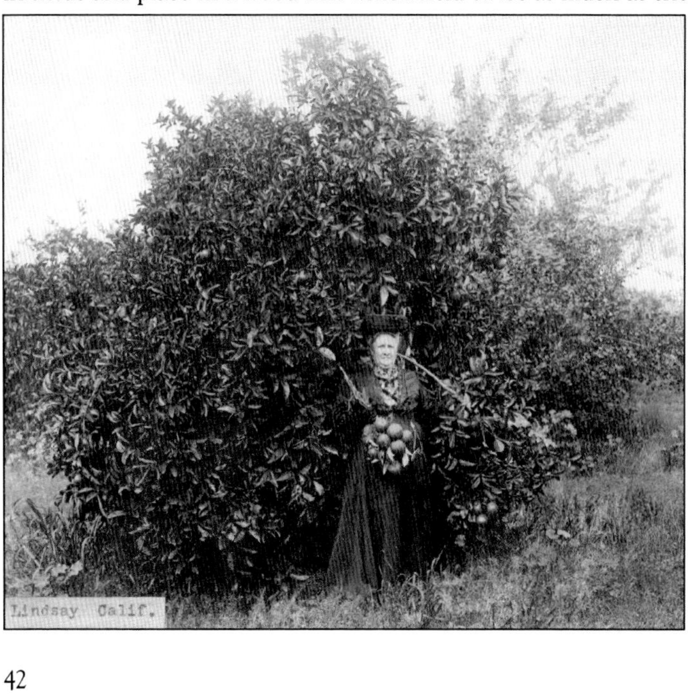

A Mrs. Platte, who owned a packinghouse, shows off some oranges from her grove. Her all-black attire indicates that she was in mourning. Throughout the Victorian era and up until World War II, it was customary for family members with a deceased relative to adopt a strict set of mourning customs that dictated behavior and clothing. (CSUF.)

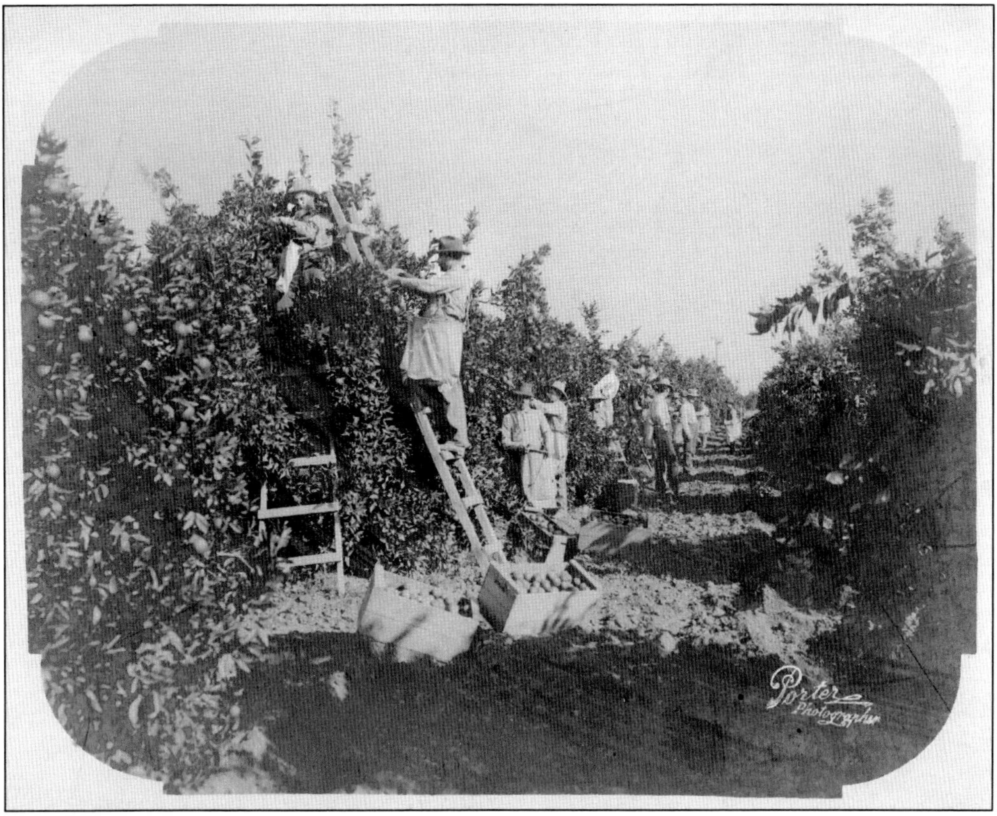

These workers are picking oranges on Basil and Dorthea Prior's Palmer Ranch in the late 1800s, when the district was just venturing into citrus farming. Those utilizing ladders would wear shoulder bags to carry the oranges. (CSUF.)

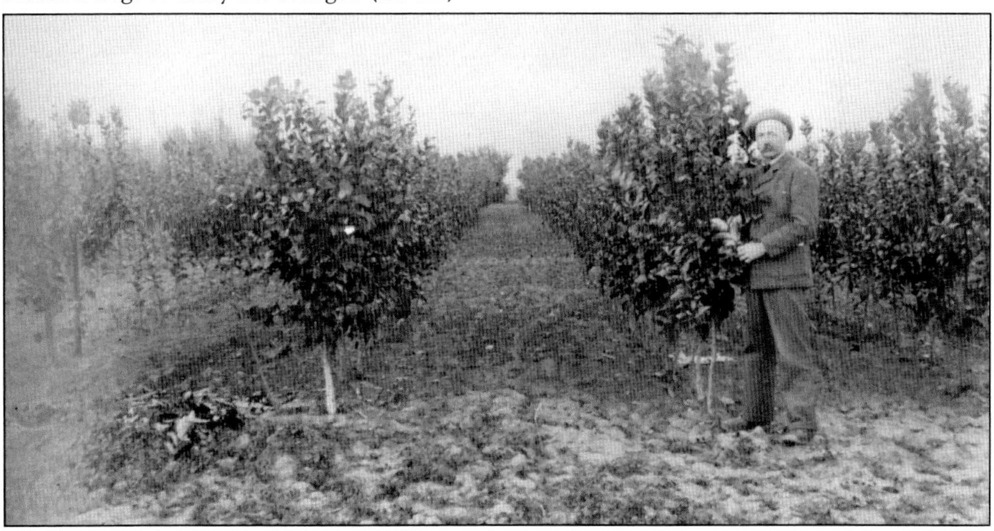

Here, a one-year-old lemon nursery flourishes in Lindsay in March 1895. A dapper gentleman proudly poses with the many lemons he has grown in his orchard. Central Valley farmers were very proud of their hard work and success and often created postcards like this to send to friends and family back home. (CSUF.)

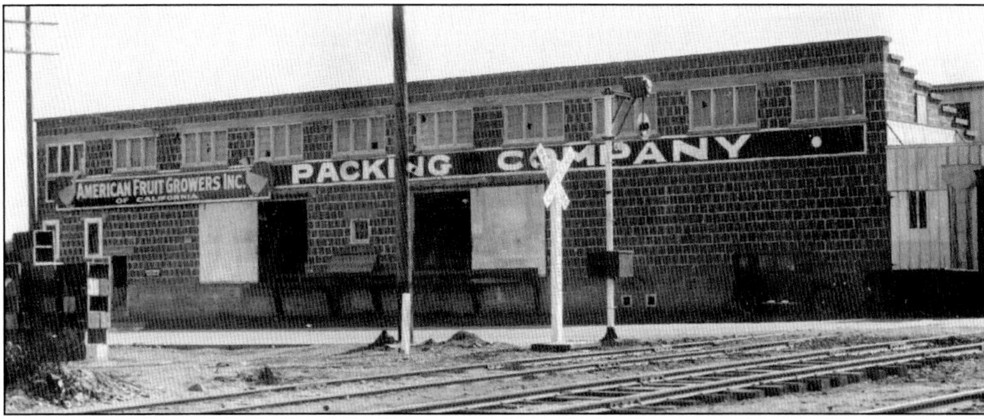

The American Fruit Growers Packing Company sits alongside a railroad crossing. By 1916, Lindsay had established an incredible 16 citrus packinghouses, more than any other place in the United States. (CSUF.)

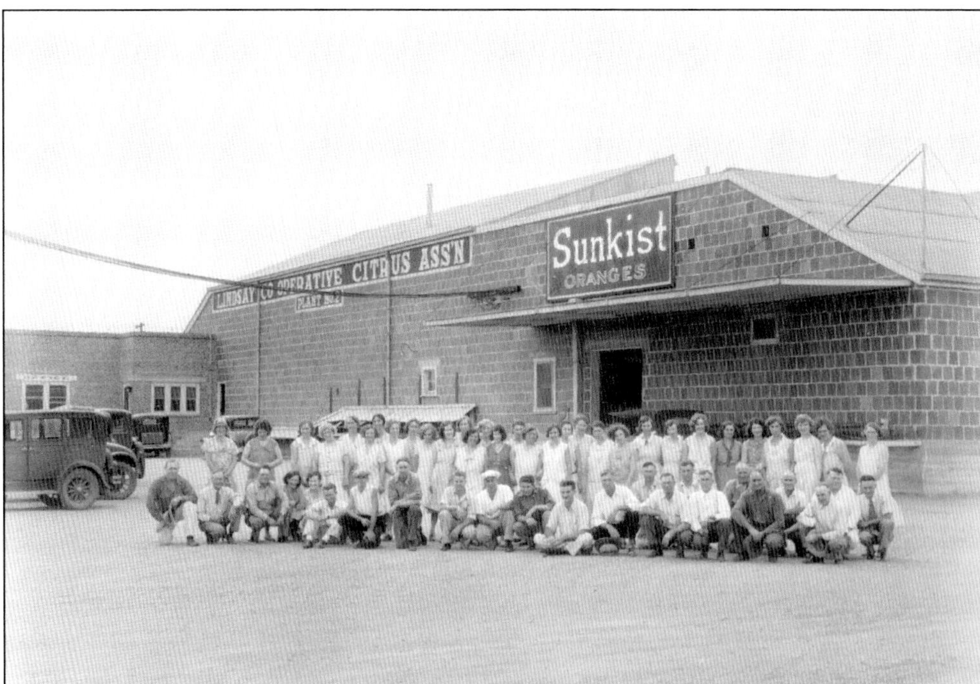

Employees of the Lindsay Cooperative Citrus Association are photographed in front of the packinghouse around 1920. Prior to the advent of Lindsay's olive industry, the citrus packinghouses employed the vast majority of the town. (CSUF.)

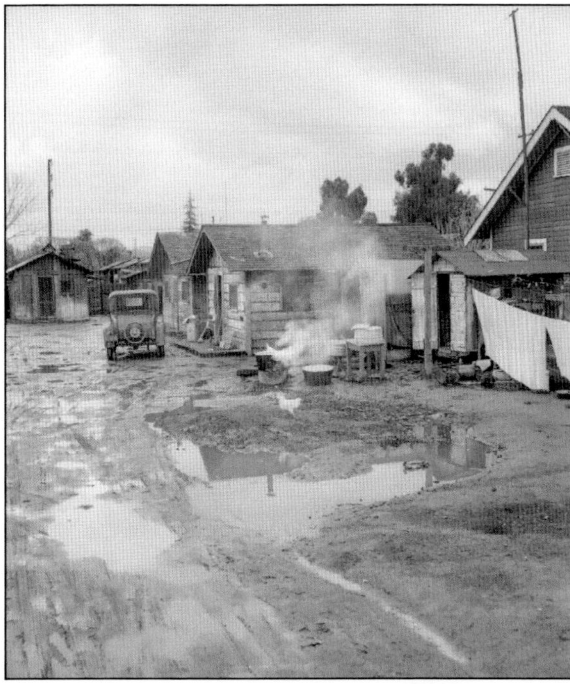

When Frederick Mills arrived in Lindsay to investigate working conditions, he was hard-pressed to find lodging, as the town was so full of people. He spent the first few nights sleeping outside on the ground or in a dirty train boxcar. Many migrant workers, which often included entire families, were provided with poor temporary housing in camps like this one. (GM.)

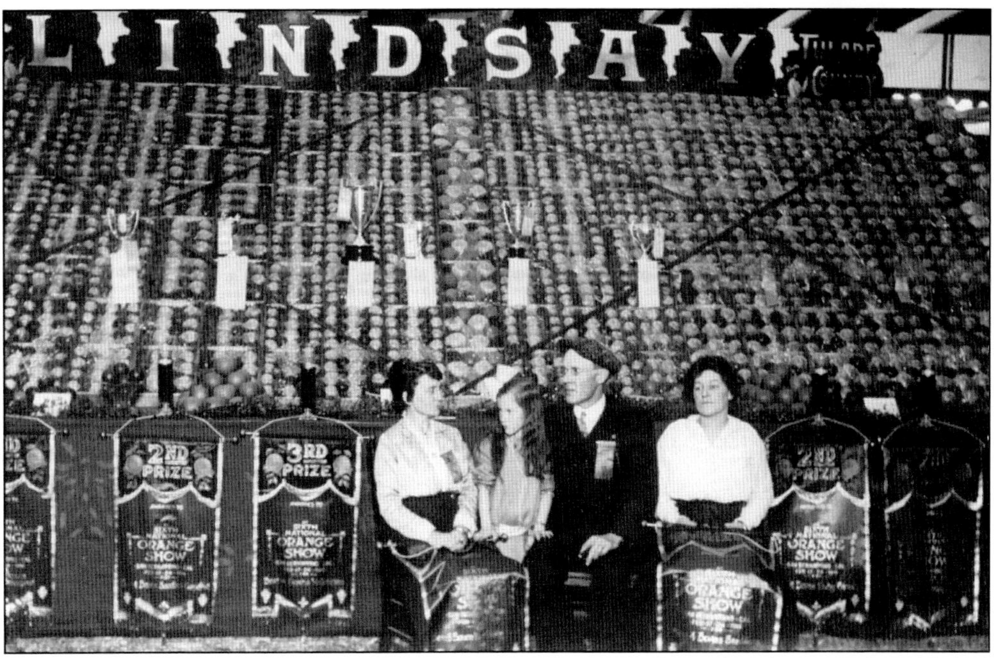

T.E. Anderson was one of Lindsay's early citrus men who opened a packinghouse and established the TEA Fancy label. The entire Anderson family worked in some aspect of the business, including traveling to promote the Lindsay citrus industry at citrus fairs and agriculture shows. They obtained immediate recognition for their elaborate displays created entirely out of citrus, dominating every category of awards wherever they went. Thanks in part to the Andersons, Lindsay has continued to become a powerhouse among citrus growers to this day. Pictured from left to right are unidentified, Pearl Anderson, T.E., and unidentified. (LMG.)

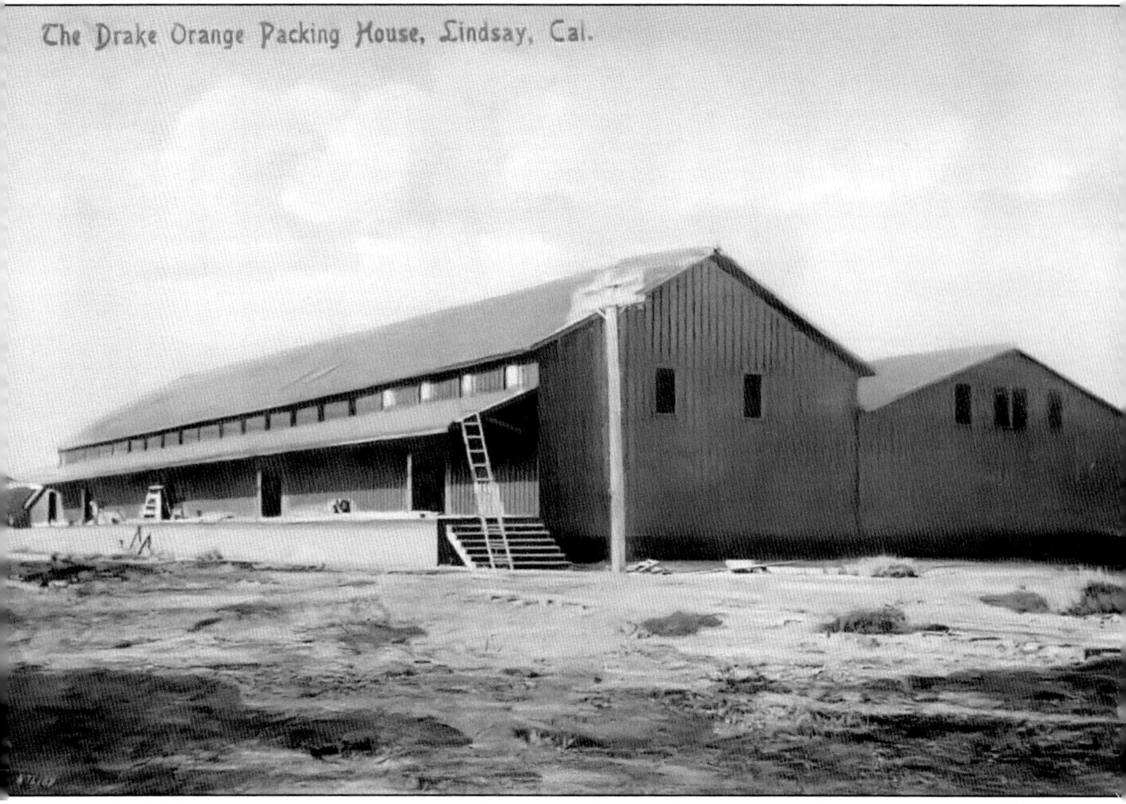

In 1914, an undercover investigator for the California Commission of Immigration and Housing was sent to Lindsay to investigate working conditions following the Wheatland Hops Riots over inhumane treatment of agriculture workers. In addition to this, ranch owners had a habit of publishing ads to lure workers to the area, promising "jobs for everyone." Entire families would spend their last pennies only to arrive and discover they had been misled. Investigator Frederick Mills worked for five days at Drake Citrus Association as a rustler. Here, the workday was 7:00 a.m. to 10:00 p.m., with a workforce comprised mostly of women. Mills found the demands of the work almost unbearable and mused in his report, "Does the organization of modern industry demand the development of a class of female workers who are worn out, ready for the scrap heap at thirty?" (GM.)

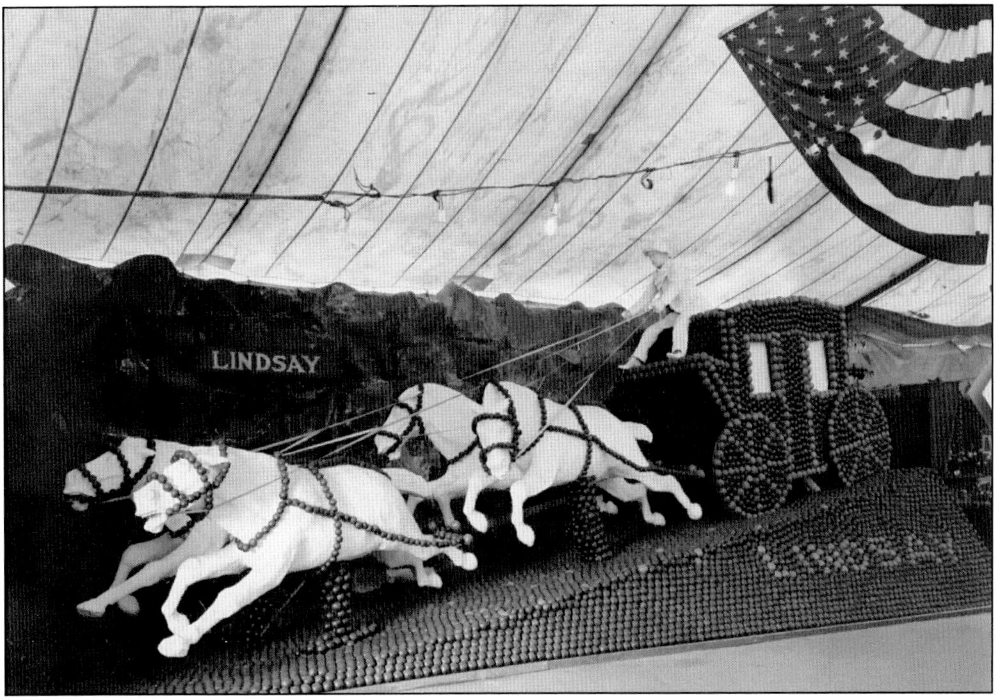

One of Anderson's more elaborate displays features this depiction of the Butterfield Stage Coach passing through Lindsay—a clever way to combine the town's history and industry at once. (PN.)

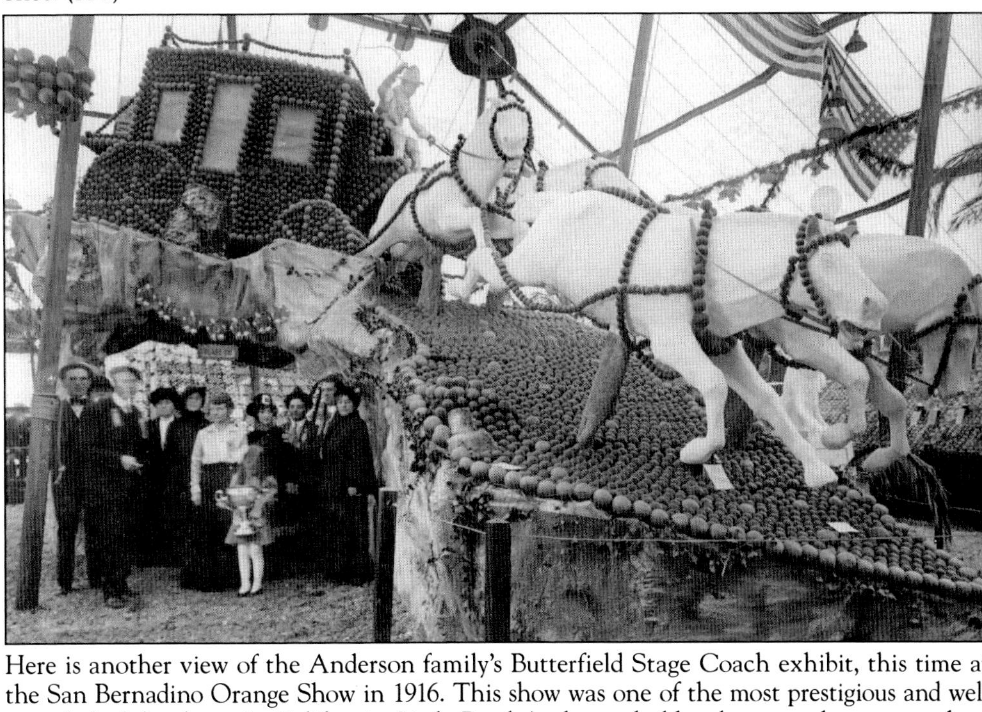

Here is another view of the Anderson family's Butterfield Stage Coach exhibit, this time at the San Bernadino Orange Show in 1916. This show was one of the most prestigious and well attended of the shows in California. Little Pearl Anderson holds a large trophy cup as others stand around her. (PN.)

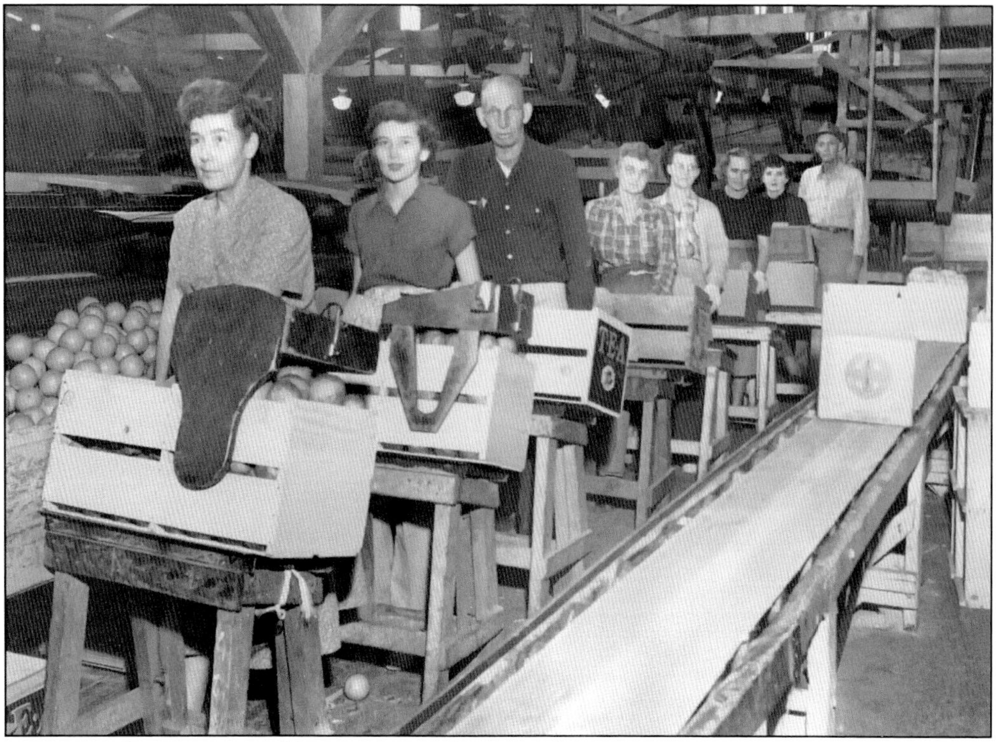

Orange packers are pictured here at the Anderson Packing Company, one of the longest-running packinghouses in town. Unfortunately, not long after this photograph was taken, the packinghouse was completely destroyed by a fire in 1932, costing $100,000 in damage. It had been the second fire in six weeks. (CSUF.)

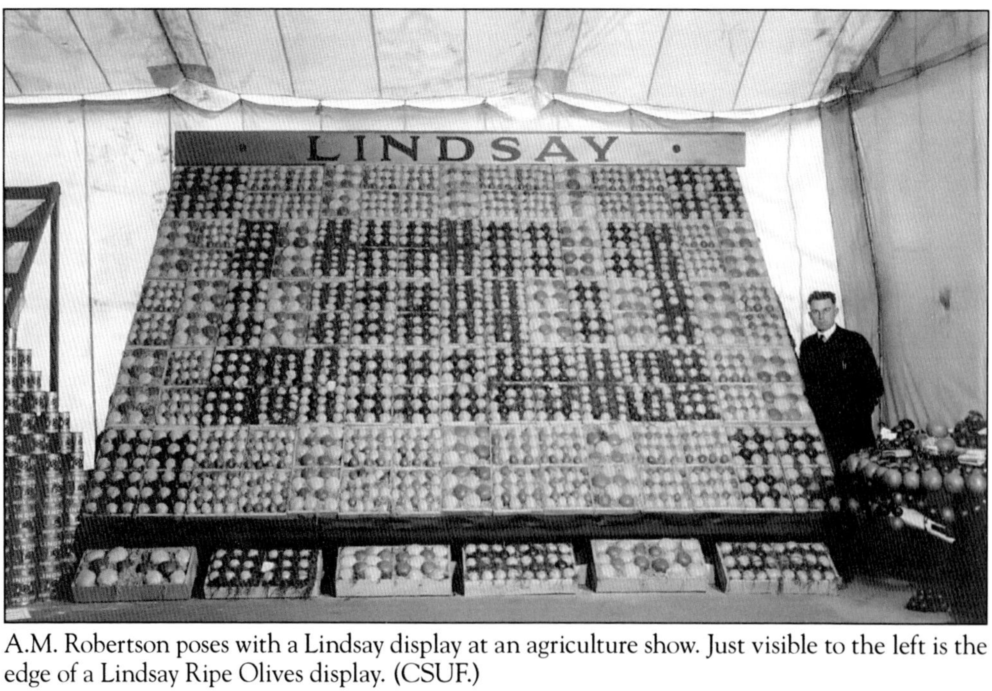

A.M. Robertson poses with a Lindsay display at an agriculture show. Just visible to the left is the edge of a Lindsay Ripe Olives display. (CSUF.)

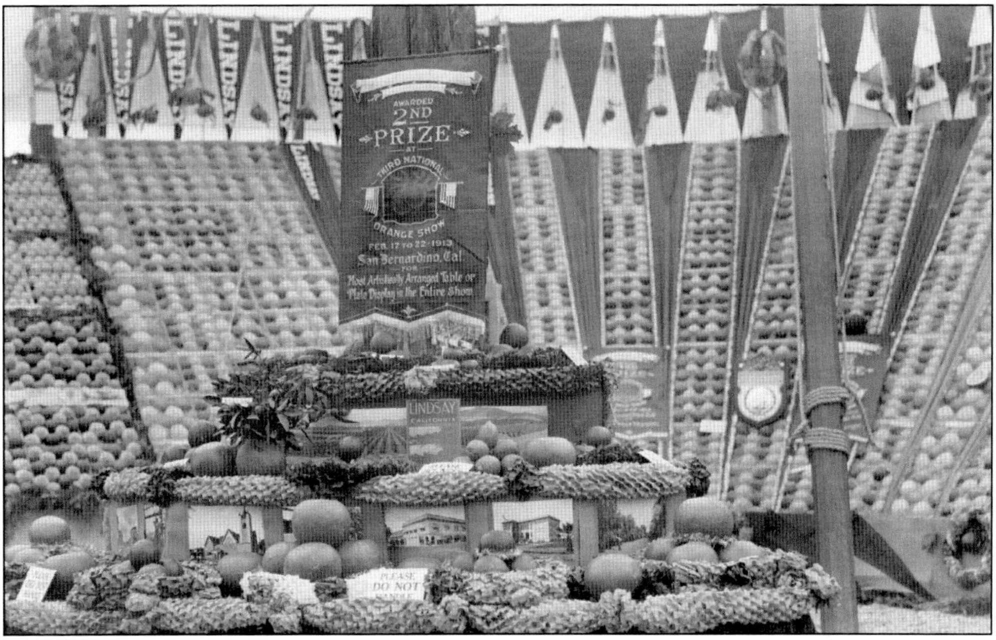

Another elaborate citrus display of the Lindsay district was created for the San Bernadino National Orange Show in 1913. Photographs of various Lindsay buildings and citrus orchards are also incorporated into the display. (CSUF.)

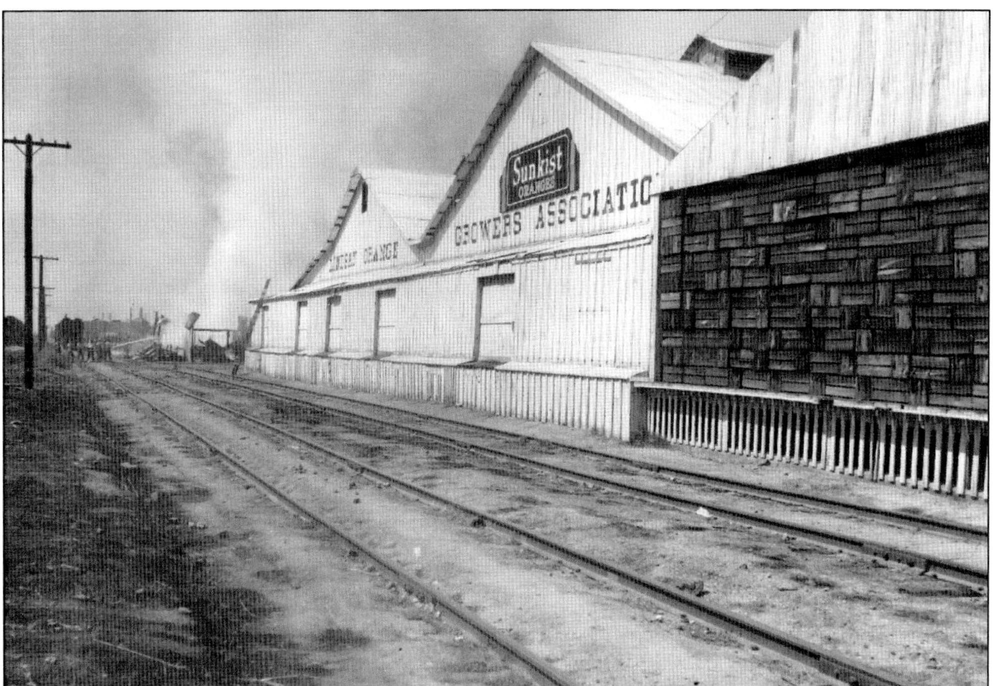

As seen here, the rear of the Sunkist Oranges Growers Association packinghouse is conveniently situated along the train tracks, as were most of the citrus packinghouses. (LMG.)

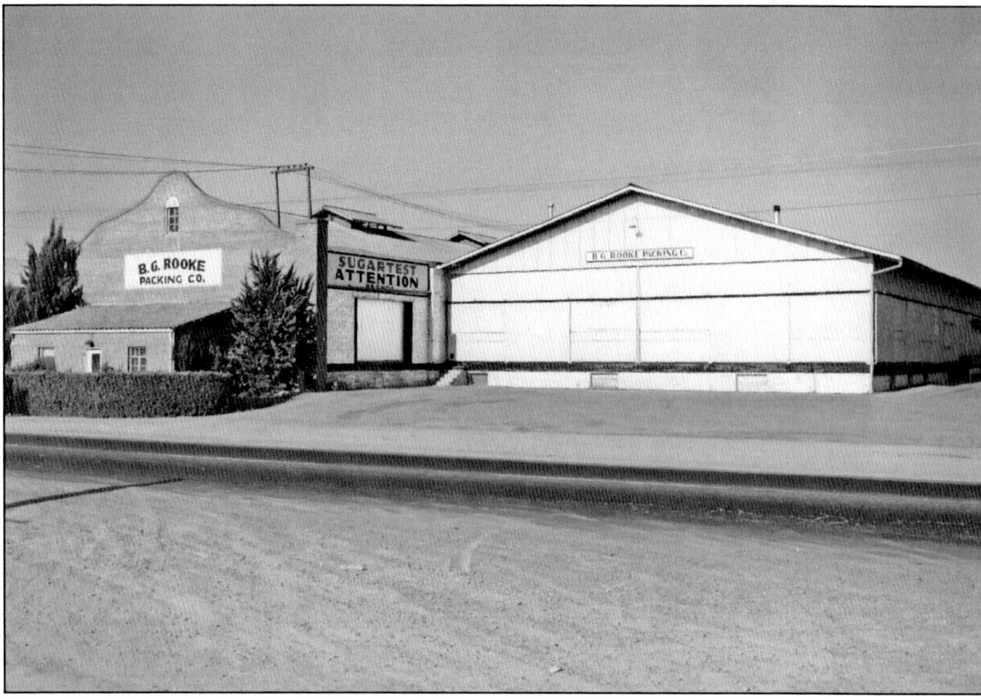

Prior to opening his own packinghouse, B.G. Rooke managed the Hillside Packinghouse in Lindsay. In the early 1900s, he made news in several citrus business publications, as well as local headlines, for driving 500 miles in 37 hours to attend a Mutual Orange Distributors meeting. (CSUF.)

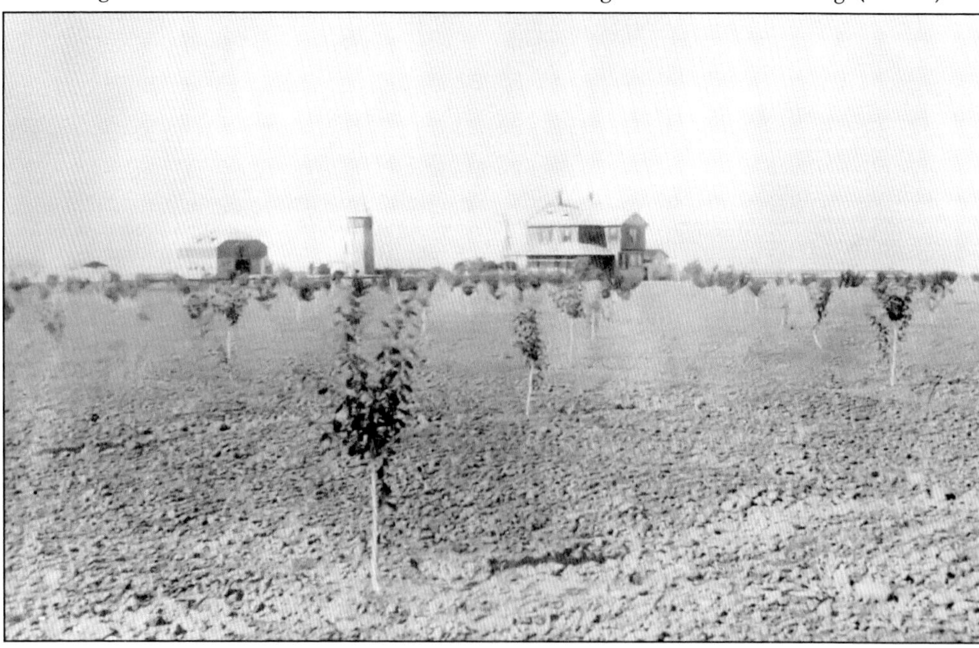

Surrounding the residence of founding family the Hutchinsons are the many acres of newly planted citrus trees, the first of which were planted by Sadie Hutchinson. It is said that she had quite a way with growing things, and she put a great deal of time and care into these first plantings that helped make the Lindsay district the heart of the citrus rush. (CSUF.)

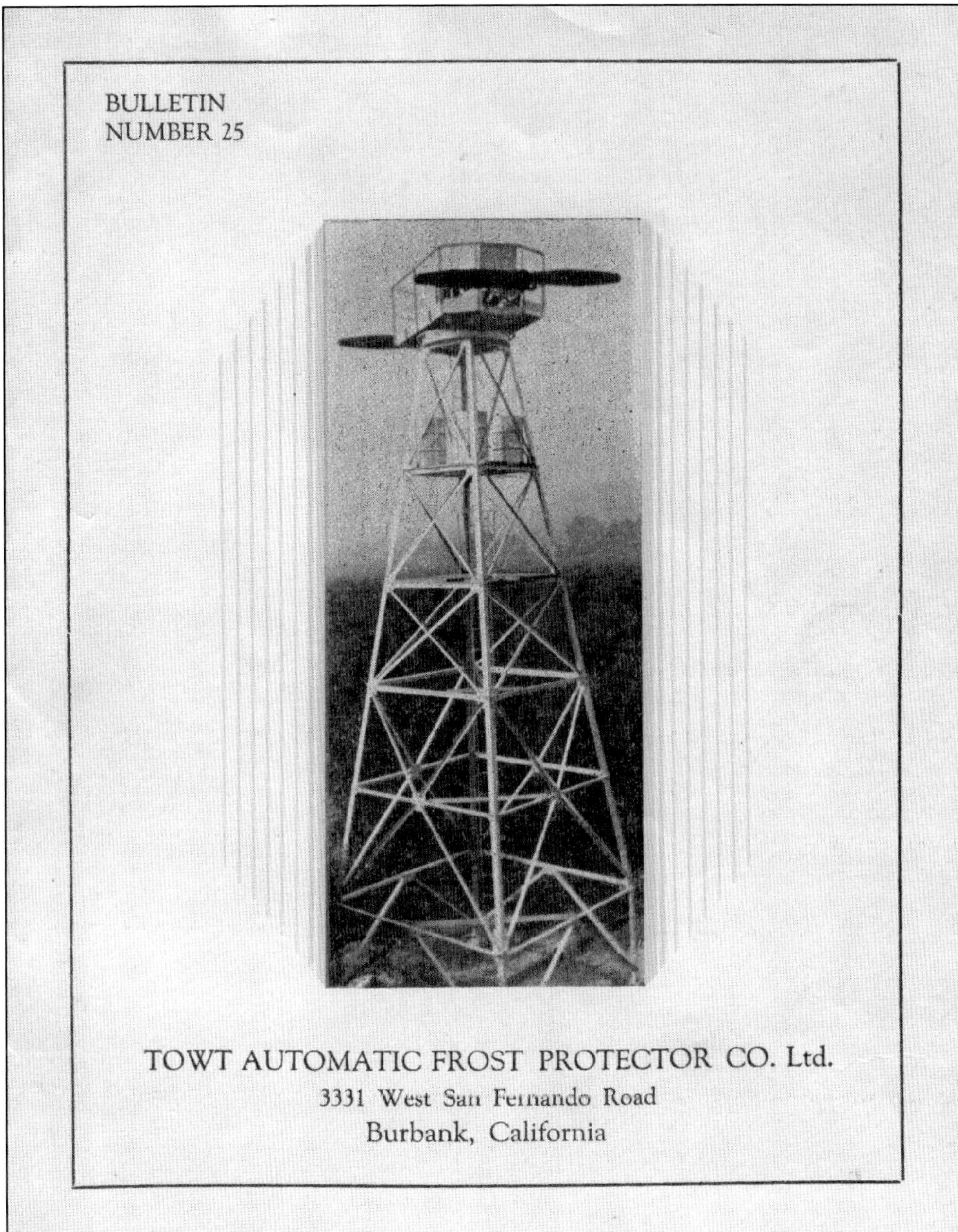

Charles Towt built the first wind machine in 1919 to protect his orange crops from freezing. In the winter of 1921–1922, a severe freeze occurred in which many growers lost most of their crops, while Towt was able to ship nearly 80 percent of his. A.W. "Doob" Jessup, a member of a prominent Lindsay family, describes what it was like to see the machine in action: "It was a monster of wood and metal nearly twenty-five feet tall. It had a large 'firebox,' in which a huge fire was built. Behind it was a large fan and when in operation, it spewed hot air and sparks out of the 'snout' and over the orchard. A magnificent sight, and one we all looked forward to seeing on frosty nights." King Gillette put $100,000 toward its development. The machines were manufactured by Kermit Nutt and Wesley Kirby. (LMG.)

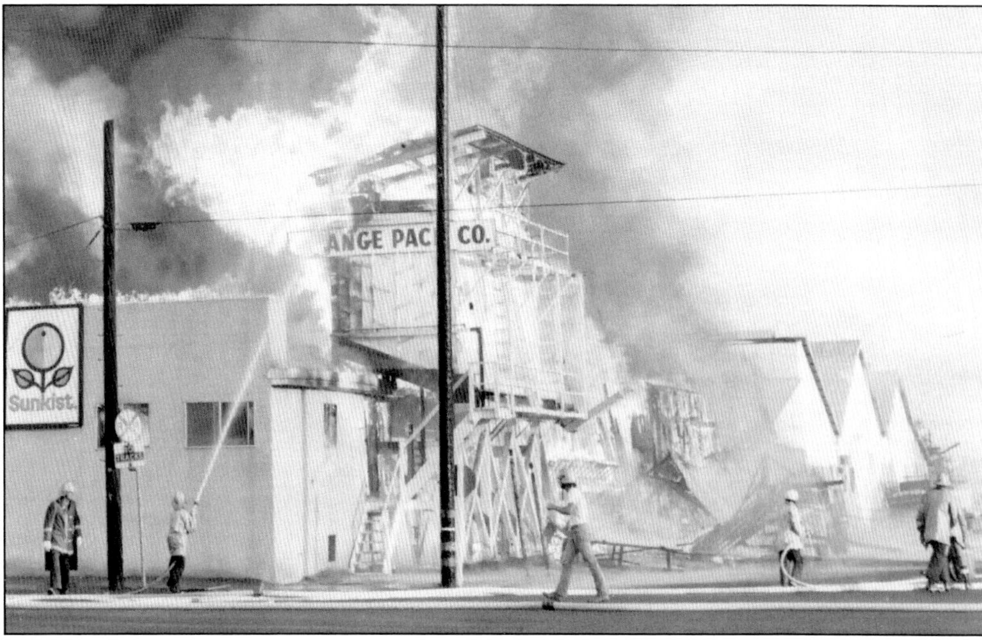

The Orange Packing Company was established in 1926 as part of the citrus powerhouse Lindsay Merryman Exchange. At its onset, the business was formed with W.S. Cairns as manager, Bart Singleterry as head of operations and hiring, and H.J. Ferry as bookkeeper, then changed hands several times until it was taken over by the Cairns sisters before ultimately changing hands again. In 1973, an electrical short in a switchboard caused this devastating fire. (CSUF.)

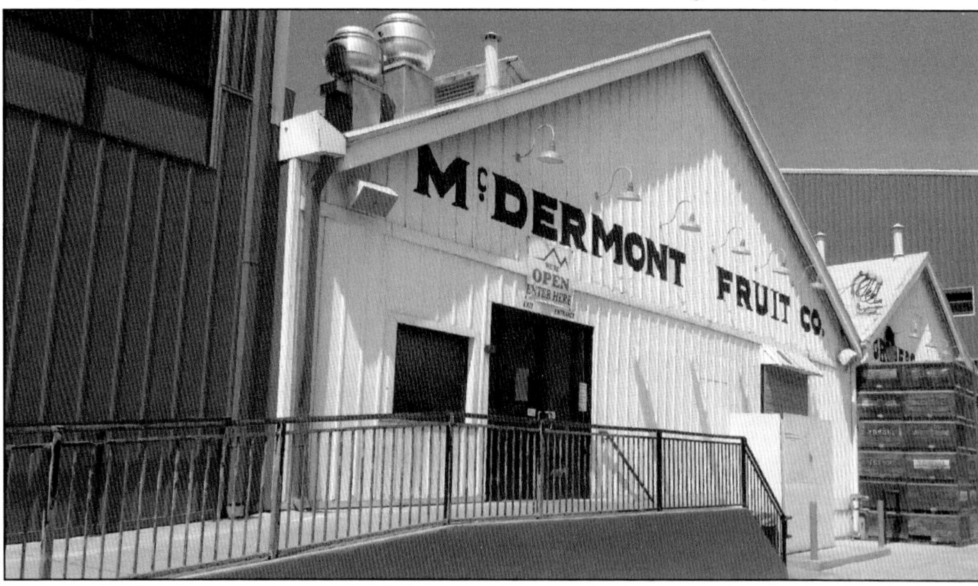

In 1955, the Cairns sisters sold one of their properties to Merwyn Arthur McDermont, a citrus man from Southern California whose grandfather had established the McDermont Fruit Company in Riverside. The facility stood empty throughout the 1990s, until the city purchased it in 2005 and created the McDermont Field House. This state-of-the-art sports and entertainment facility features a rock climbing wall, a FlowRider surf machine, an indoor skate park, basketball courts, and laser tag, among other attractions. (Photograph by DeLea Davis.)

Three

A Nice Town, A Great Olive

It is believed that Franciscan missionaries first brought olives to the state of California; however, the preservation of the fruit and the complicated process of canning is attributed to Freda Ehmann, who is considered "the Mother of the California Olive Industry." In 1895, Ehmann, widowed and penniless, was determined to make a living from her only asset: an olive orchard at her residence in Oroville, California. After much trial and error, Ehmann invented a process to cure ripe black olives and effectively preserve them in cans. A number of farmers in Lindsay and the surrounding area quickly adapted her process. By 1916, there were so many olive growers seeking a way to market their olives that they decided to come together to establish the Lindsay Ripe Olive Company, a processing and marketing initiative. The company's success was so great that it expanded extensively throughout the 1920s, becoming the largest olive packinghouse in the world. As with many long-standing businesses, Lindsay Ripe was not without its struggles and controversies over the years. The first bout of controversy began during the Depression era when it was discovered that manager W.O. Johnson had been taking more than his fair share of the profits. This conflict ended with a lawsuit resulting in favor of the packinghouse. Decades later, in the 1970s, controversy over field laborers' working conditions emerged, a fire destroyed part of the packinghouse, and a contract dispute resulted in a labor strike at the olive plant—the first and only in its history. The final blow came at the end of the company's reign as the olive industry's powerhouse, leaving Lindsay with a $30 million environmental cleanup bill. The company was sold in 1992, but the Lindsay name continues to be associated with the world's best ripe olives. They were even mentioned in an episode of one of television's longest-running shows, *Seinfeld*, when character Kramer regarded them as a "staple." Households across America consider their family gatherings incomplete without these olives, and eating them on holidays is a common childhood memory of many Americans.

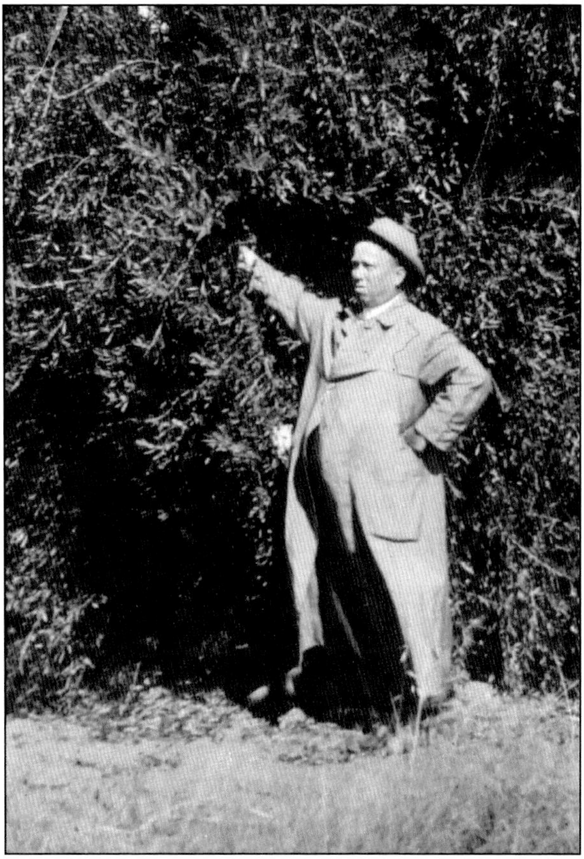

Here, an unidentified man stands among the olive trees on the Gillette family ranch on October 26, 1909. Although the Gillettes primarily grew citrus, particularly lemons, they had several acres of olive groves as well. (CSUF.)

This photograph provides a good view of the rear of the Lindsay Ripe Olive Company plant during the early 1920s. Two employees pose at the entrance for office employees and receiving. To the right, a man in an early automobile transports boxes of olives. (LMG.)

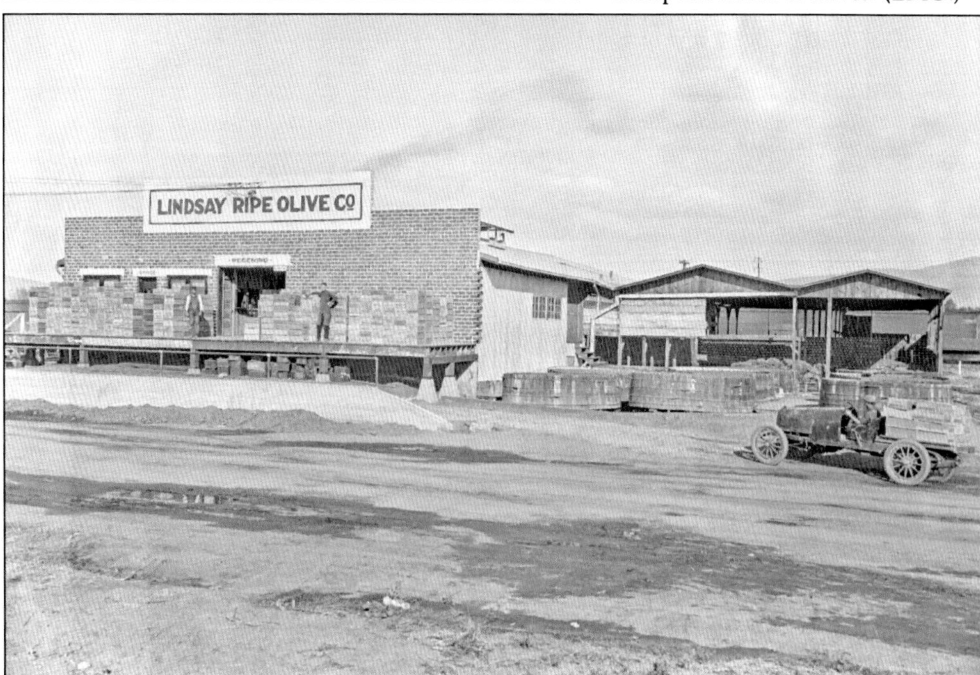

The Lucca Olive Oil Company, seen in an aerial view from the early 1920s, ships its products nationwide. Aerial photographs, newly available during this era, became very popular. There were several local outfits that provided this service. (LMG.)

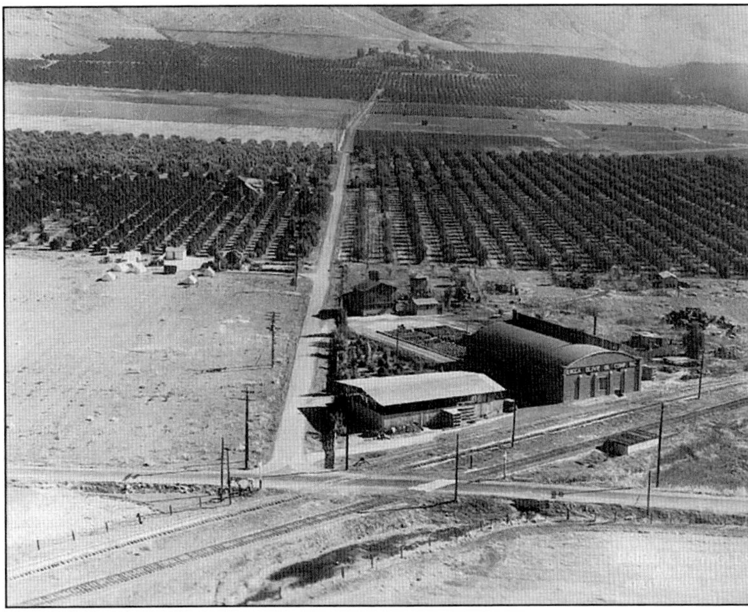

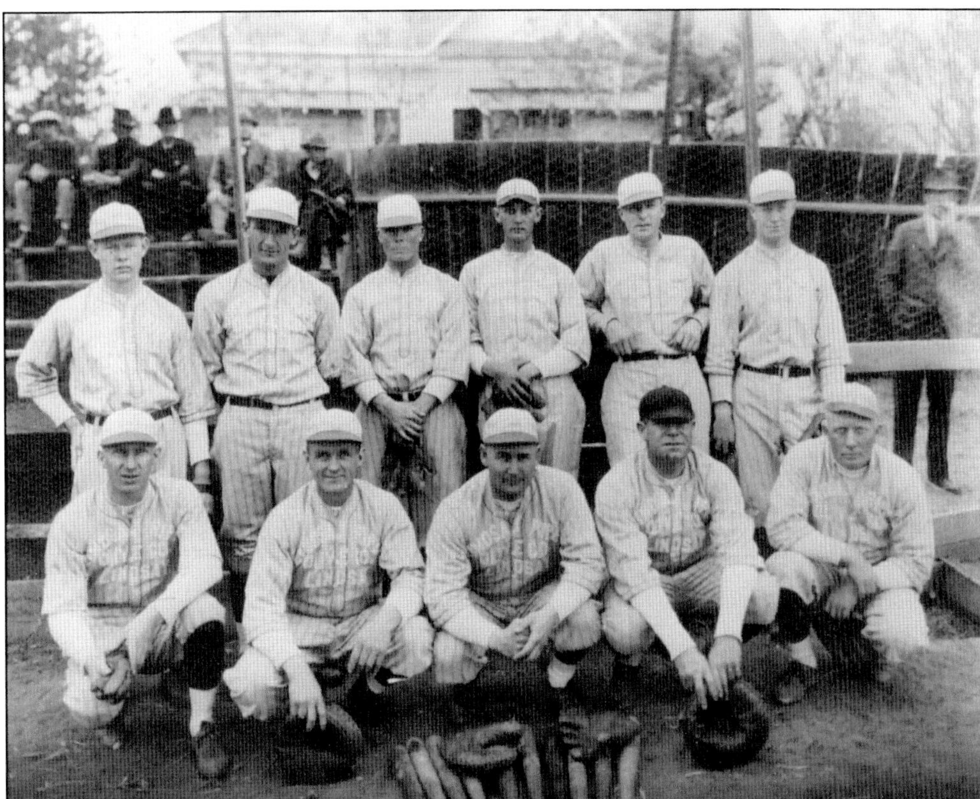

During the 1930s, the Lindsay Ripe Olive Company had a baseball team managed by Natt Handy. One of the players was Frank Skadan, a popular athletics coach at Lindsay High School during this period. The vast majority of local teams would be disbanded when the United States joined Word War II. (LMG.)

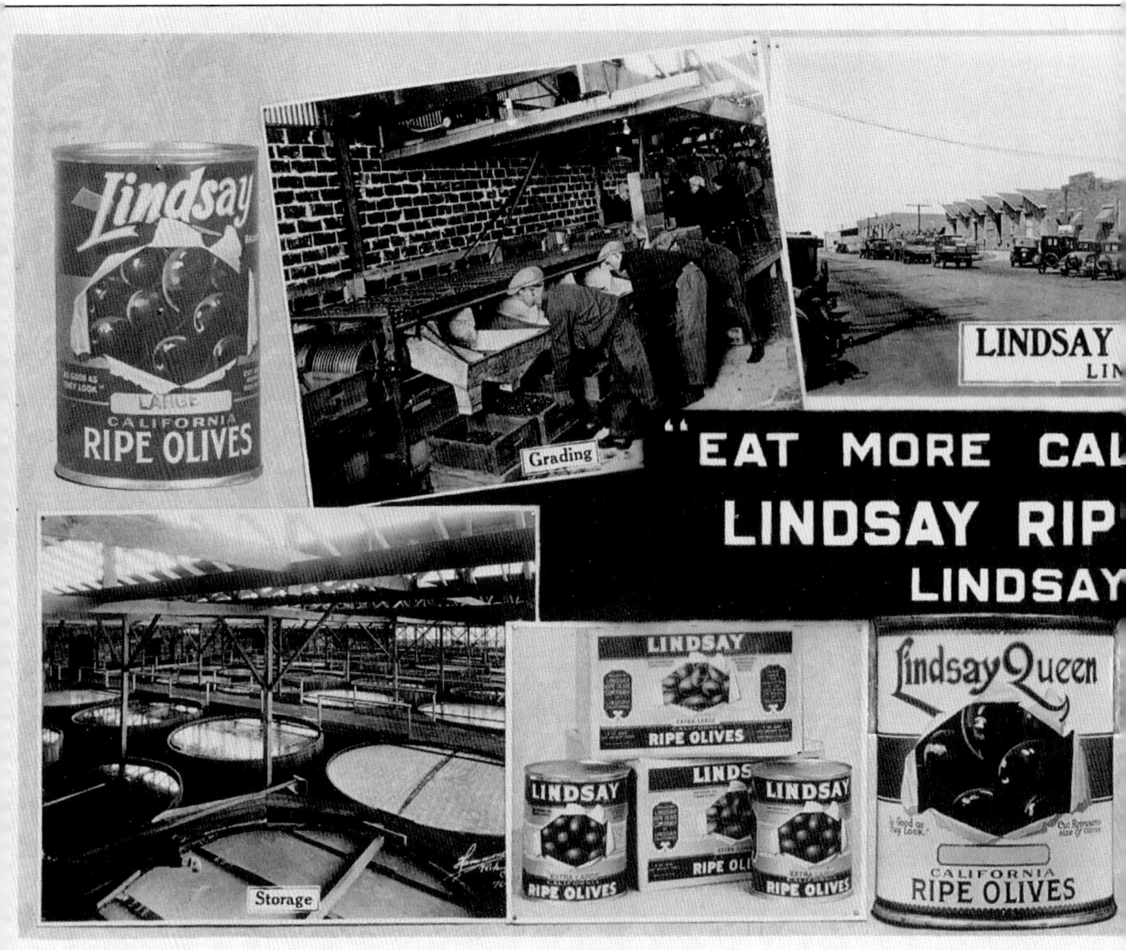

An early postcard for the Lindsay Ripe Olive Company urges Americans to "Eat More California Ripe Olives." Featured at the top center is the first home of Lindsay Ripe Olives, surrounded by collage

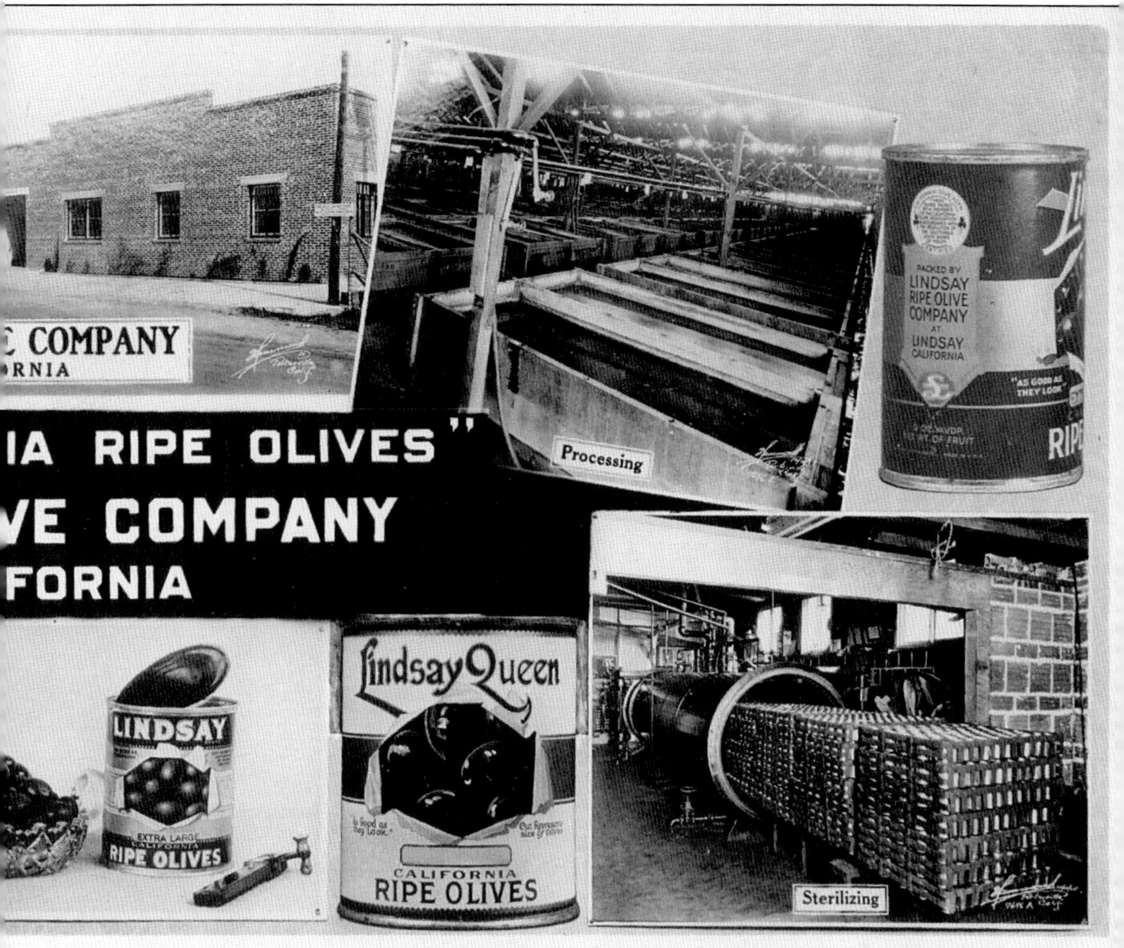

of promotional photographs of the various workrooms at the plant. The processing, sterilization, grading, and storage facilities are all pictured, as is the finished, canned product. (LMG.)

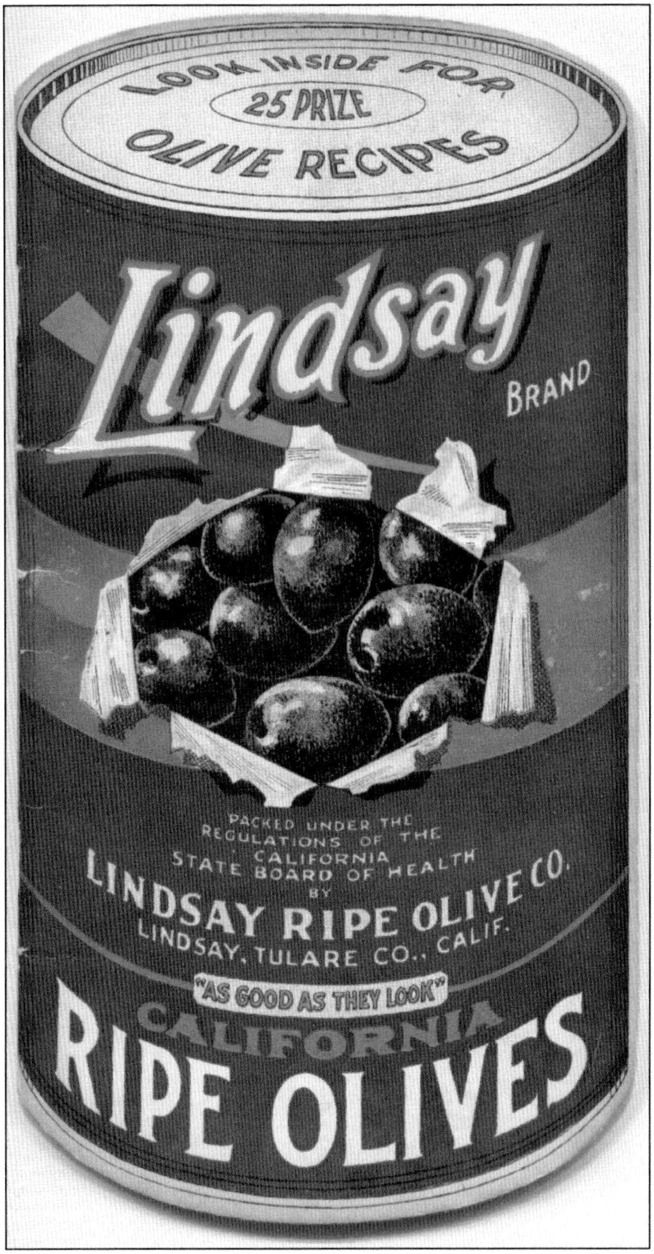

Possibly the earliest example of promotional merchandise produced by the Lindsay Ripe Olive Company was this can-shaped booklet from 1928. Titled "The Lindsay Ripe Olive Way to Welltown," it featured a brief history of the olive industry, as well as recipes with olives since they were not yet a commonly used ingredient. Health, wellness, and sanitization were garnering a great deal of attention in the United States during this time, and this little book took advantage of the current trend of focusing on one's health. One section boasts, "Since California Ripe Olives have been put on the market the sanitariums and hospitals, and the leading physicians are using them extensively." It also goes so far as to say the olives are "a food which is giving our captains of industry, our statesmen, our writers and thinkers supremacy over those of excessive meat-eating nations." (LMG.)

This 1920 photograph was included in "The Lindsay Ripe Olive Way to to Welltown" informational booklet, along with the accompanying caption: "Largest olive tree in the world. 50 feet high, 25 years old, Lindsay, California." (LMG.)

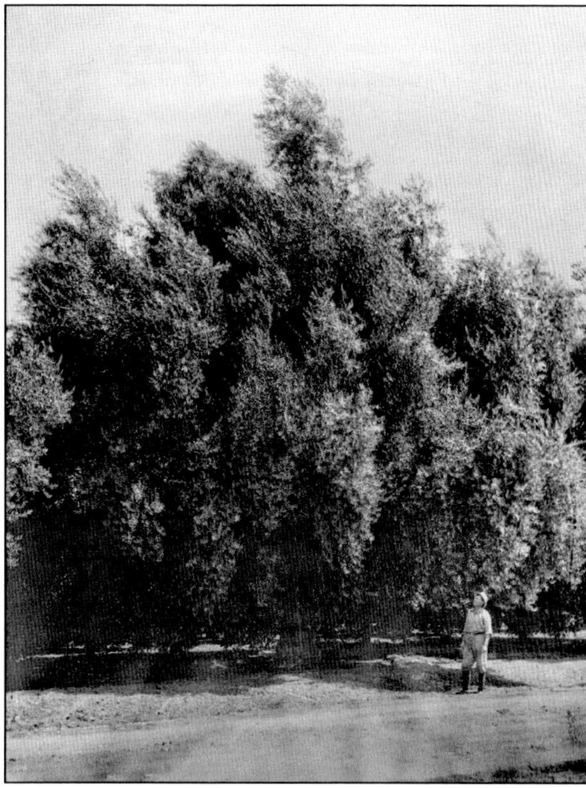

In the Chemistry Room at the Lindsay Ripe Olive plant, chemists worked on maintaining and improving the preservation process. Various tests were run on the products, along with some experimentation with ideas for new recipes. Some of the many items on view in this 1933 photograph of the lab are beakers, Bunsen burners, jars of olives, cans of olive oil (also processed at the plant), a plethora of chemicals, and common pantry items like nutmeg and mustard. (LMG.)

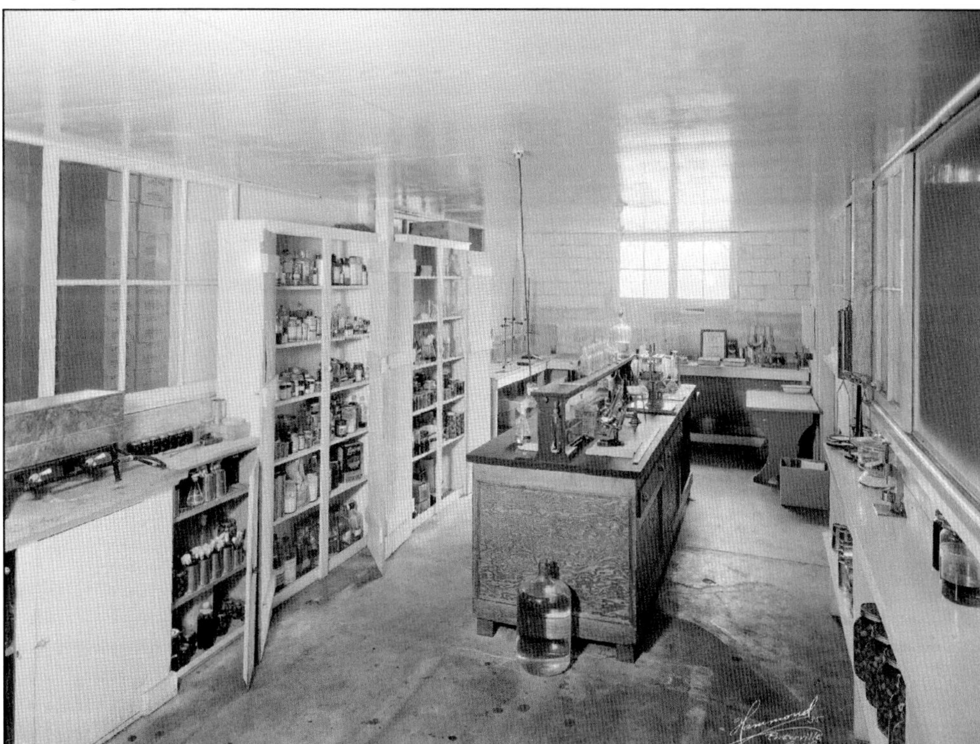

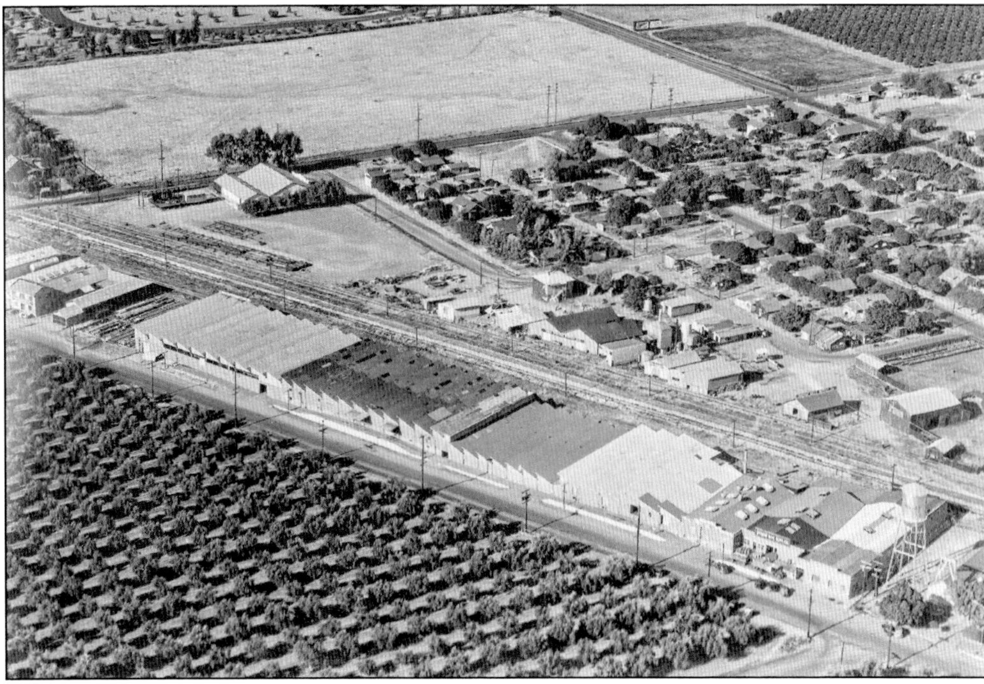

Here is another aerial view, this time taken above the Lindsay Ripe Olive plant in the 1930s. This photograph demonstrates the enormous success of Lindsay's olives in a relatively brief period of time through its growth. A massive processing plant is flanked on one side by an olive grove and residences on the other side. (LMG.)

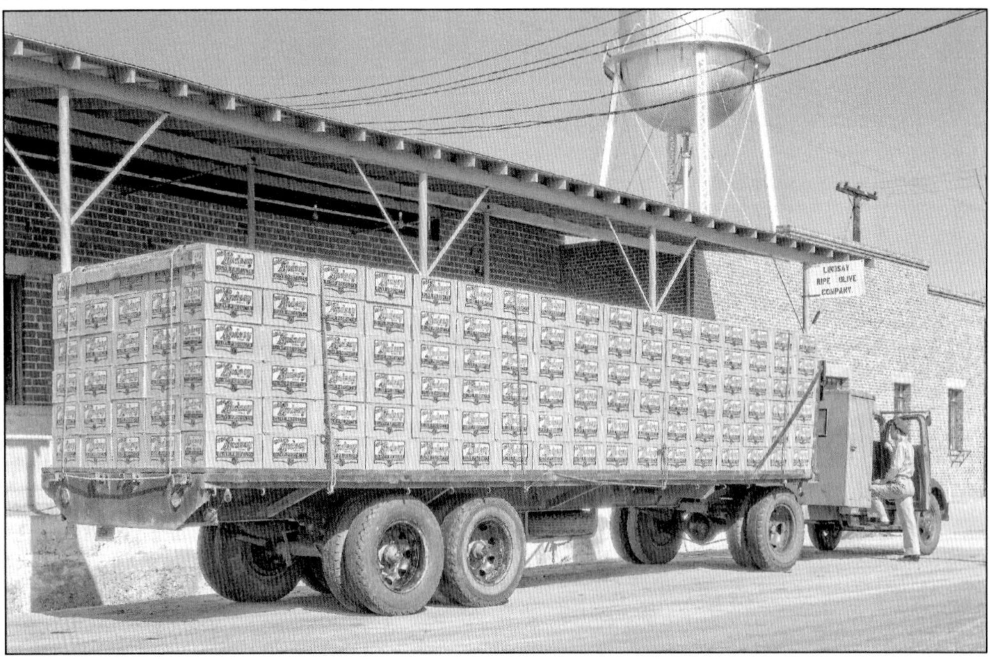

A fully loaded truck with boxes of olives ready to be shipped all over the United States is pictured in front of the Lindsay Ripe Olive Company in the 1930s. Just visible above the building is a portion of the Lindsay water tower. (LMG.)

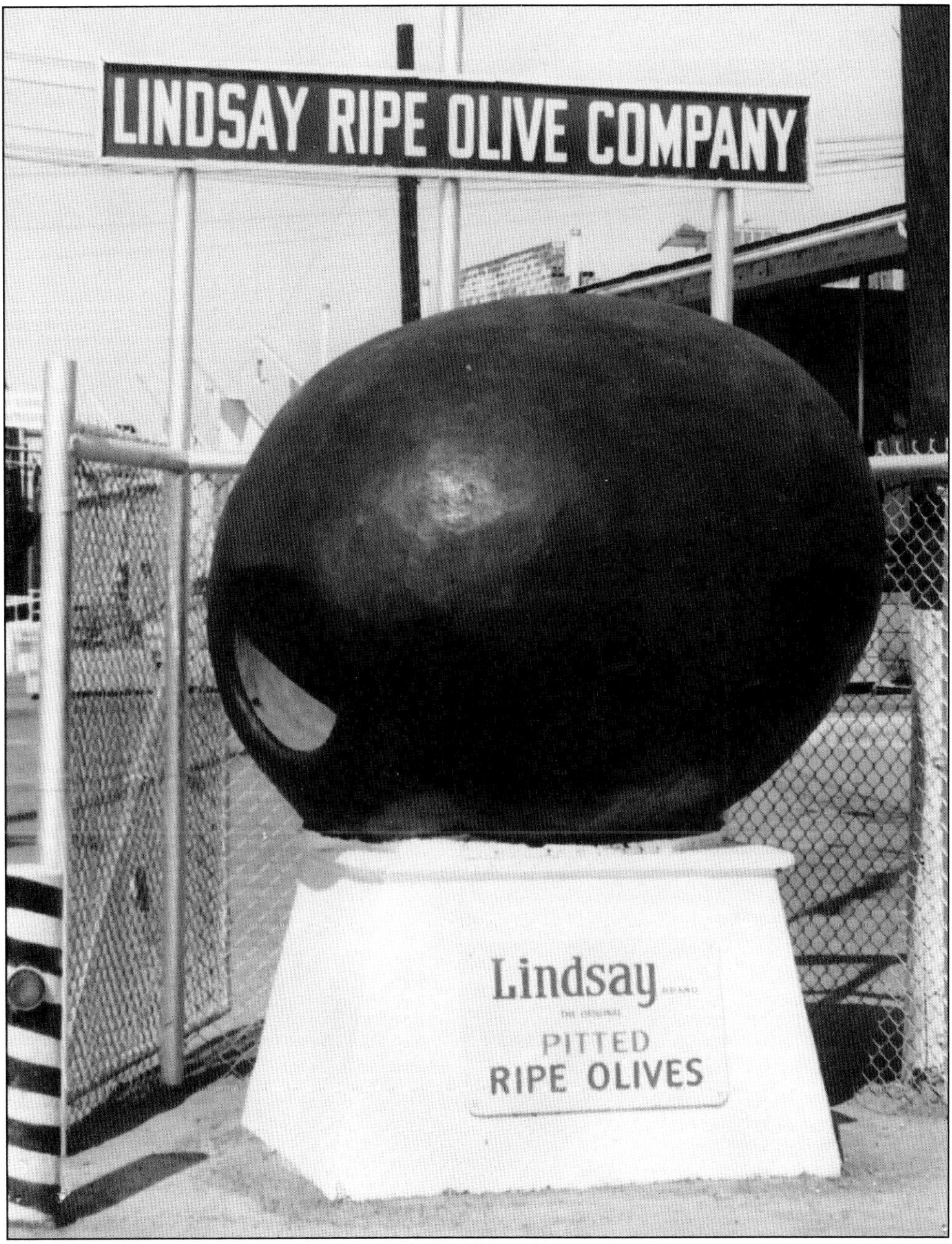

This giant olive is now a well-known roadside oddity, featured in books and apps concerning the subject. It was originally constructed by Lindsay Olive employees in the mid-1930s to commemorate the success of their invention of the world's first olive pitter. Prior to this, olives were pitted by hand. The first eight prototypes could pit 850 olives per minute. The giant olive made its first appearance as a prop on an Orange Blossom Festival float. Afterward, it remained in storage at the plant until 1945, when it was refurbished and put on display near the doorway to the cannery and sales office. When the plant caught fire in the 1970s, the olive survived and was moved to the new plant. It currently sits on Highway 65, where people often stop to take pictures with it and children climb inside. (LMG.)

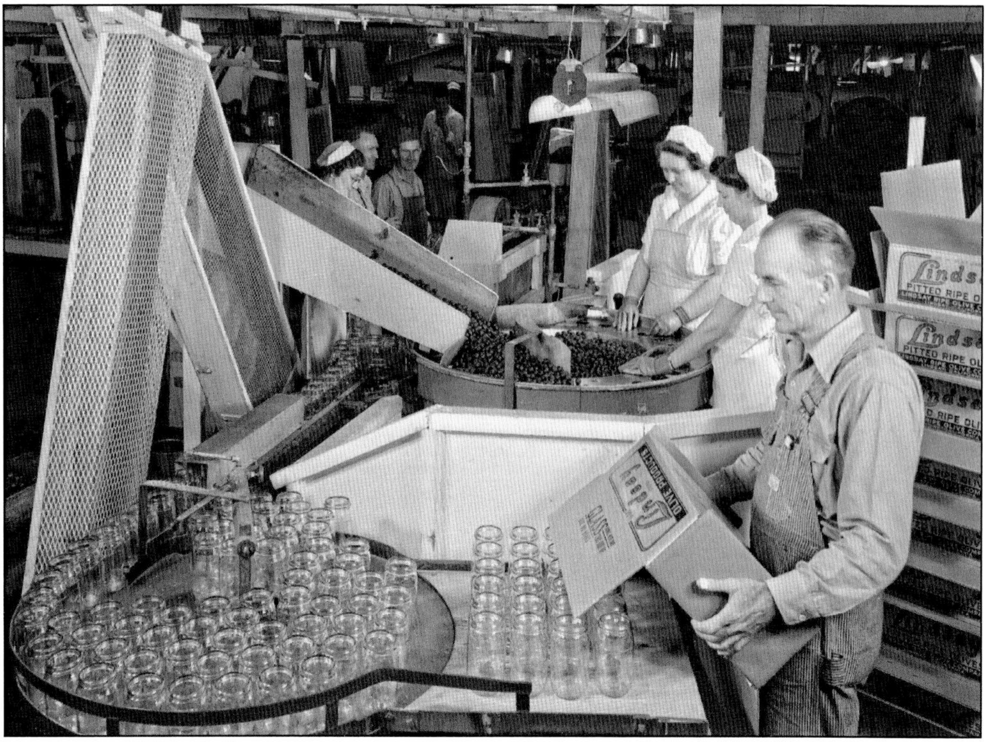

A man stands in the foreground with a packing box for Lindsay Olive Products while women work to jar olives in the background in 1943. The olives are placed by hand into glass jars, which are filled with juice and sealed by a machine. Workers monitor this process, then place the jars onto a conveyor belt for labeling. (LMG.)

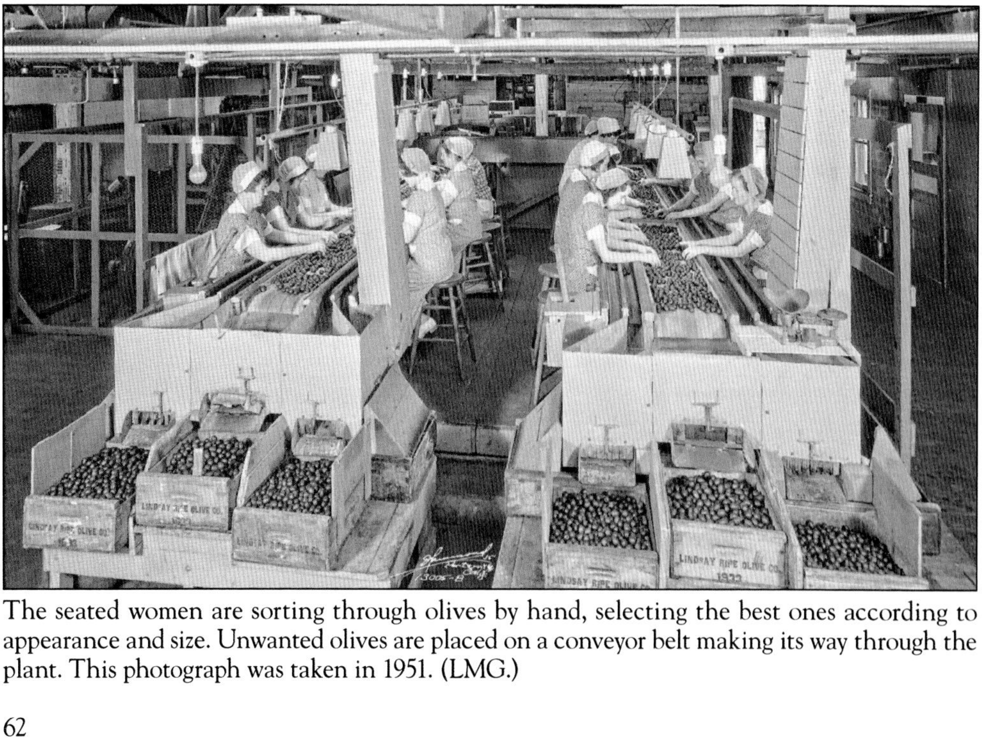

The seated women are sorting through olives by hand, selecting the best ones according to appearance and size. Unwanted olives are placed on a conveyor belt making its way through the plant. This photograph was taken in 1951. (LMG.)

With an imaginative space theme, this 1939 display for Lindsay Ripe Olives would have especially appealed to the store's younger customers. An astronaut and spaceship, with a sign promising the olives are "out of this world," hover above a huge rocket ship sculpture constructed from cans of olives. (LMG.)

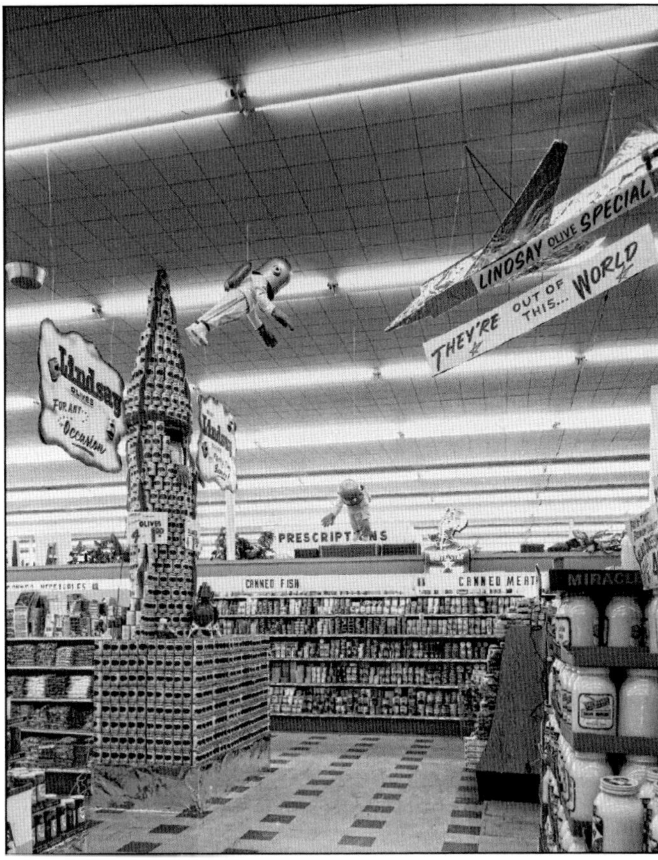

On March 23, 1962, the large group of unidentified gentlemen below gathered for a photograph in front of a truck bearing the Lindsay Ripe Olives logo. (LMG.)

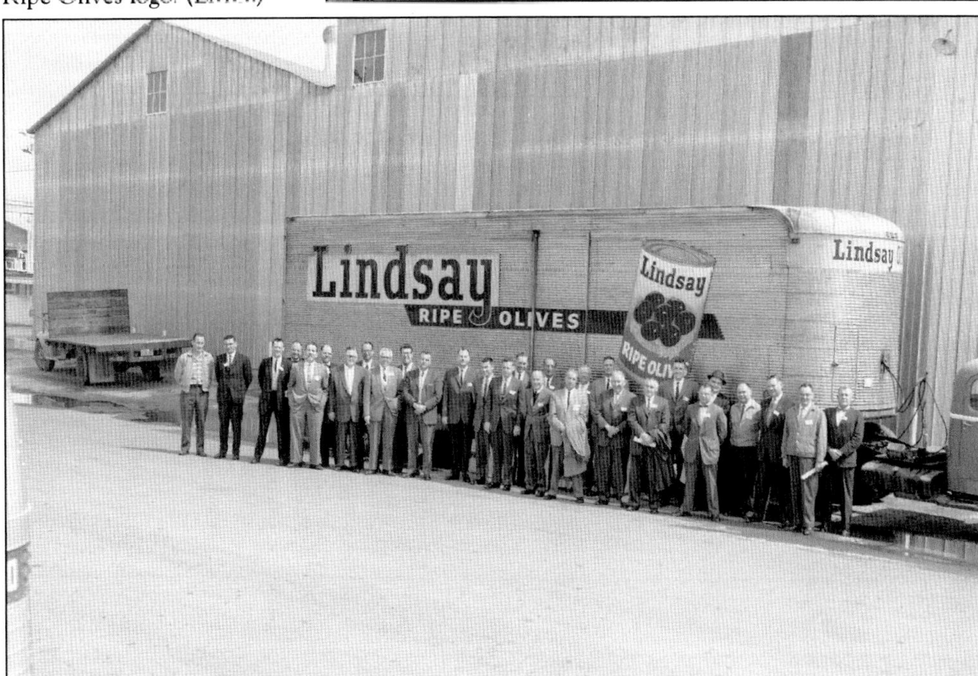

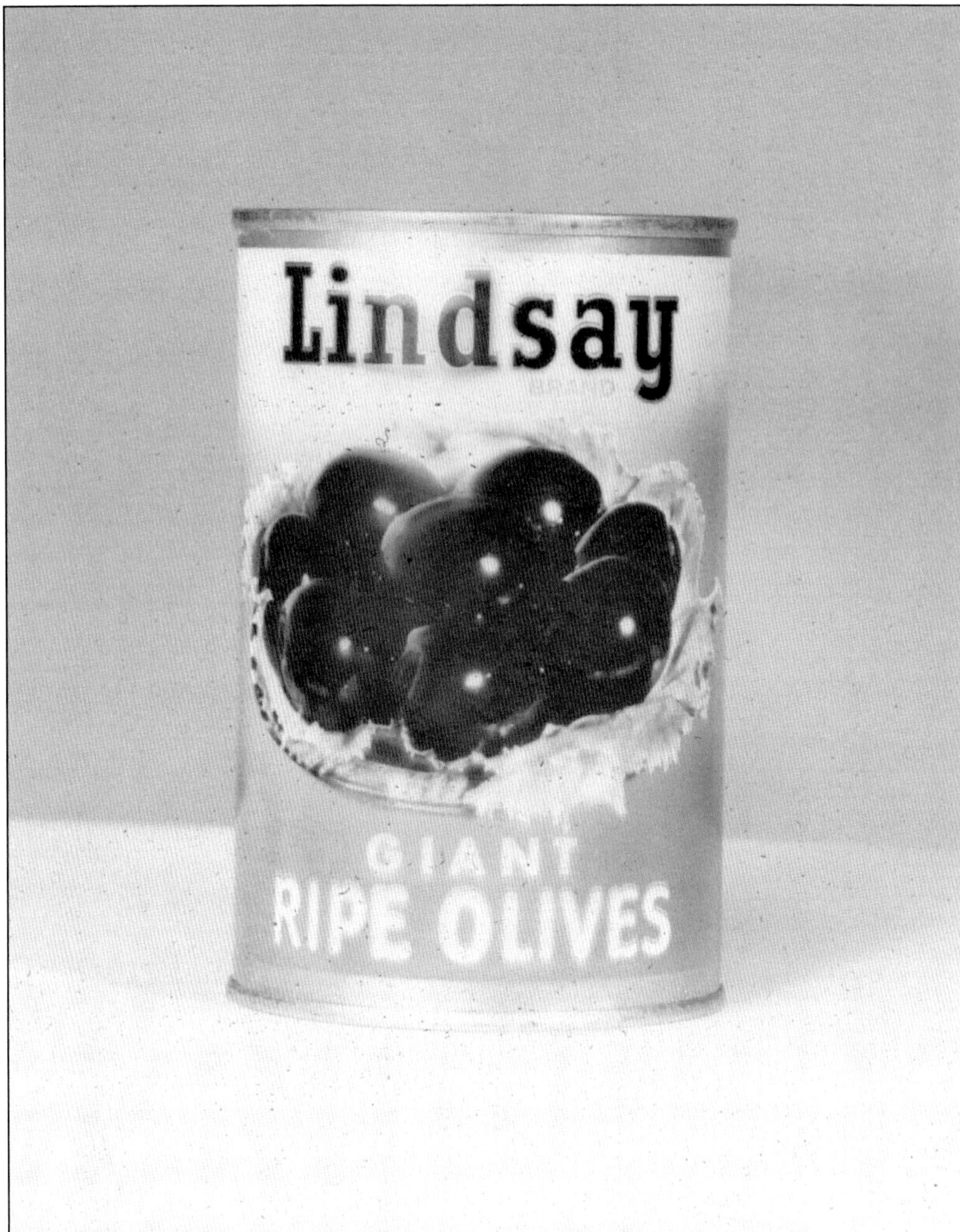

In 1962, Lindsay Ripe Olives launched a marketing campaign in the town of Lindsay. The television and radio ads, which ran nationwide, were filmed in Lindsay and featured local residents. The campaign was conceived in an effort to introduce the consumer to the small, unknown town of Lindsay. The first ad—print, radio, and television—featured Greta Stewart, features editor of the *Lindsay Gazette*. In the ads, Stewart could be heard saying, "There's a little country town in the Central Valley of California. It's a town where you can still hear crickets at night and smell the soft summer afternoons—the town is Lindsay. I live there." The campaign was far more successful than anyone had anticipated and made Lindsay famous for a time. The residents who appeared in the ads received fan mail from around the country. (LMG.)

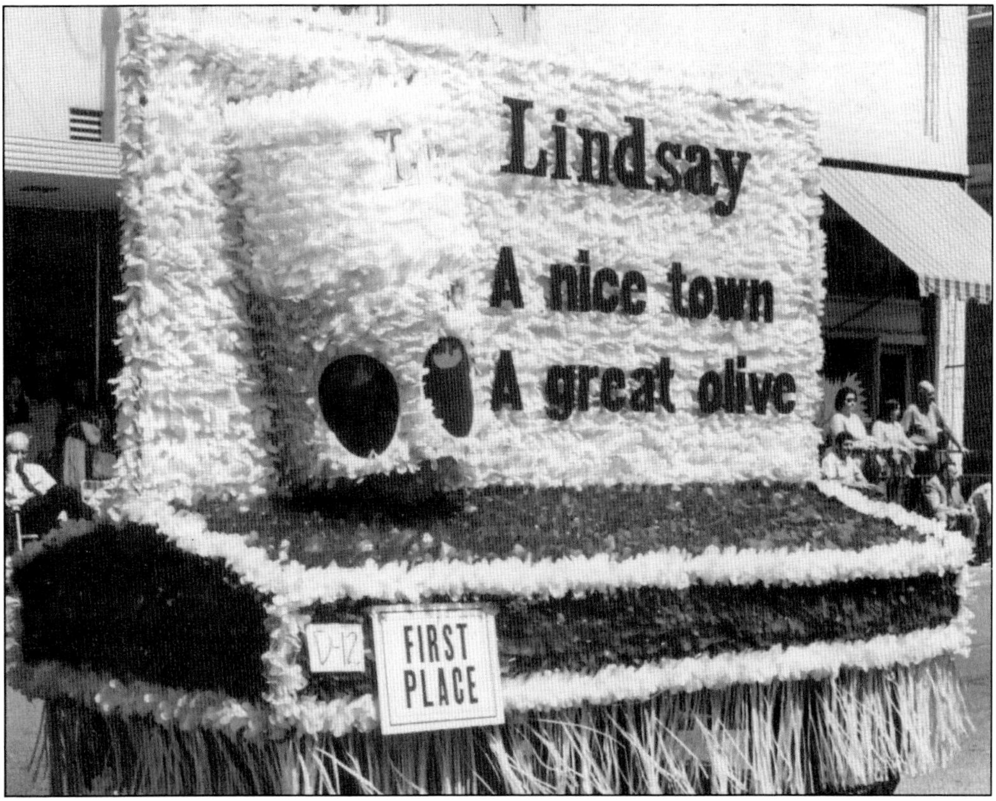

Walter Kimball, director of industrial relations for Lindsay Olive Growers, created the slogan for the 1962 campaign: "Lindsay. A nice town. A great olive." It is seen here on the Lindsay Olive Growers' prize-winning float, which appeared in the Orange Blossom Parade that year. Kimball also served as mayor of Lindsay. (LMG.)

In response to the sudden popularity of Lindsay and the influx of tourists, there was an increase in the number of plant tours. A large billboard was erected on Highway 65 to direct visitors to the plant. A favorite memory of many Tulare County residents was a class trip to tour the olive plant. Children were given paper hats with the Lindsay Brand Olives logo, along with a small can of olives to take home. (LMG.)

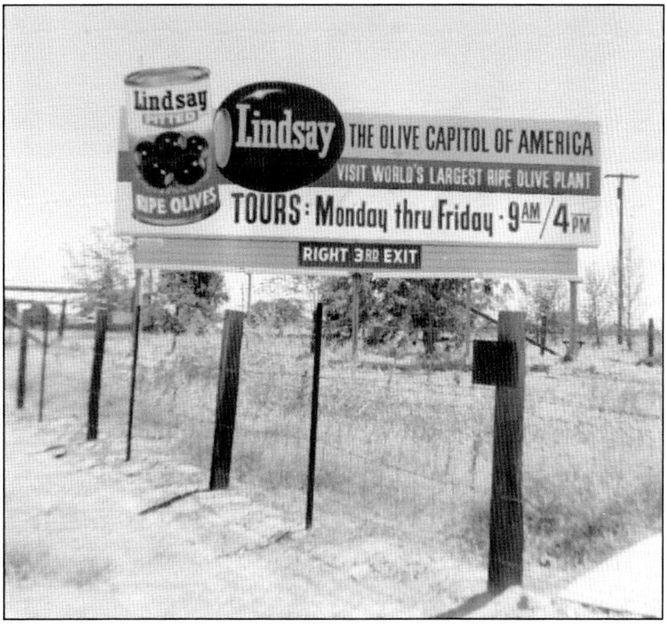

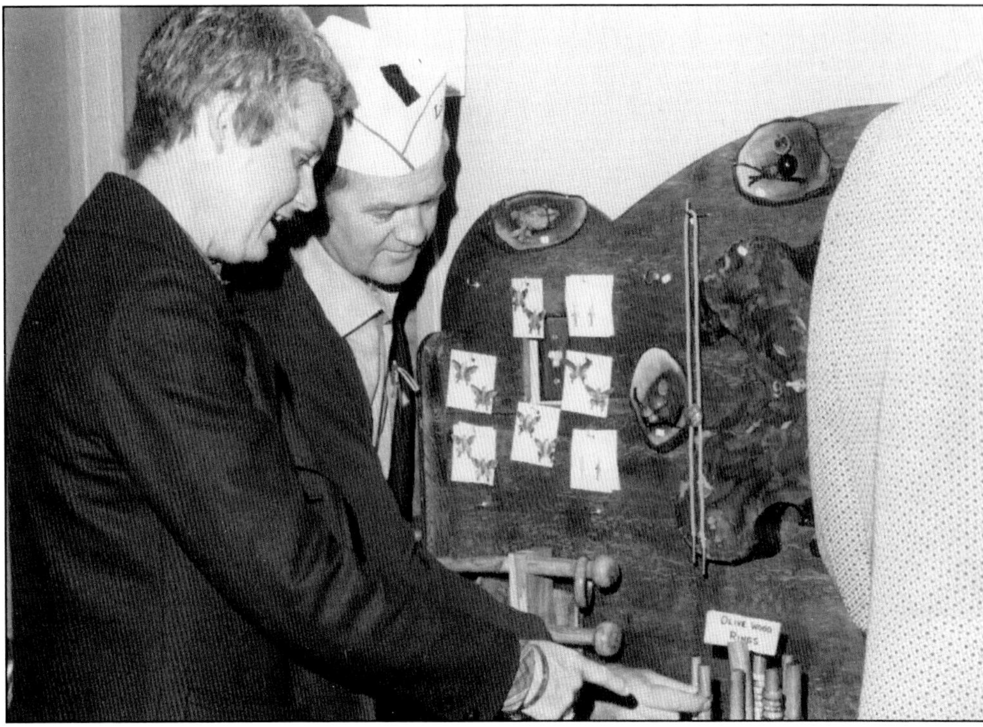

Some of the most popular items for sale in the gift shop were Burl Wood's olive wood carvings. Many locals had one of Wood's natural-style clocks hanging in their home or office. Wood's unique name earned him notoriety in light of his chosen profession as a wood carver, and he was even featured in a *Ripley's Believe It or Not!* newspaper segment. Other gift shop items created by Wood were rings and bracelets, bolo ties, and butterfly or crucifix pins. (LMG.)

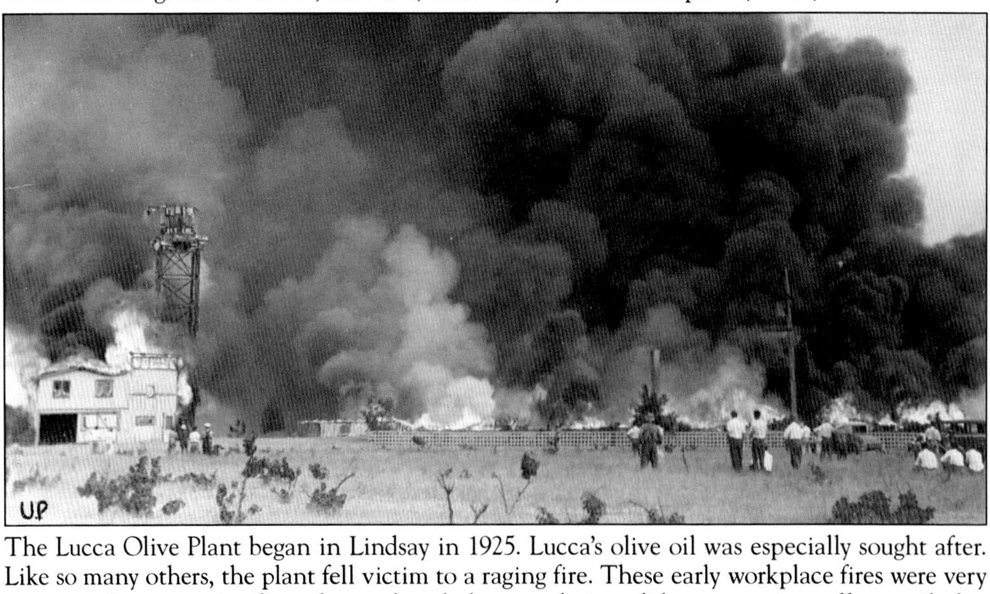

The Lucca Olive Plant began in Lindsay in 1925. Lucca's olive oil was especially sought after. Like so many others, the plant fell victim to a raging fire. These early workplace fires were very common. Laws ensuring fire safety and workplace regulations did not come into effect until after 1911, prompted by one of the most horrific and tragic events in the nation's history: the Triangle Shirtwaist fire in New York. (GM.)

Four

ORANGE BLOSSOM FESTIVAL

In hopes of boosting morale during the Great Depression, Lindsay Chamber of Commerce manager R.I. Clearman created the Orange Blossom Festival as a celebration of the community and the citrus industry on which the town had been built. A joint effort between the towns of Lindsay and Strathmore, the first festival was held on April 23, 1932. The events of the day began with the crowning of the Orange Blossom Queen in Strathmore, followed by a procession of decorated cars down the Orange Belt. In the afternoon, a cast of nearly 400 presented *The Pageant of the San Joaquin*, written by Lindsay teacher Valda Prizer. The pageant came to life in a natural amphitheater between Lindsay Peak and Elephant's Back for an audience of almost 4,000. The pageant depicted scenes from Lindsay's past, including the Yokut Indians, the Gold Rush, and as a finale, a veritable river of oranges flowing down to the audience from the top of the hill. After the initial pageants, it was deemed too costly to continue, and the festival as it is known today began to take form, with the crowning of a new Orange Blossom Queen and a parade remaining the centerpiece of the annual fete. Throughout the years, a number of activities have been part of the festival: an orange-packing contest, fishing derby, circus and carnival, horse show, Hollywood air show, street dance, homecoming picnic, baseball game, orange crate stock car race, Queen's Ball, Wiskerino contest, and much more.

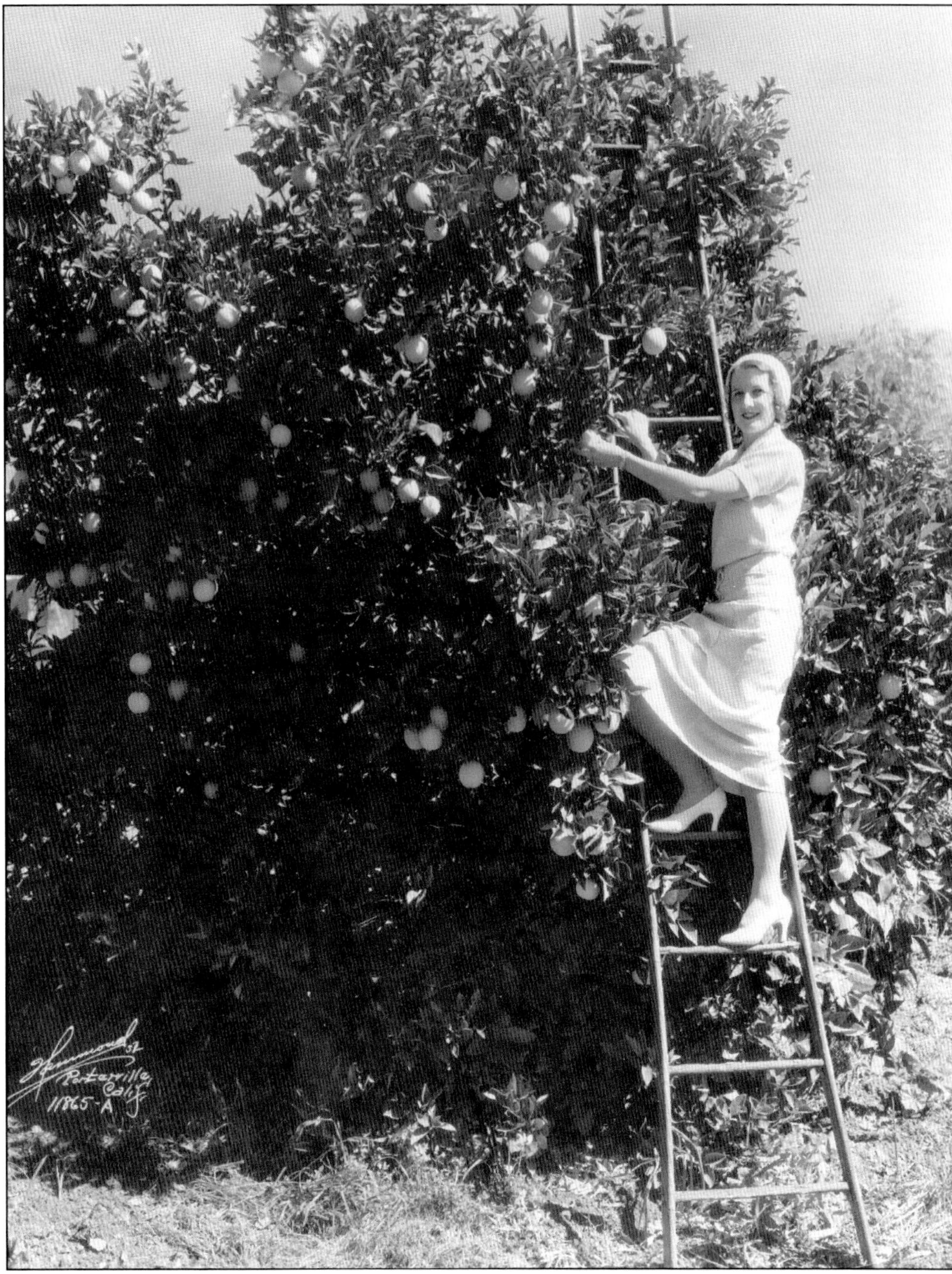

Winifred Cowles was the first in what would become a long line of Orange Blossom Queens. Here, she poses among Lindsay's celebrated orange trees. (LMG.)

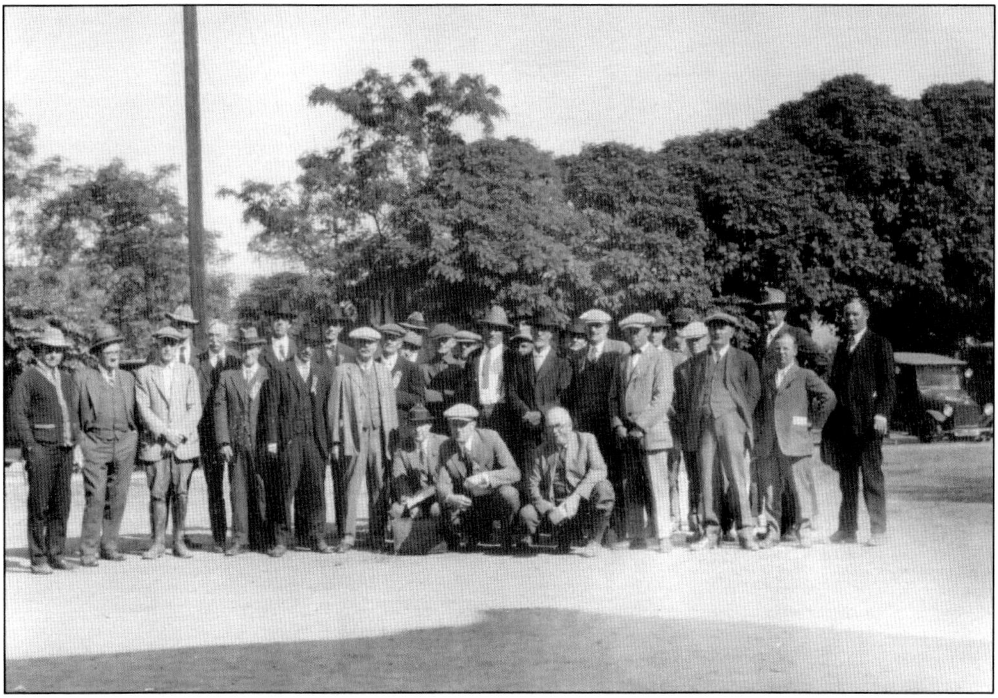

A group of drivers in the first Orange Blossom Festival parade gather for a picture in 1932. The parade route along the Orange Belt Highway would have been a beautiful drive, with the air heavily scented with orange blossoms. (LMG.)

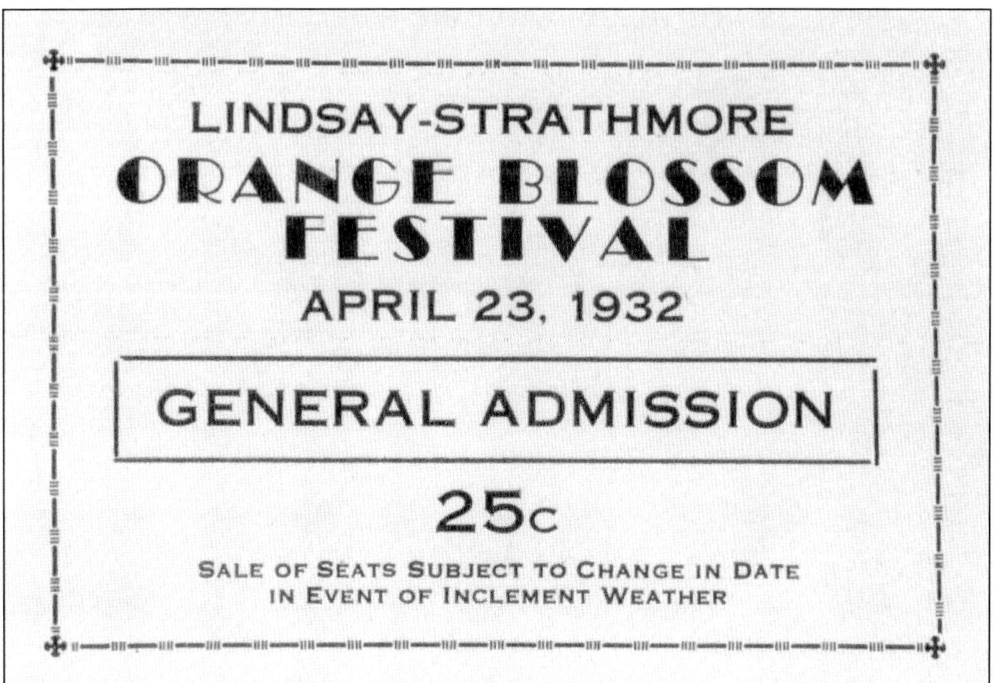

A general admission ticket to the first Orange Blossom Festival in 1932 cost a mere 25¢. This would have admitted ticket holders to the many main attractions of the day. (LMG.)

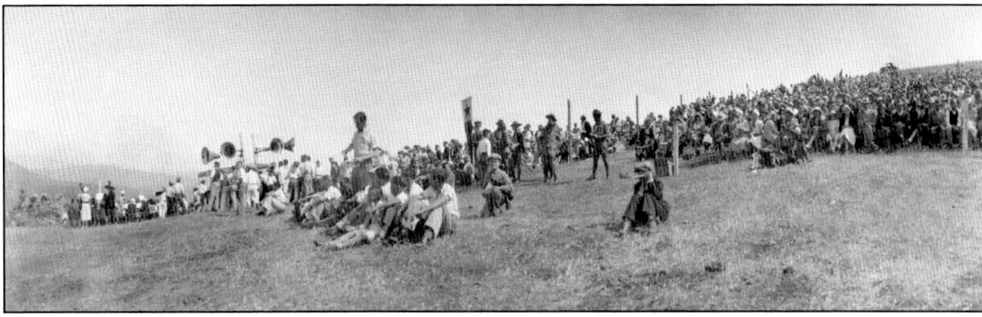

As noted on the back of the photograph, an audience gathers "on the hill near where Lewis Creek enters the valley" to watch the first *Pageant of the San Joaquin* in 1932. Locals later referred to the location as "Legion Farm," according to a 1938 article in the *Lindsay Gazette*. (LMG.)

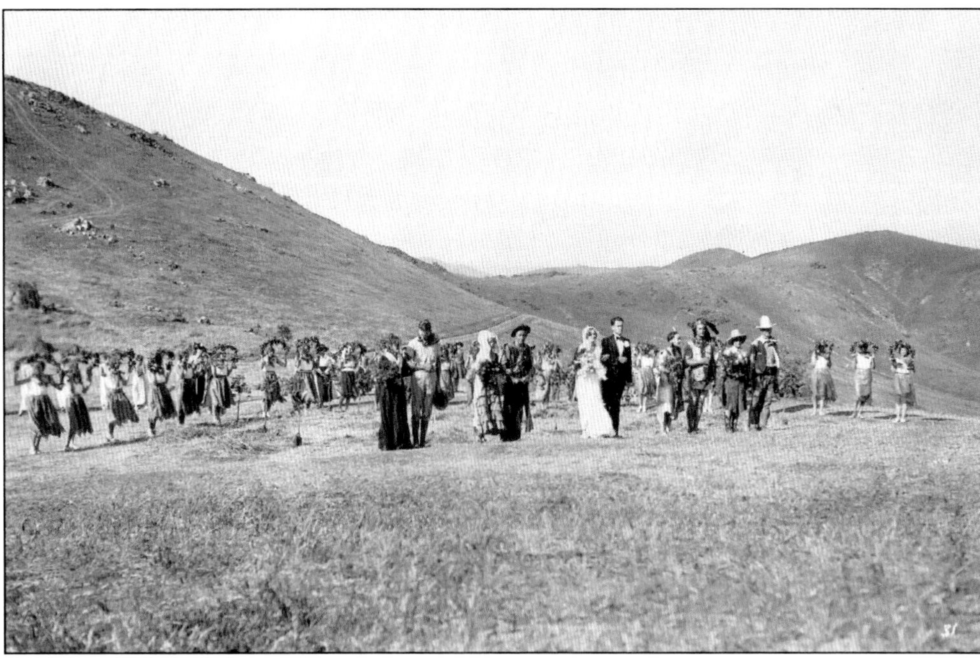

A scene from *The Pageant of the San Joaquin* is seen here in 1932. The pageant was billed as "an accurate and graphic portrayal of the history of this great California valley." At the time, pageants like these were popular attractions in California. A couple of original pageants can still be seen in the state of California, including the famous *Ramona* pageant, based on the popular novel by Helen Hunt Jackson. (LMG.)

Elizabeth Peery portrayed an Indian in the first and second pageant. Her great-grandfather, who worked as an interpreter, was a noted chieftain of the Peoria Tribe of Indians of Oklahoma. In addition to speaking multiple Indian languages, he was fluent in French, English, and American Sign Language. Peery's own father, a graduate of Notre Dame University, worked on a government-appointed business committee before moving to Lindsay with his family. (LMG.)

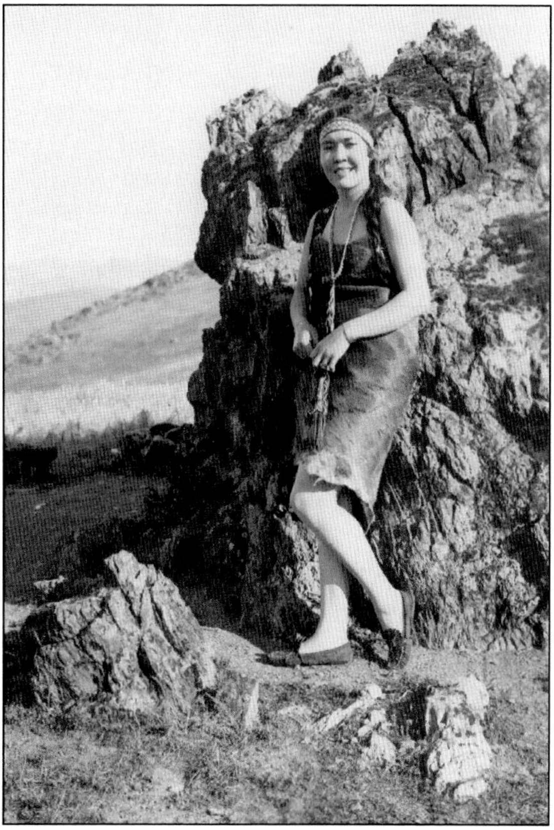

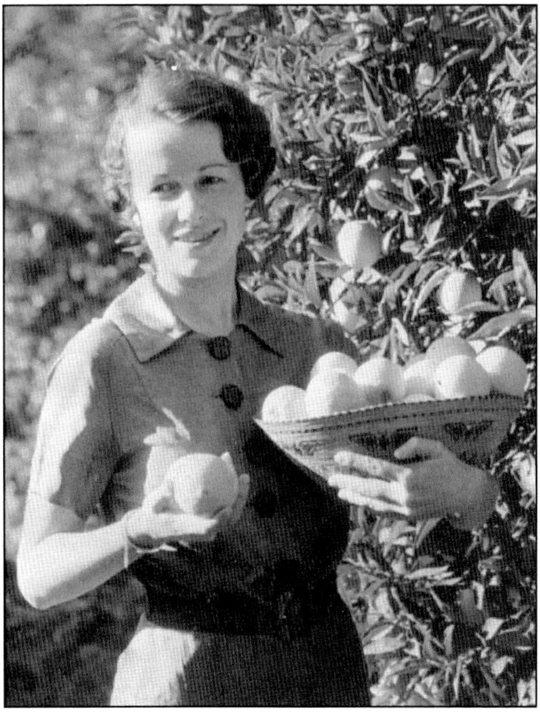

In 1934, Charlotte (Bequette) Chrisman was Lindsay's second reigning Orange Blossom Queen. The Bequettes were ranchers and one of Lindsay's most prominent families. Queen Charlotte's great-grandmother was Mary Graves, a surviving member of the famously ill-fated pioneer migrants of the Donner Party. Shortly after her rescue, Graves married Edward Gant Pyle. They lived in San Jose, where she became the first female teacher there. Sadly, their joy was short-lived when Pyle was found murdered. When his killer was discovered almost a year later and subsequently imprisoned, Graves tended his wounds, fed him, and watched over him just so she could see him hang for the crime. Graves wed a second time, then moved to the Tulare County area. There, she had seven children, but only two of them survived. Mary Graves passed away in 1891 and is interred in the Visalia Public Cemetery. (LMG.)

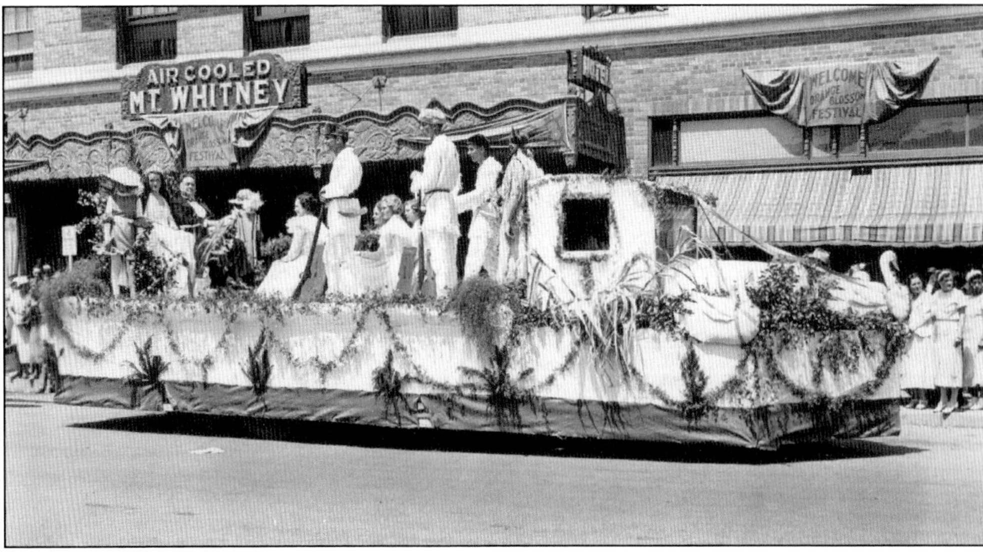

Queen Charlotte Bequette's coronation was a special event for numerous reasons. Her arrival through the streets of Lindsay and neighboring Strathmore in a covered wagon was preceded by a band of Indians and scouts. Bequette is pictured seated on the royal float, which paid homage to her Donner Party ancestor, Mary Graves. As Lindsay mayor Charles F. Burr was giving Bequette the key to the city following her crowning, the event was interrupted by a Mrs. Henry, the wife of special guest at the festival, M.R. Henry, who was the president of the California Newspaper Publishers' Association. The couple had been visiting from Los Angeles. Mrs. Henry came on-stage during the proceedings, exclaiming, "Why my own Grandmother was Nancy Graves, Mary Graves' younger sister!" This unexpected and rather exciting encounter was the first time the two descendants had ever met, and it was quite the highlight of the festival that year. (LMG.)

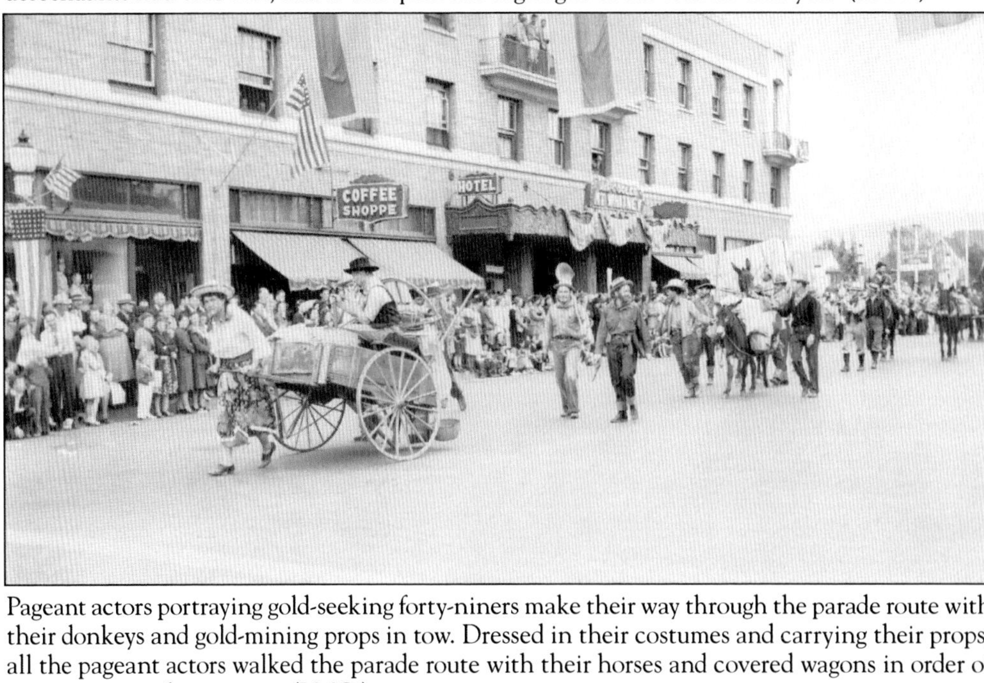

Pageant actors portraying gold-seeking forty-niners make their way through the parade route with their donkeys and gold-mining props in tow. Dressed in their costumes and carrying their props, all the pageant actors walked the parade route with their horses and covered wagons in order of appearance in the pageant. (LMG.)

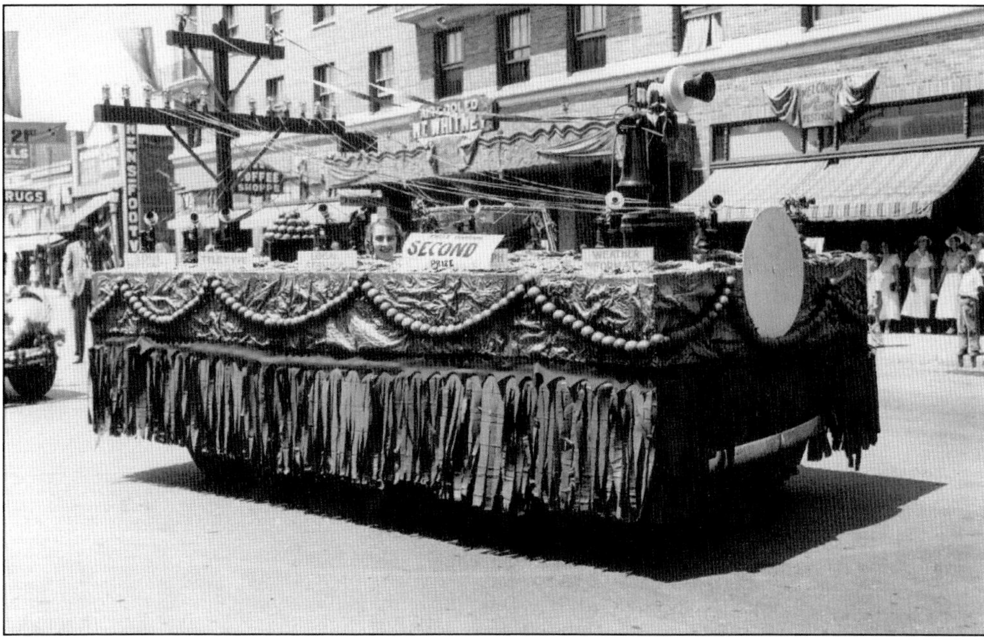

A 1934 parade float promotes Lindsay Home Telephone and Telegraph services, complete with a giant telephone and telephone pole. In Lindsay's early years, the phone switchboard was first located in postmaster Billy Grace's tobacco and stationary shop, then later moved to the Awbrey family's store. At this time, the phone line was first built from Tulare, utilizing fence wires along the route. (LMG.)

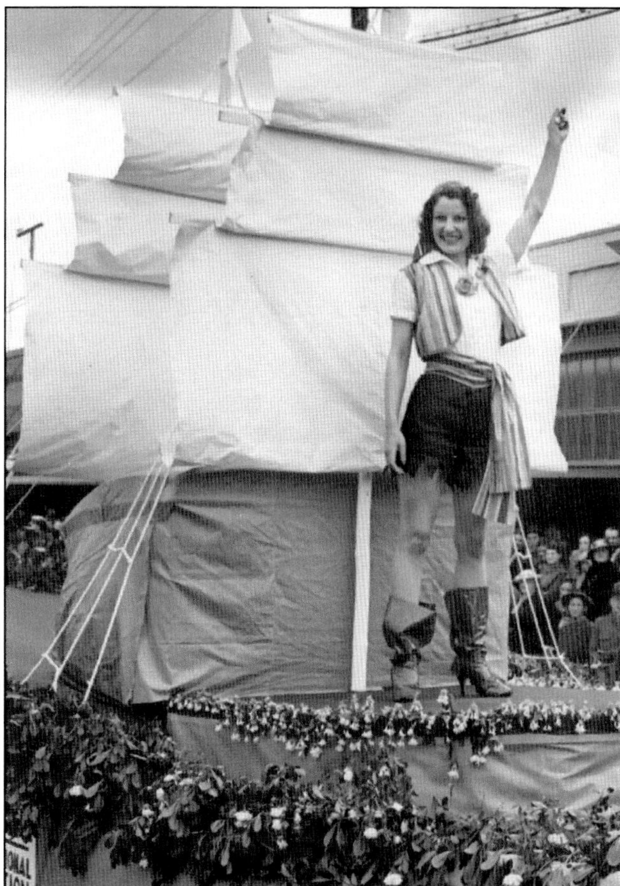

The Golden Gate International Exposition's "theme girl," Marie McDowell, was a special guest at the 1938 Orange Blossom Festival. She dressed as a pirate to promote the upcoming world's fair, hosted by San Francisco on Treasure Island. The theme girl was welcomed by Lindsay mayor Charles F. Burr at the Orange Blossom Queen's coronation and rode atop a pirate ship float in the parade. (LMG.)

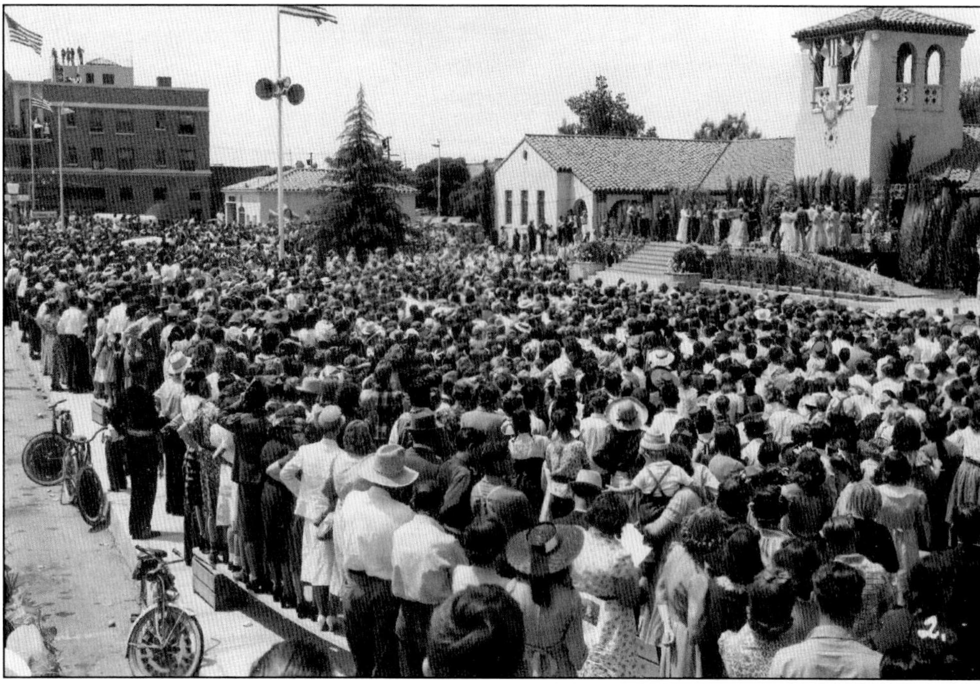

In 1940, an ample crowd gathers in front of Lindsay's new city hall to watch the coronation of the Orange Blossom Queen. This portion of the Orange Blossom Festival remains popular today and is looked forward to by all with much anticipation. (LMG.)

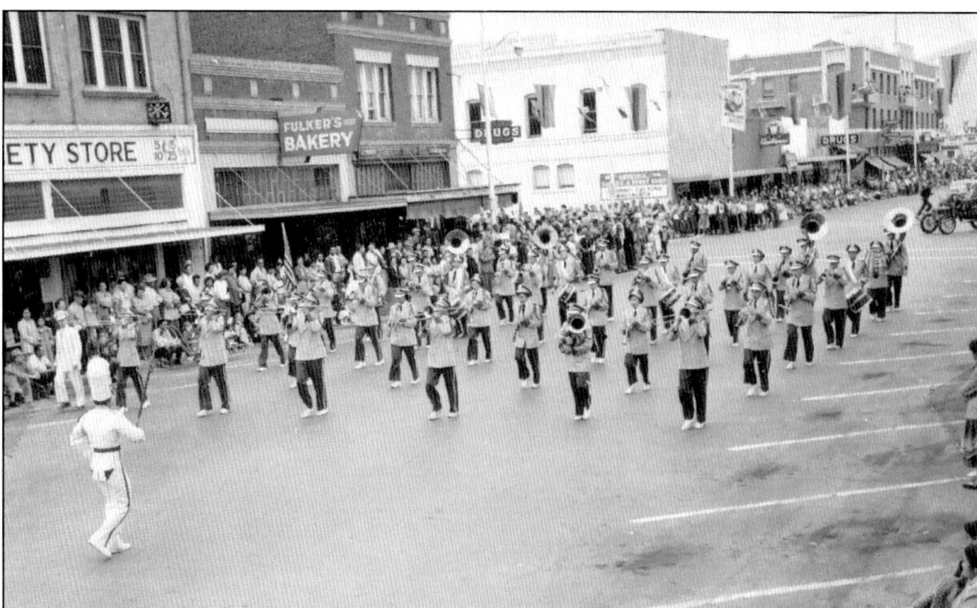

A local band entertains Orange Blossom Festival parade goers. Marching bands like these have been a staple of American parades as long as they have existed. Typically, high school bands from all over Tulare County participated in the parade portion of the festival. (LMG.)

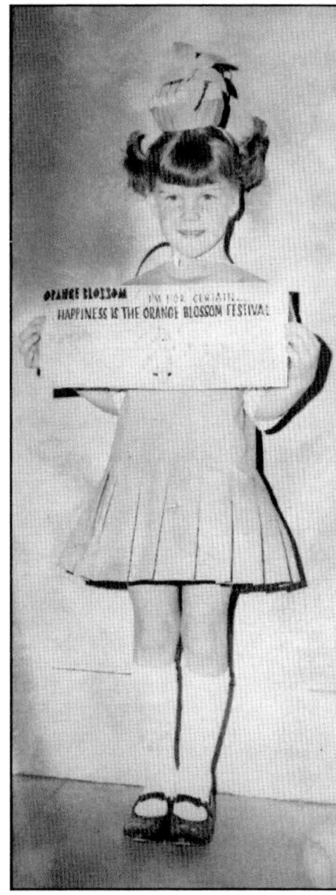

Young Julie Barlow shows off an illustration of a little girl in Lindsay who bears a striking resemblance to herself. This might have been a piece of art entered in the annual Orange Blossom Art Show, hosted by the Lindsay Art Association. The art show is yet another festival mainstay that has endured through many decades. (LMG.)

Two young boys ride their horses past the Lindsay Post Office in the 1949 parade. Behind them, a ghost sign, a hand-painted advertisement on a building that still exists, can be seen, promoting "20-Mule-Team" Borax soap chips. It is painted on the side of a grocery store next to the former Mount Whitney Hotel on Honolulu Street. This sign can still be seen today. (LMG.)

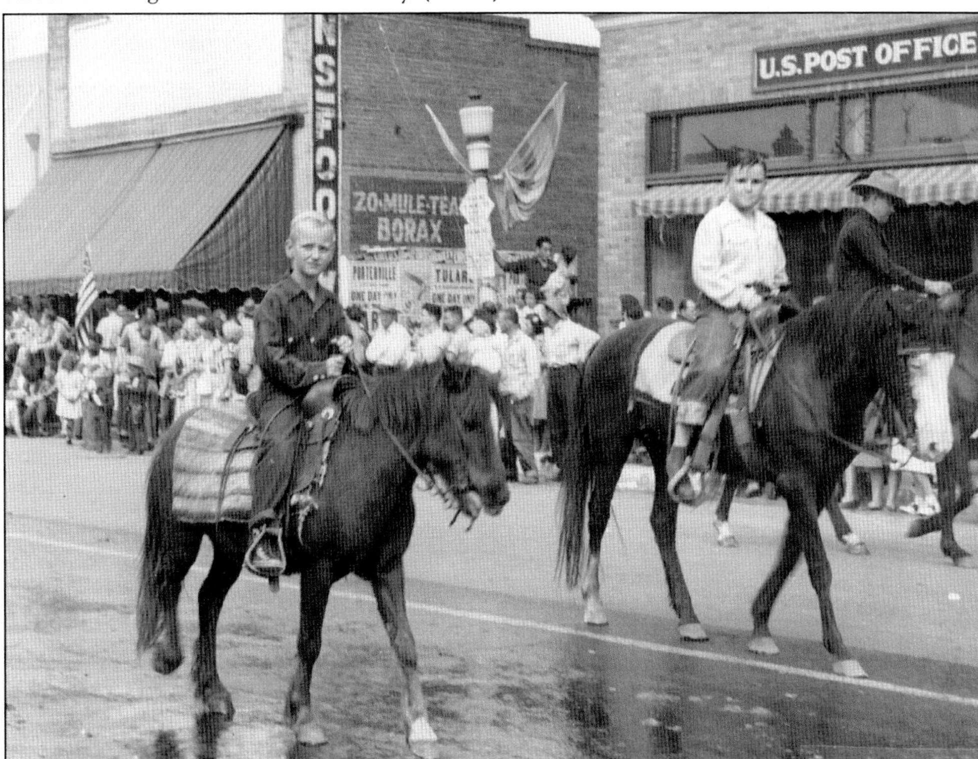

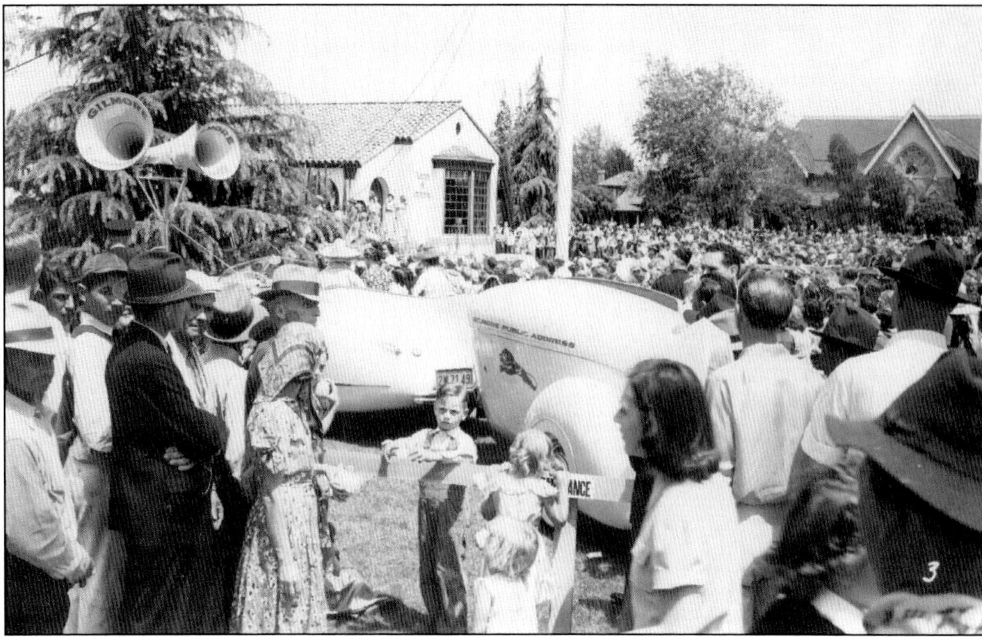

People fill the streets surrounding Lindsay City Hall in hopes of catching a glimpse of 1946 Orange Blossom Queen, Ina Mae Redmond. At the height of the Orange Blossom Festival's popularity, it drew crowds of over 40,000 attendees, including radio, film, and television celebrities. (LMG.)

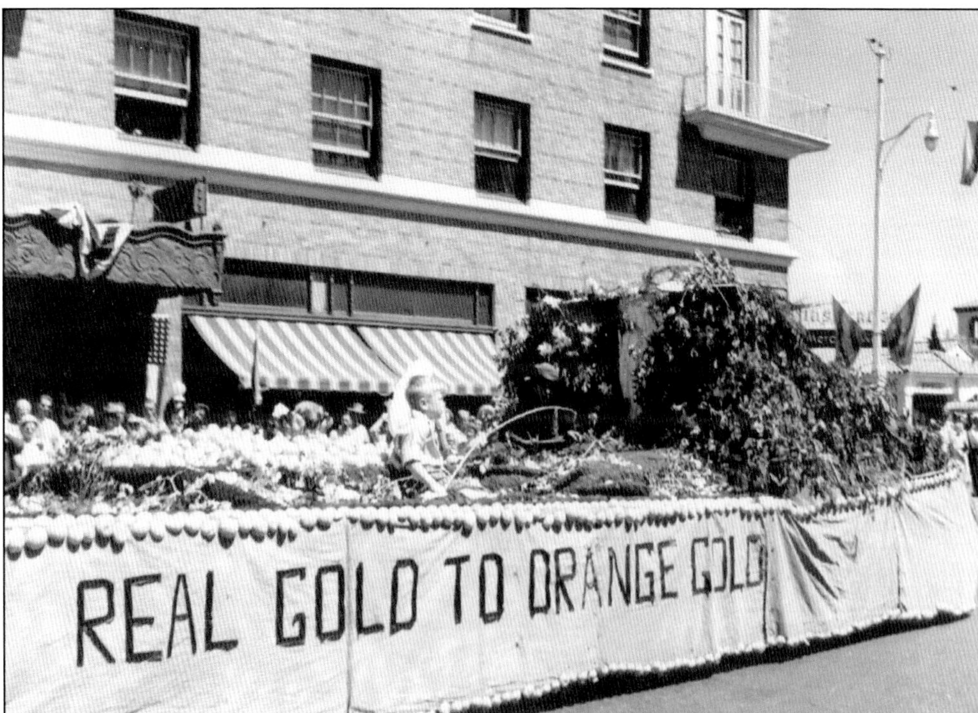

This parade float acknowledges that Lindsay and Central California's version of "gold" is oranges. Although the town later became famous for its olives, it was literally built upon the success of its citrus, an industry the town is still known for. (LMG.)

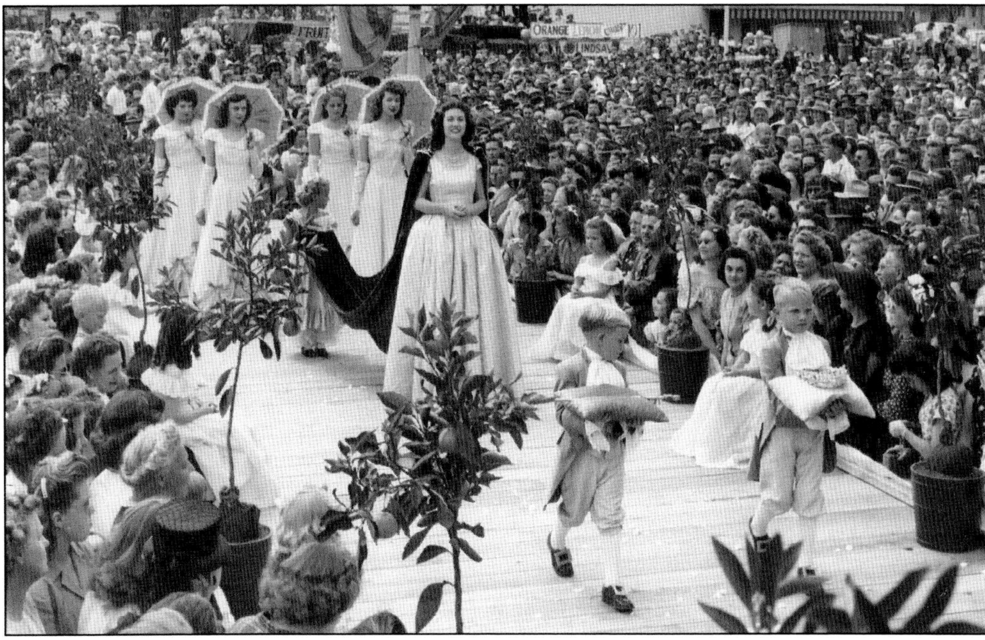

Queen Wanda Lassetter and her court make their way to the coronation. They are preceded by two young gentlemen acting as crown bearer and scepter bearer as thousands of onlookers anticipate the official beginning of the 1948 Orange Blossom Festival. (LMG.)

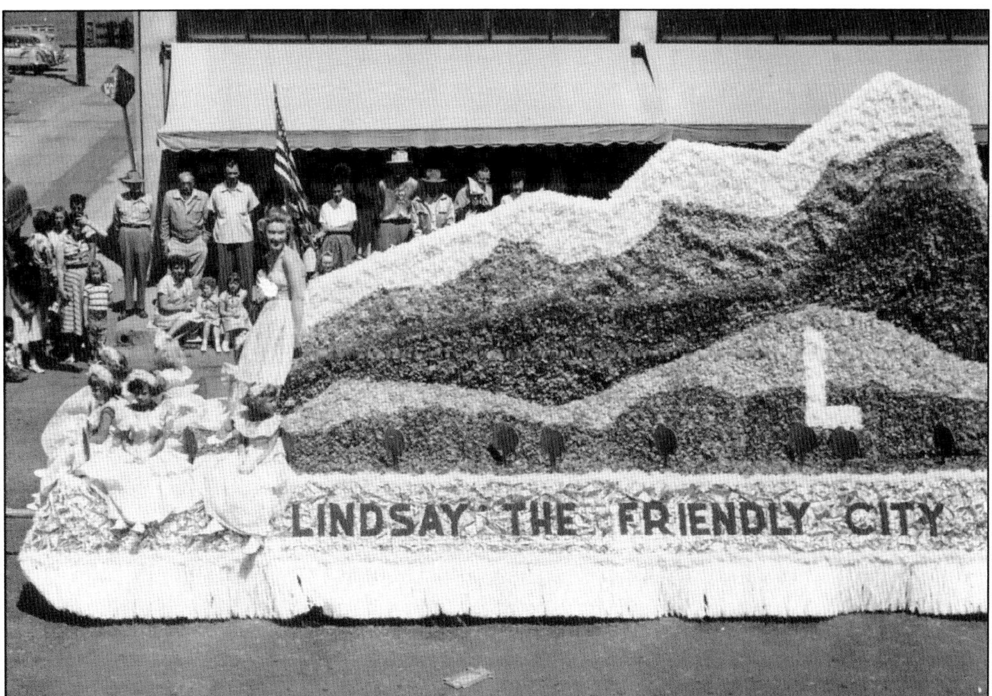

An Orange Blossom parade float displays the town motto, "Lindsay, the Friendly City," and the trademark "L" on the hill overlooking the town. (LMG.)

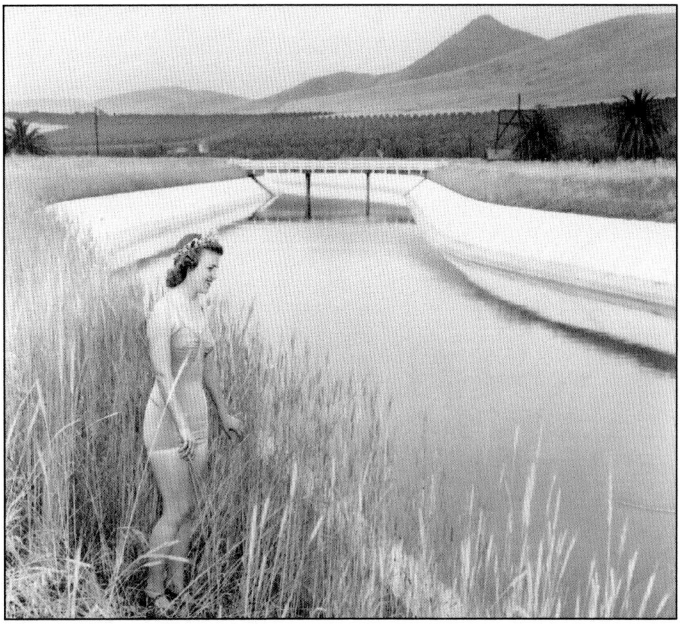

Sue Depew Lady, the 1951 Orange Blossom Queen, looks out over the Friant-Kern Canal. Orange groves, palm trees, and the surrounding foothills, what locals call the Elephant's Back, depict the picturesque landscape Lindsay is known for. (LMG.)

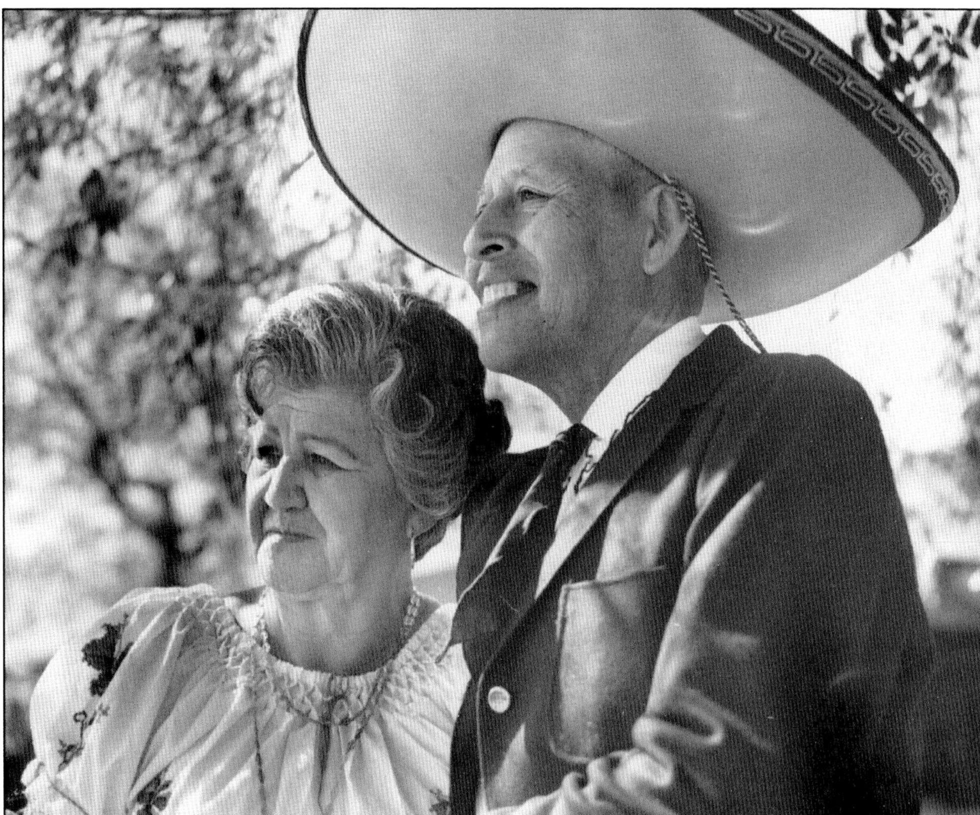

In 1956, a tradition was added to the Orange Blossom Festival of recognizing an "Honored Couple" from Lindsay who had greatly contributed to the community through the years. Pictured here are Mary and Tony Hernandez, Honored Couple of 1979. (LMG.)

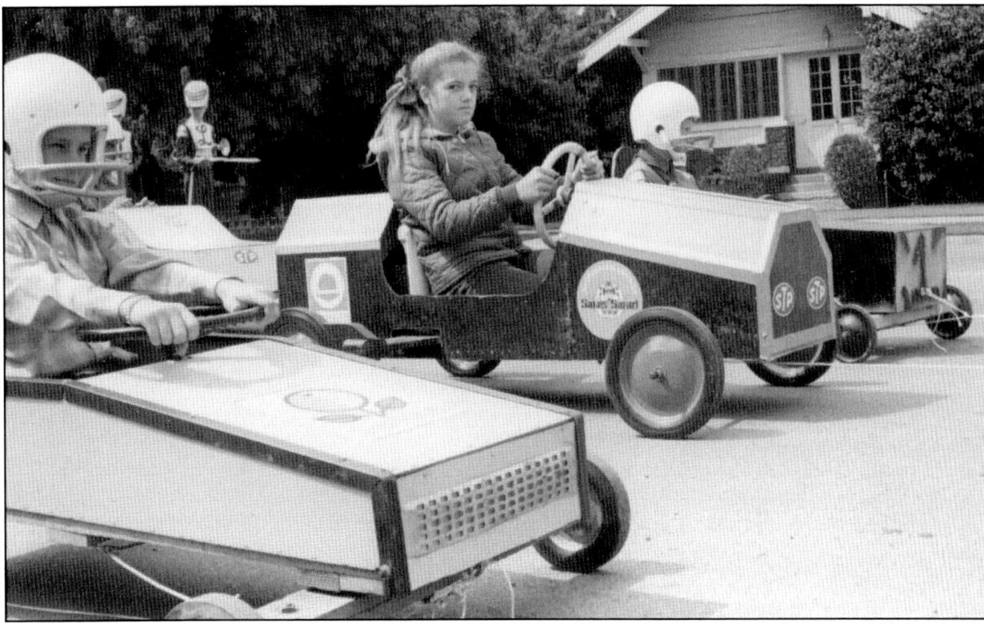

Participants of the Orange Crate Derby prepare to race as Lindsay High School band members look on in the background. The races were held on Towt Hill, close to the home of the Towt family, citrus ranchers who were responsible for a wind machine that would heat the orchards during cold winter nights. (LMG.)

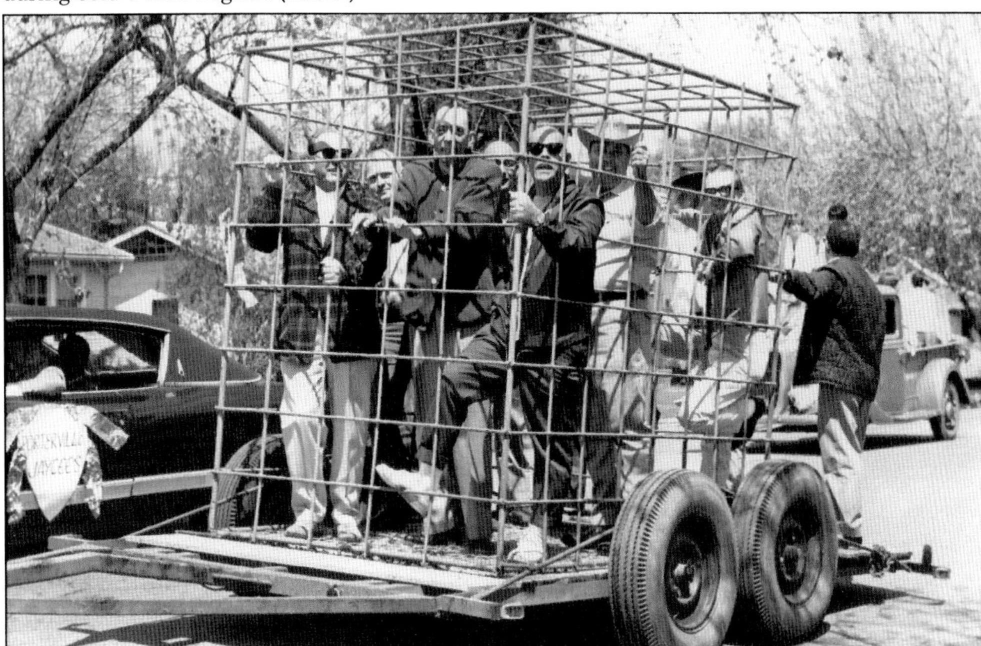

One of the most beloved Orange Blossom Festival traditions was the Slick Puss fundraiser, hosted by the Jaycees. Local men who were clean shaven or possessed "slick pusses" were subject to numerous penalties, including monetary fines and social ostracism, as well as capture and subsequent imprisonment in this portable jail that was carted around town. Penalties could be avoided by purchasing a special ribbon and wearing it during the festivities. (LMG.)

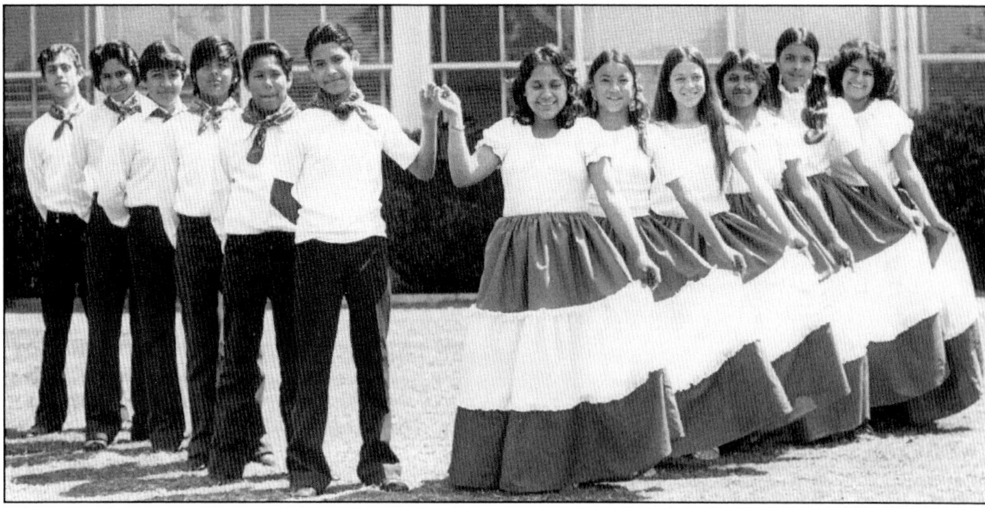

The La Bamba Dancers delight Orange Blossom Festival audiences with traditional folk dancing. (LMG.)

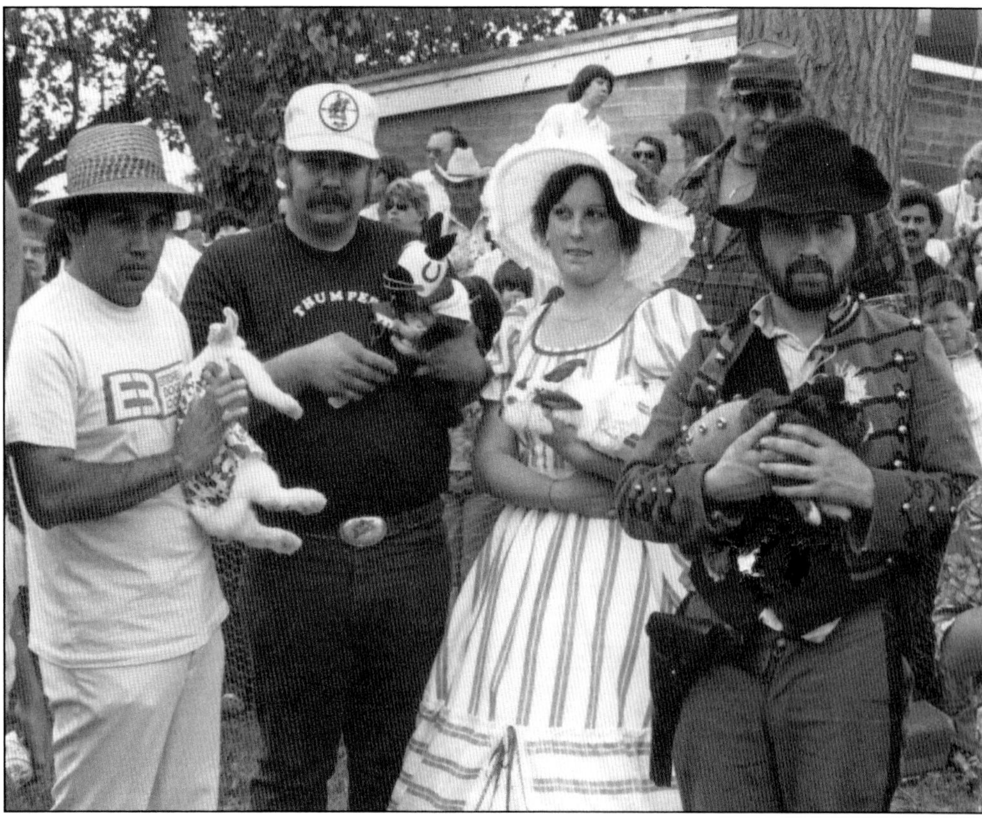

Lindsay resident Lupe Castro (far left) and other unidentified competitors hold their costumed rabbits, participants in the popular Rabbit Race. (LMG.)

Five

The Heart of Lindsay

A.L. Evans once said, "When we first saw Lindsay in the Springtime . . . oranges ripe on the trees, flowers everywhere and heavy snow dusting the sierras, our first dream of Heaven was realized." As it has been described for years, Lindsay and its community have captured the hearts and dreams of many an American seeking a home and a better life. Throughout the years, Lindsay and its inhabitants have been the epitome of the word *community*, with neighbors helping one another and the community at large uniting together to overcome its many hardships time and time again. This sense of community has even been recognized on a national level when the town was given the All-America City Award. This award is the oldest community recognition program in the nation, established in 1949 to recognize and celebrate communities whose inhabitants "work together to identify and tackle community-wide challenges and achieve uncommon results." The following pages feature some of the imaginative, inventive, tenacious, and courageous people who were the heart of this small town.

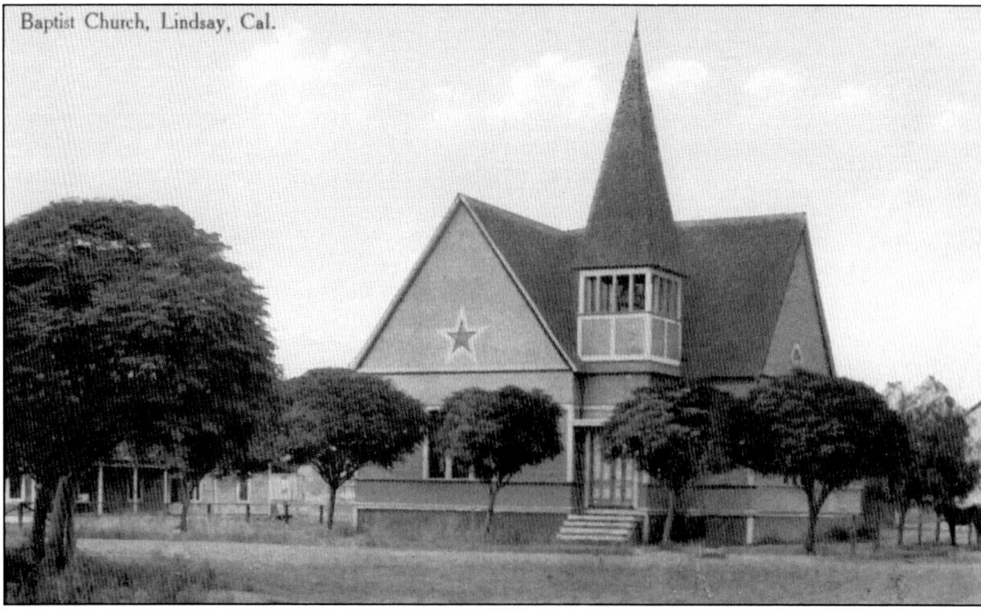

Lindsay's first church was part of a Christian missionary program started by the American Baptist Home Missionary Society, renowned for establishing 27 historically black colleges. Early missionaries risked their lives spreading the gospel and establishing organized, albeit temporary, structures utilizing colporteur wagons, railroad cars, and "gospel boats" along American waterways. Lindsay's chapel car was dubbed Emmanuel in 1884, and shortly thereafter, the First Baptist Church of Lindsay came to fruition. (GM.)

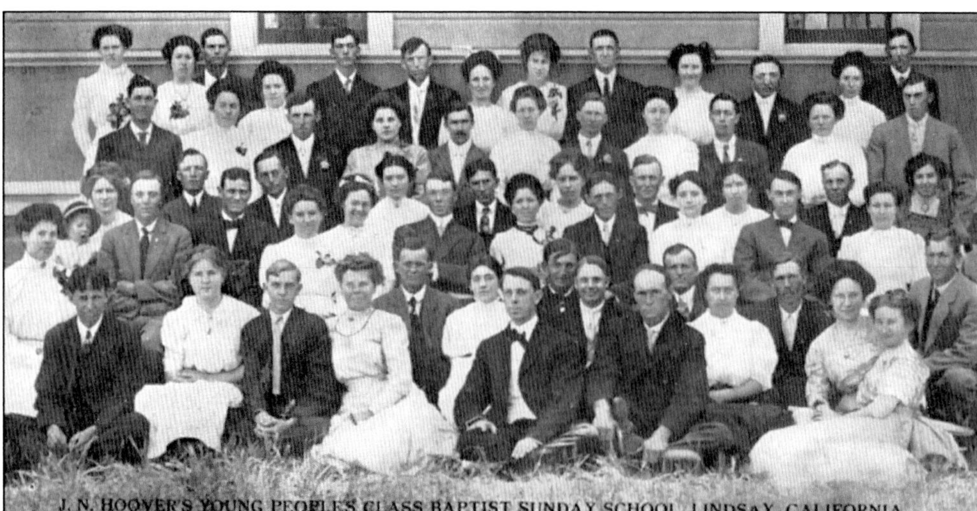

Rev. J.N. Hoover came from Wichita, Kansas, to become the pastor at Lindsay's first church, whose congregation grew rapidly. A 1906 publication states that there were 300 students in their Sunday school program, and the Young People's Class, pictured here, had 95 students led by Jonas Williams. (GM.)

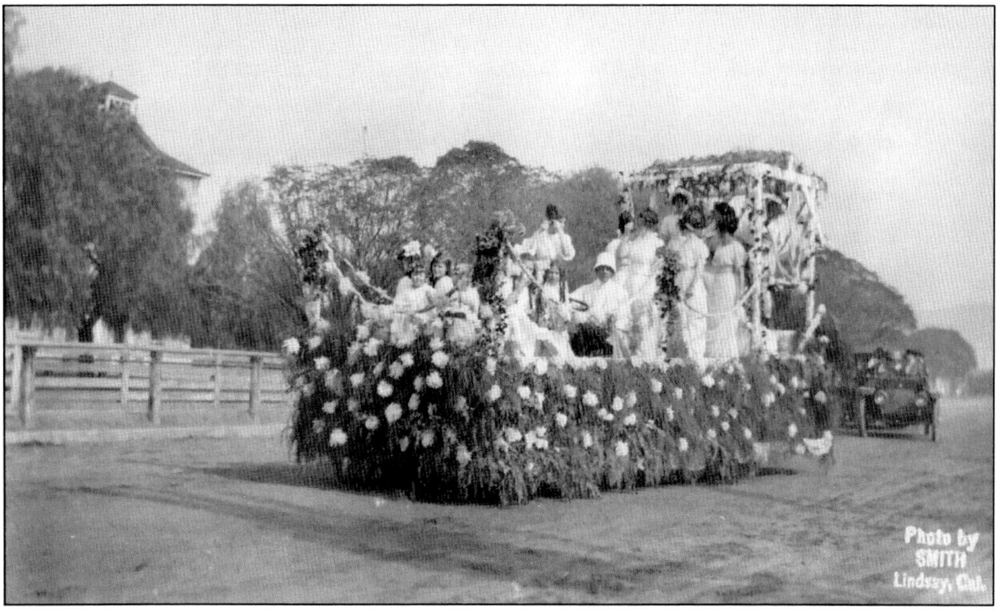

A beautifully decorated float with many passengers dressed all in white is en route to some local festivities. In the center, a steering wheel is just visible. To the left is a glimpse of the Little Red Schoolhouse. (PK.)

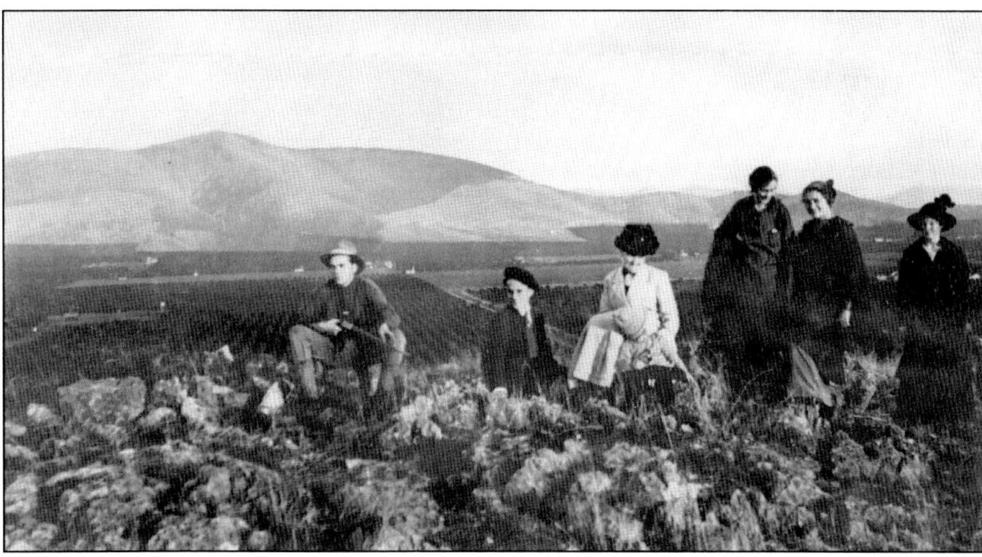
This photograph, taken around 1906, shows a group of friends or family pausing after a hike. Behind them, the town of Lindsay, full of citrus orchards and new homes, spreads out in the distance. (LMG.)

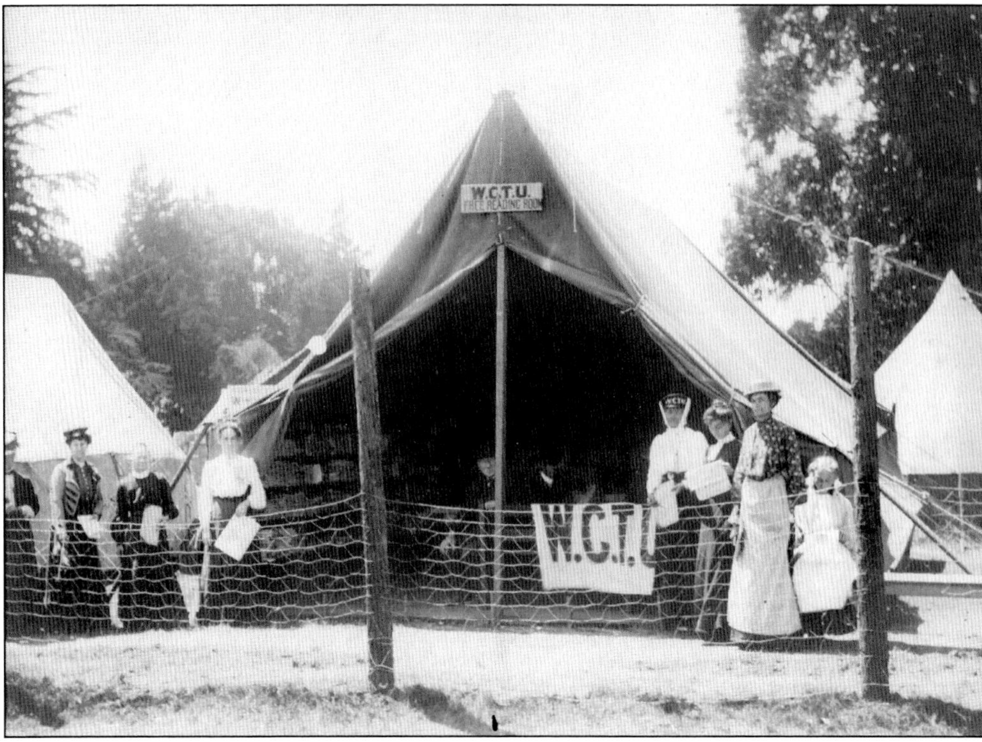

Members of Lindsay's branch of the Women's Christian Temperance Union (WCTU) are pictured outside a tent being utilized as a reading room. While the main goal of the WCTU was to advocate for a "sober and pure world," they were interested in numerous social reform issues, to boot. One of these was encouraging women to get involved in politics and supporting the women's suffrage movement. (LMG.)

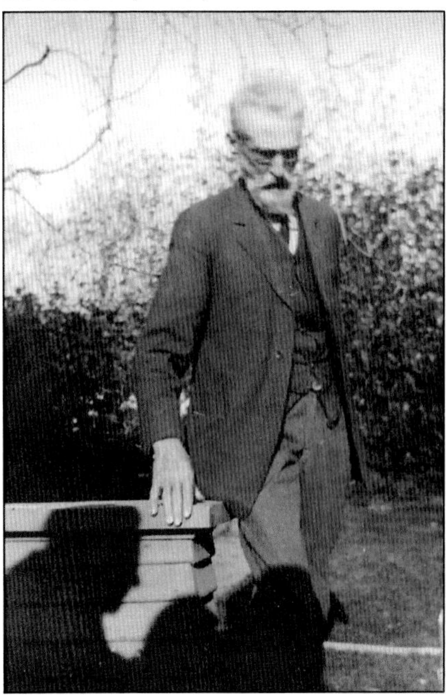

George Kirkham Hostetter and his wife, Margaret, purchased land in Lindsay in the 1800s. Their home on Tulare Road, like many of the town's pioneer homes, is still standing. One of the most prominent pioneer families, the Hostetters' early domain was the town's largest store, the Lindsay Mercantile. Throughout the decades, the Hostetter family has significantly contributed to the community. (GH.)

Helen Ford stands alongside Jenny Barnes, who is seated atop a prop ostrich. Both ladies are at the height of late Victorian fashion in their shirtwaists. As the Victorians were huge nature enthusiasts, ostriches were very popular for a time, often seen pulling ornate passenger carriages or their lush feathers adorning living rooms. (LMG.)

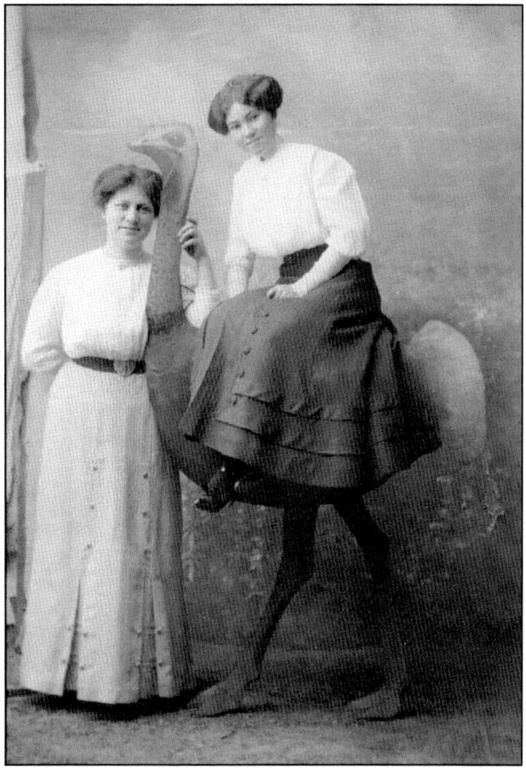

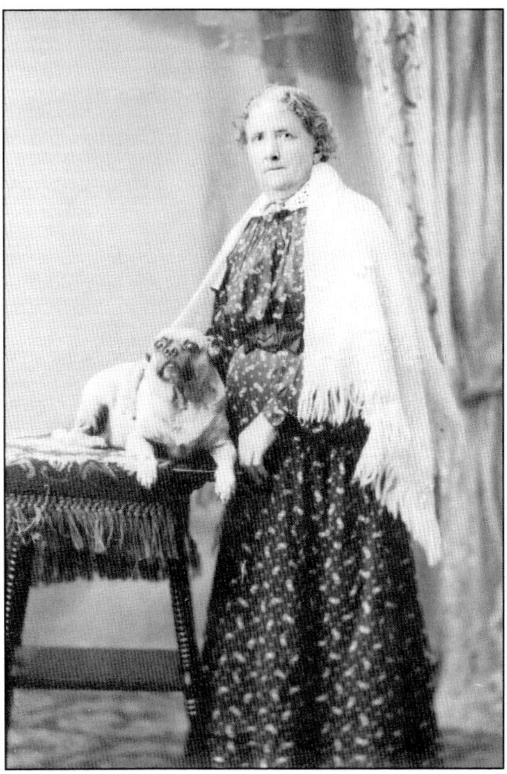

As loyal companions, indispensable workers, and guardians of the farm and ranch, pets have always been a cherished part of Lindsay's families. A Lindsay resident poses for a portrait with her dog, Roscoe, in 1910. (LMG.)

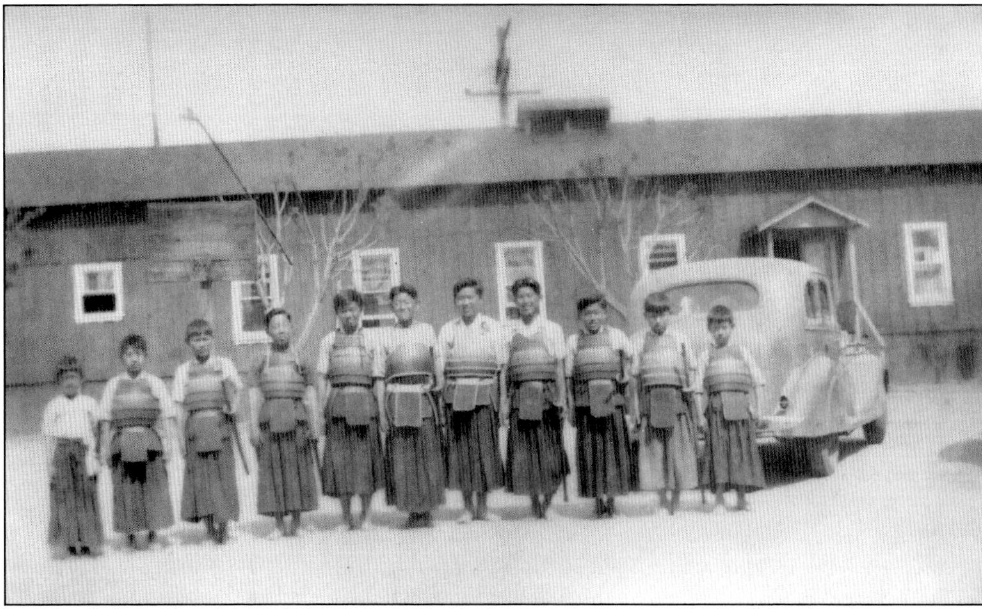

Japanese immigrants made up a significant percentage of Lindsay's pioneers, so much so that a thriving Japantown existed within its borders. There was a hotel, saloons, restaurants like the Noodle House, and a market run by George Kaku and his family. The Kakus' store served the community for over 60 years. In addition to these establishments, there was also a beautiful Japanese school, pictured here. (LMG.)

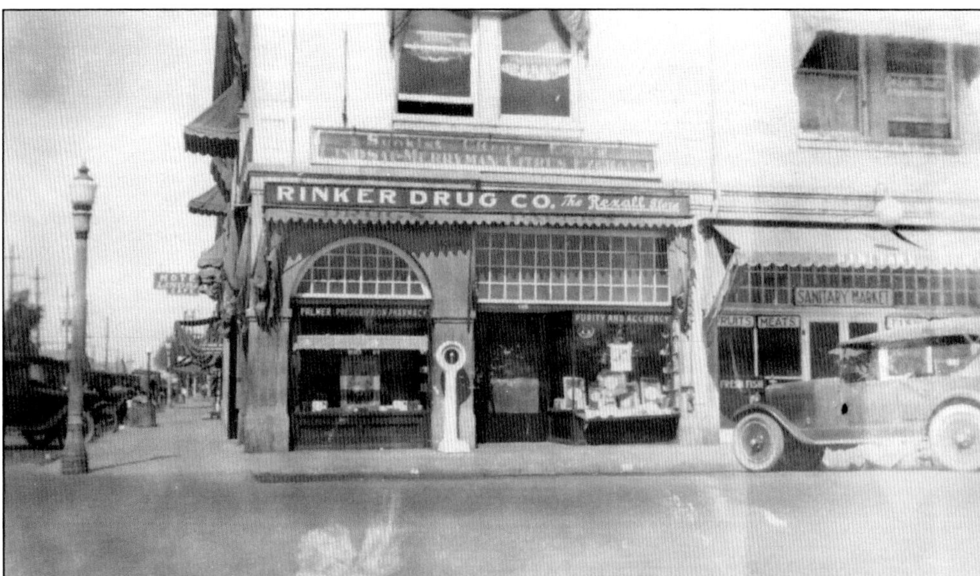

Certainly one of Lindsay's busiest locations during its early years was this corner. Above Rinker Drug Company were the offices for the citrus powerhouse Lindsay-Merriman Citrus Exchange, purveyor of the well-known Sunkist brand. Jutting out to the left is the sign for Hotel Lindsay, which was frequented by newcomers and established citrus men alike. (CSUF.)

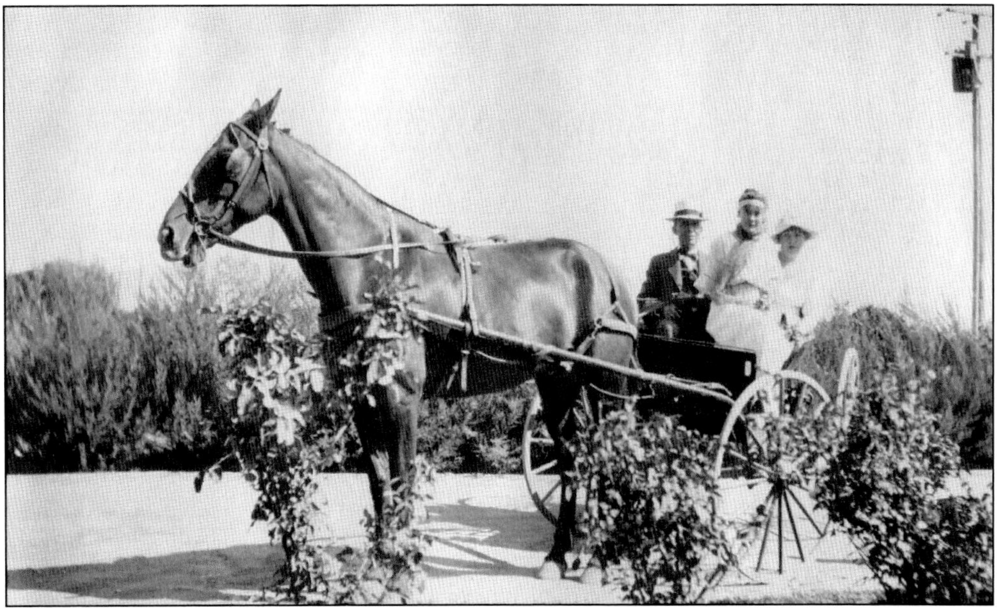

Local girls Anne Keeley (right) and Carol Brady (center) would often tend to the Gillette family property when the family was away. Here, the girls have taken the liberty of hitching up the Gillette horse to a carriage and decorating it to ride around the expansive estate. (LMG.)

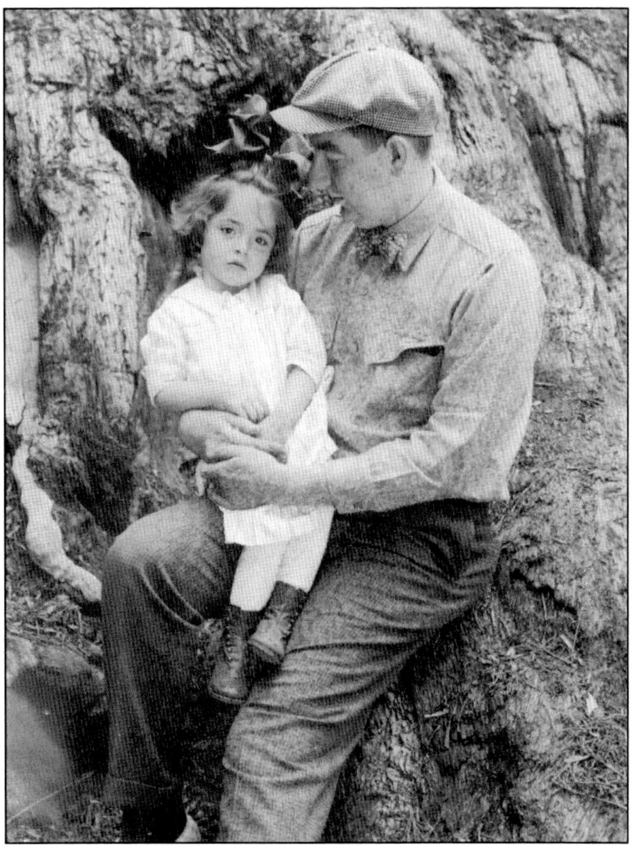

King Gillette Jr. is pictured here with daughter Celeste. The Gillettes of Gillette razor fame owned property in Lindsay and Strathmore and invested in numerous local businesses, including a failed broom company. Gillette Jr. and his partners had intentions of making Lindsay the "broom capital of the world." This venture proved to be a poorly thought-out plan, as the expense to ship the necessary materials, from Lindsay, Oklahoma, proved too costly. (LMG.)

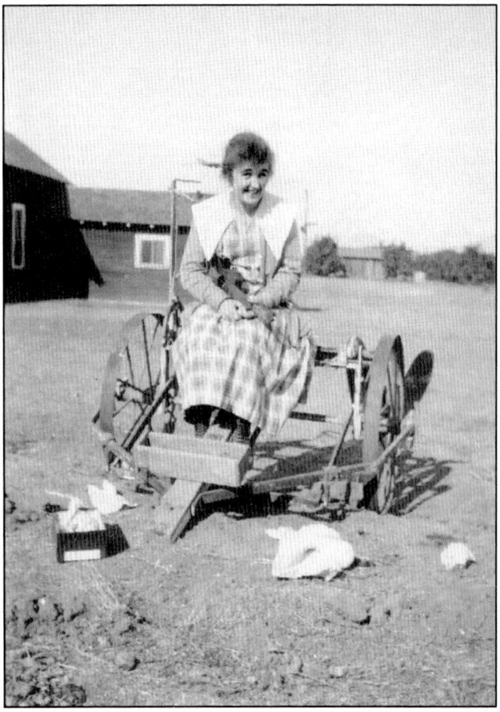

Anne Keeley often cared for little Celeste Gillette and spent a great deal of time with the family on the Gillette properties, as well as the home built by King Gillette's sister and her husband, C.A. Gaines. In later years, the residence was referred to as the Waddell House when the Waddell family occupied it. (LMG.)

A photograph taken for the *Lindsay Gazette* shows, from left to right, Harry Purcell, W.H. English, Charles F. Burr, P.E. Lynch, and Buel Williams in front of the Lindsay jail. According to some of the locals, the jail was constructed utilizing bars from the original Visalia jail in 1890. Both the Lindsay jail and the original Visalia jail, which is now a dining establishment, are still standing. (CSUF.)

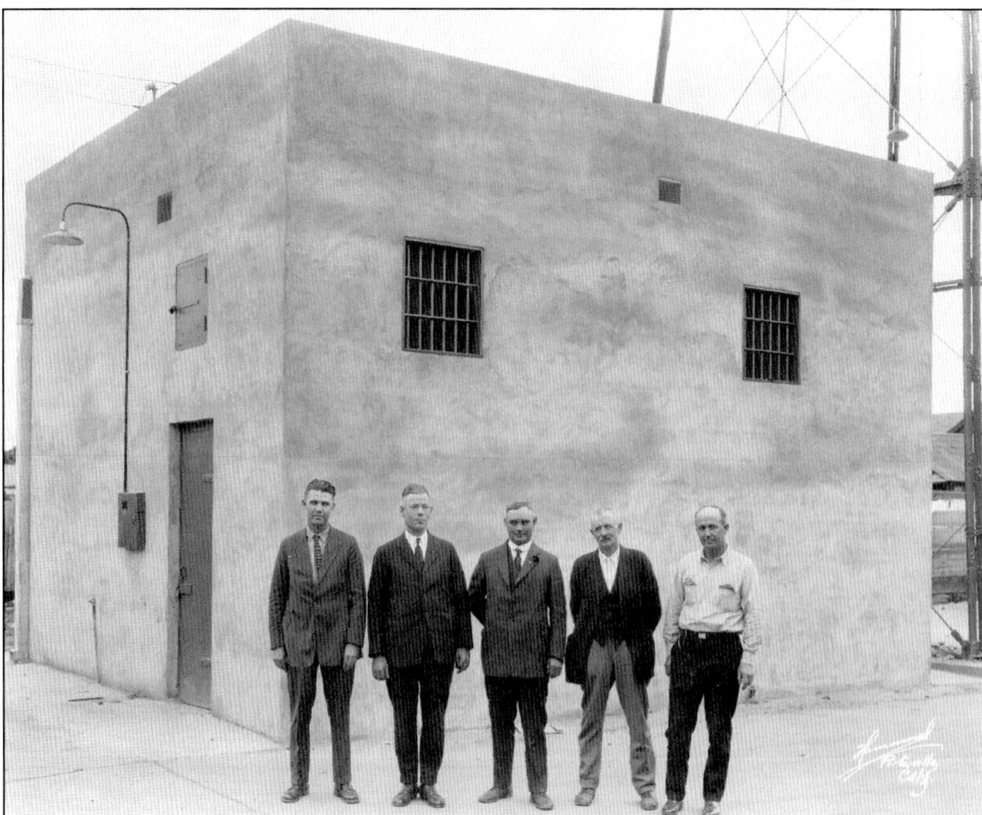

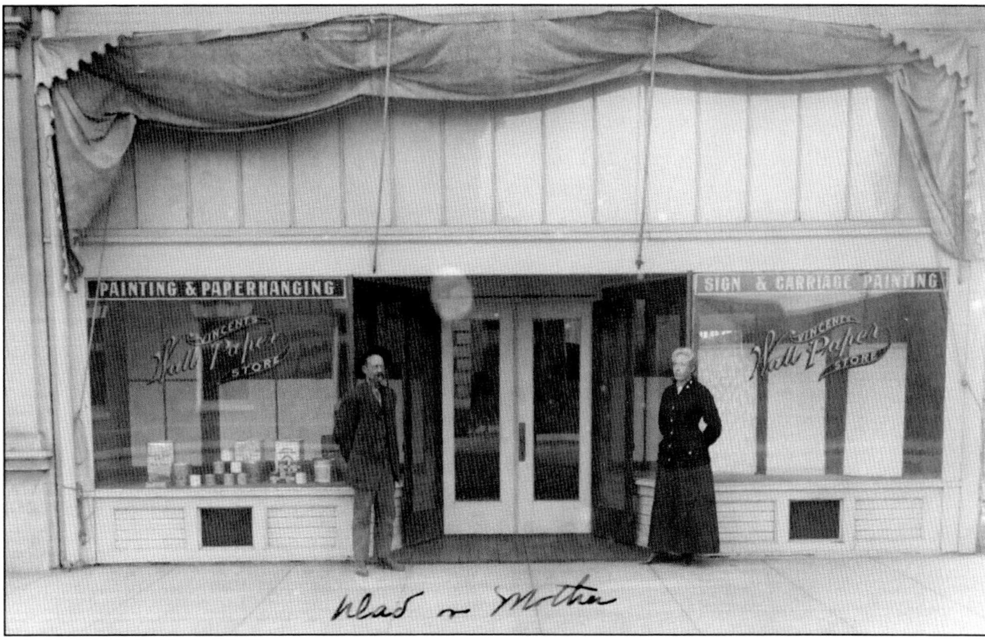

Vincent's Wallpaper Store was located on South Elmwood Avenue, next door to what was once the Lyon Insurance office. Wallpaper could be hazardous or even deadly during this era if it was colored using the popular Scheele's Green, a pigment derived from arsenic. The color was used in everything from clothing to toys to food, leading to many painful deaths. (CSUF.)

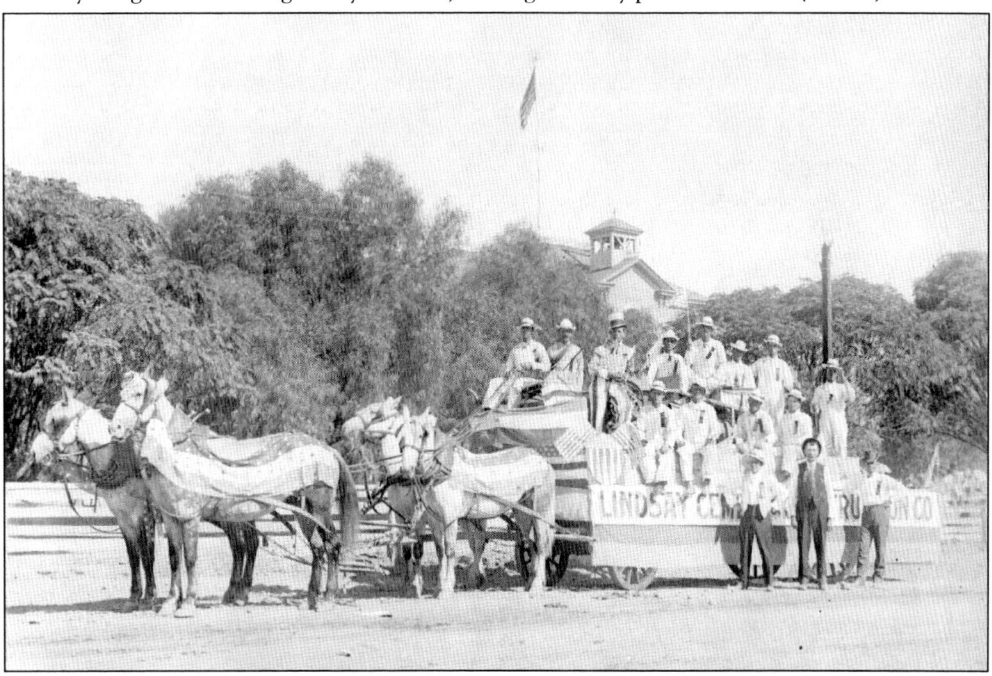

Here is a float entry from the Lindsay Cement and Construction Company for a fair that took place in 1910. Behind them is the original Little Red Schoolhouse. The horses are outfitted in patriotic finery, as is one gentleman in particular astride the float in a star-studded vest and striped trousers. (GM.)

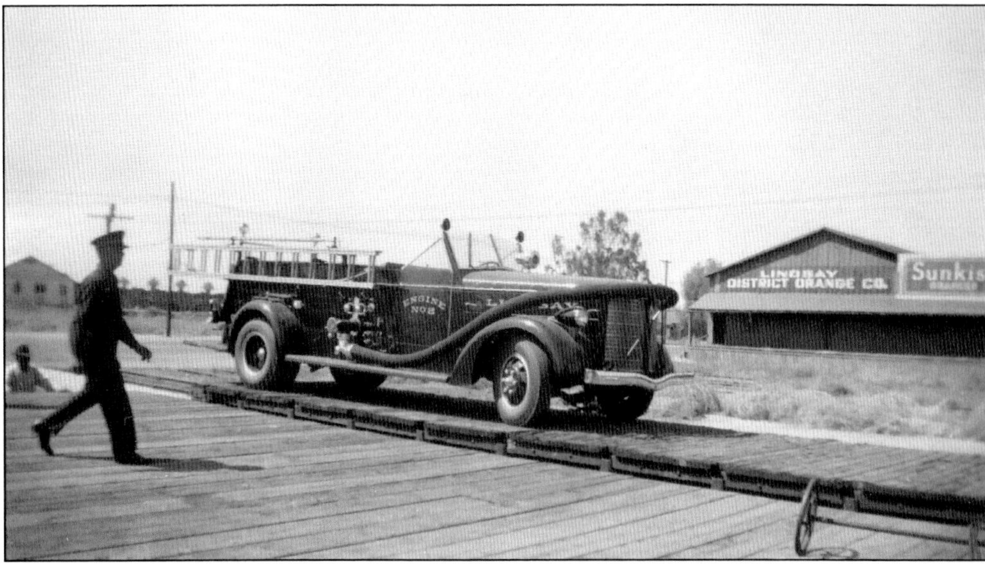

The Lindsay Fire Department was established in 1910 when a meeting was held in McGregor's Garage. The first fire chief was Clint Roberts, who had been elected by the town trustees when Lindsay was officially incorporated. A firefighter is seen here walking toward a fire truck in 1940. In the background, the Lindsay District Orange Company building can be seen with a Sunkist oranges sign displayed on it. (GM.)

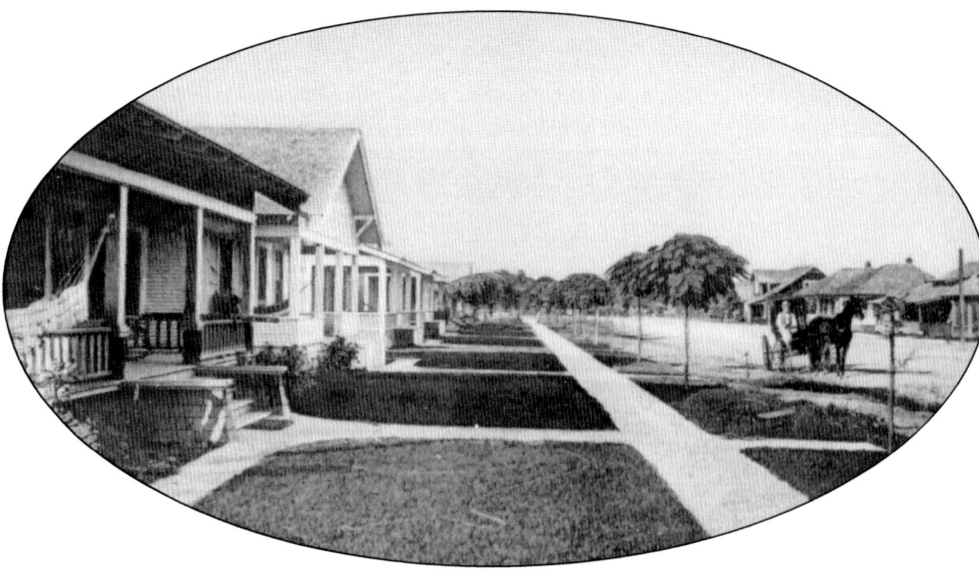

In this view from about 1910 is a residential street referred to as Bungalow Row. To the right, a man is driving his horse and buggy down the unpaved street. Some of the porches have hammocks hanging on them. Many homes were built with porches to accommodate family members with tuberculosis, as the clean California air was thought to be the best remedy. (GM.)

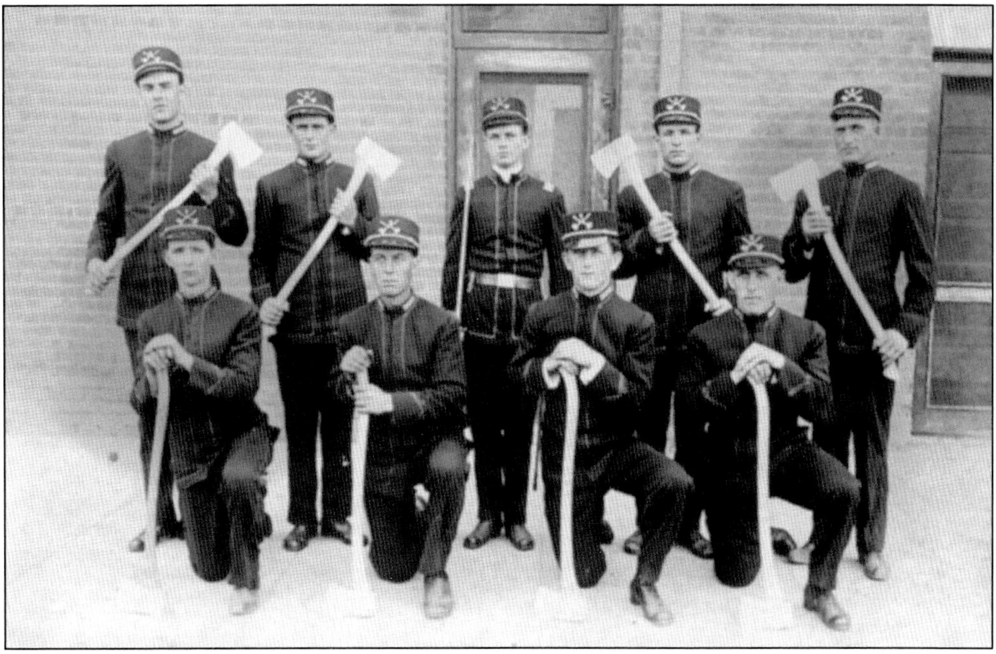

Here is a portrait of the Lindsay branch of Woodmen of America. These organizations served as benefit societies that provided private insurance. Their women's auxiliary, Royal Neighbors of America, was popular in Lindsay. Although progressive in their women's rights stance, their bylaws were not favorable to all women, forbidding membership to "women of color." Also denied were individuals with occupations deemed hazardous, such as wild animal trainers, glassblowers, and chimney sweeps. (LMG.)

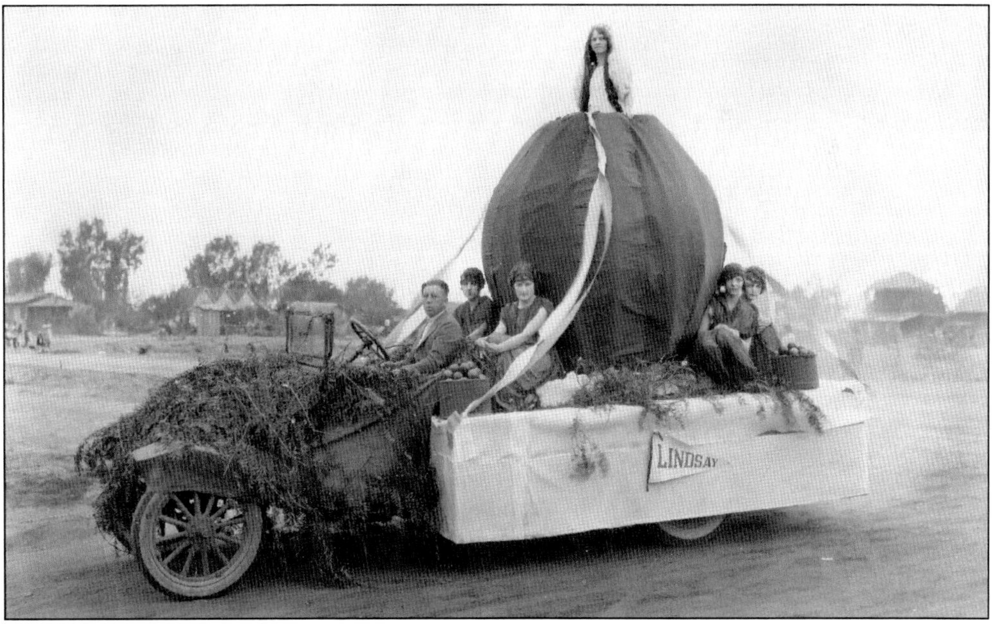

Representing Lindsay and the orange industry it was known for, this wonderfully imaginative float features a giant orange with a lady emerging from the center. Around it are more ladies with buckets of oranges, which they likely distributed along the parade route. (LMG.)

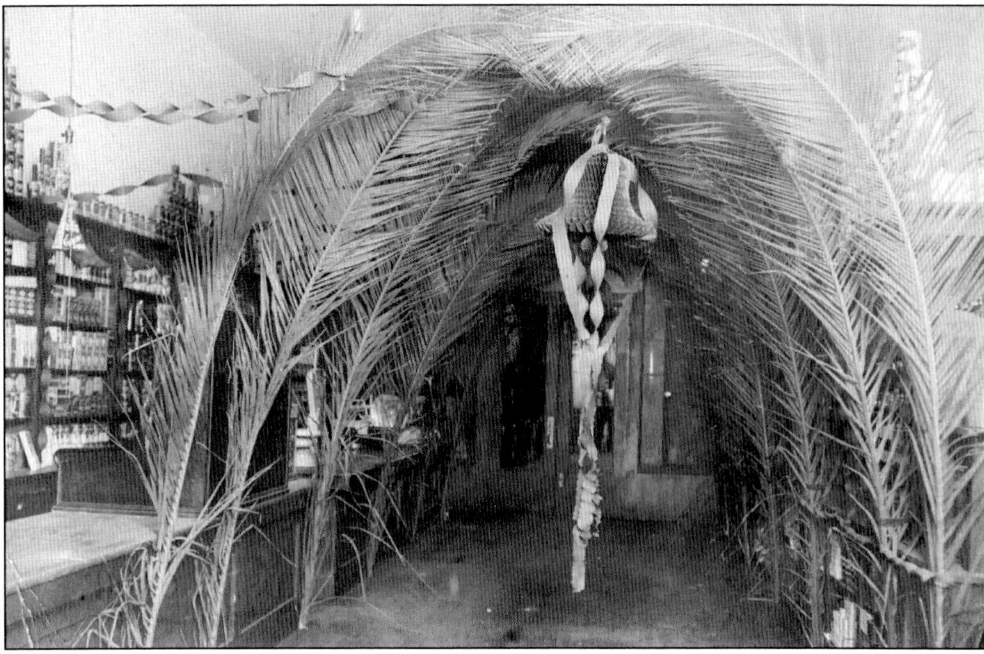

The Orange Front Cash Grocery, owned by E.C. Graham, is decorated with palm fronds and a pole adorned with a crepe paper bell. Such decorations were typical of this period, and they still find a place at celebrations and festive occasions today. (CSUF.)

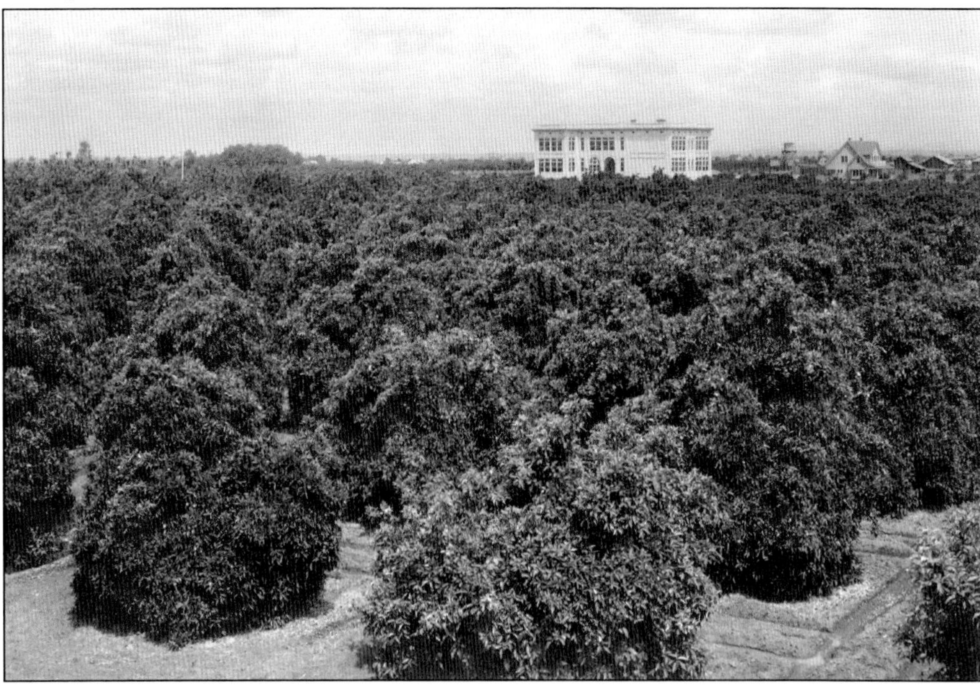

The Jefferson school opened in February 1911. The new facility had a total of nine classrooms and employed five teachers. This is a wonderful shot of the school, which sat deep within the orange groves. It reveals the beauty of not only the location of the school, but also of Lindsay itself. (CSUF.)

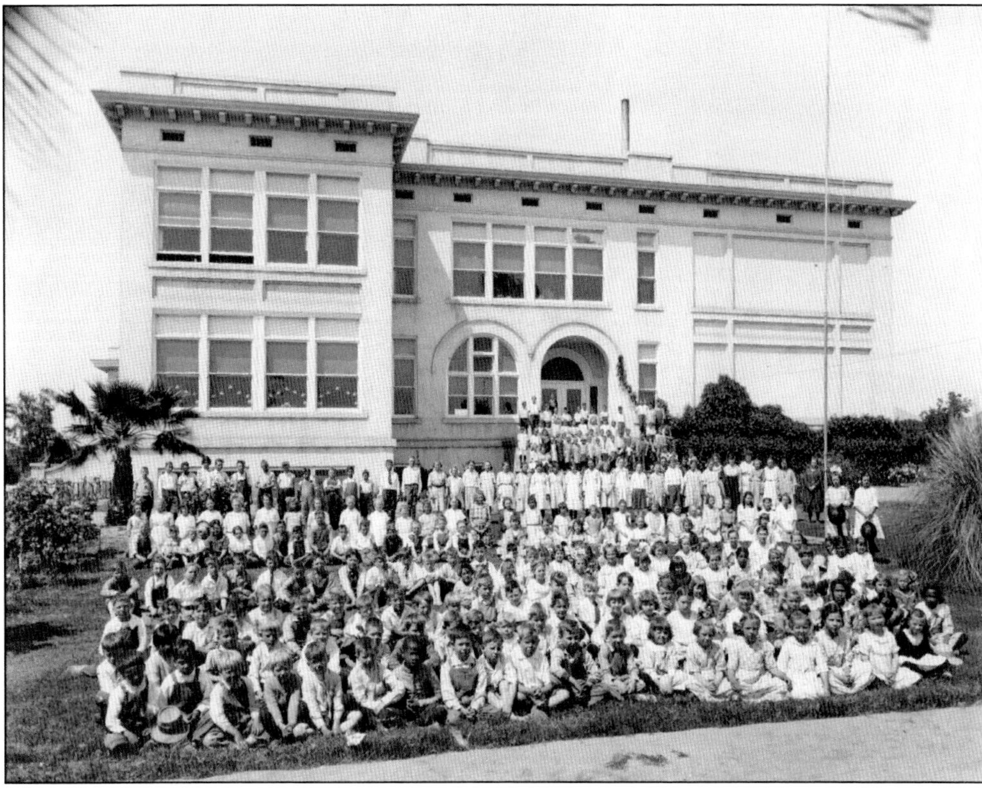

Jefferson schoolchildren, dressed in their Sunday best, are gathered together in front of their school. This photograph was taken by B.P. Cole. (CSUF.)

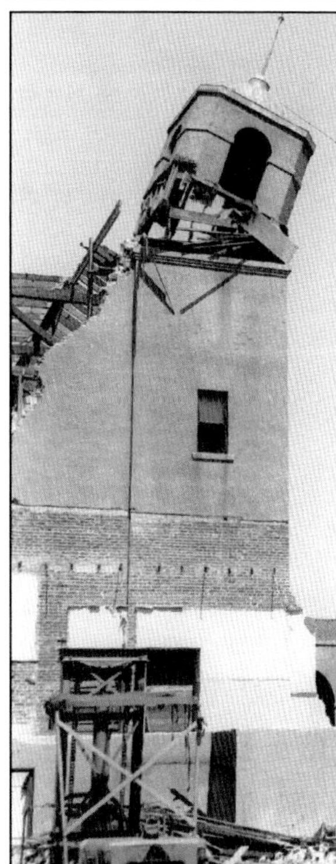

This is an undated photograph of the demolition of the Little Red Schoolhouse. The town's population had grown so much that a new schoolhouse was necessary to educate the many school-age children now residing in Lindsay. (CSUF.)

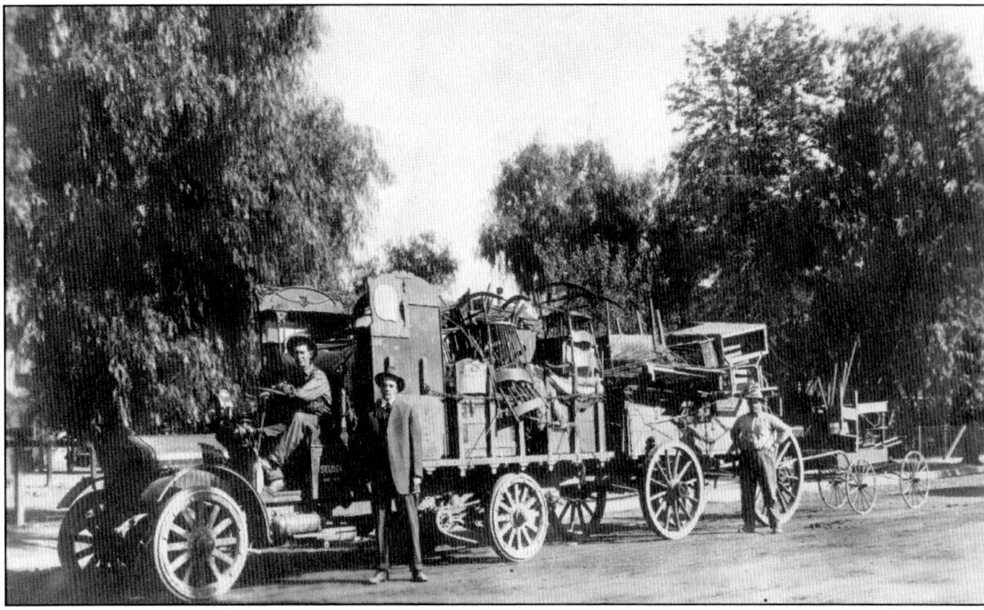

Clare Brady stands just to the right of the driver's seat of his one-ton truck loaded up with furniture. Brady was a salesman for Selden trucks for a period of time. Selden was an automobile manufacturer founded in 1905. Salesmen like Brady would be provided with a truck for use in promoting sales of the vehicles, a highly desirable item for citrus farmers in the area to transport their goods. (LMG.)

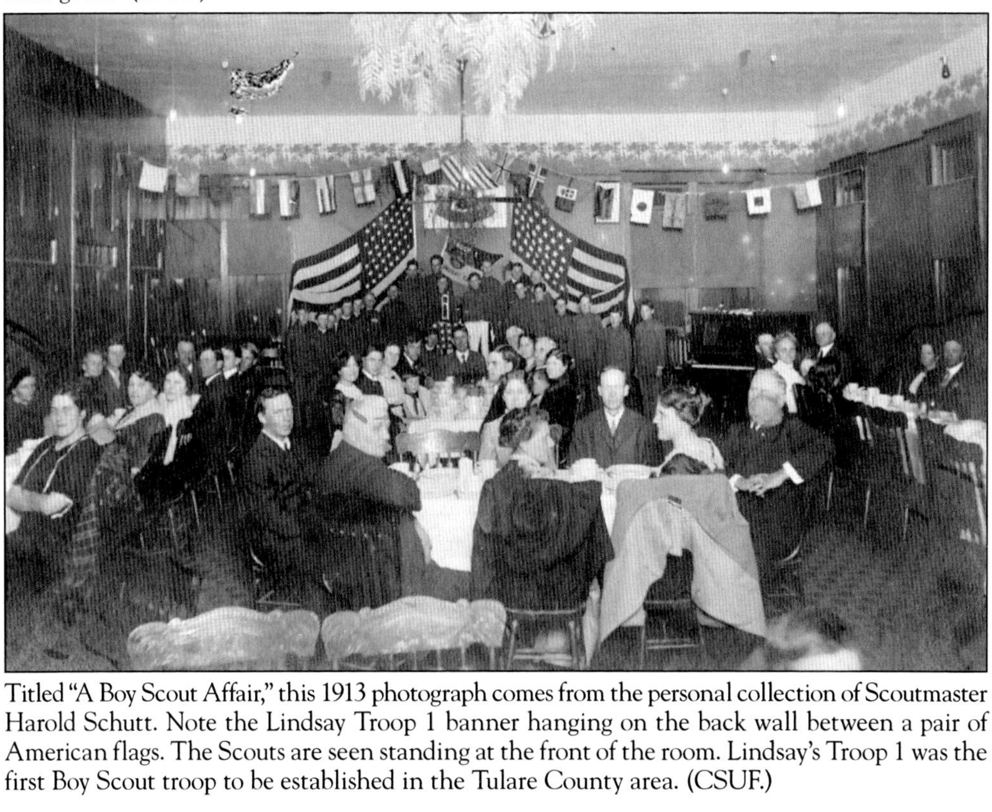

Titled "A Boy Scout Affair," this 1913 photograph comes from the personal collection of Scoutmaster Harold Schutt. Note the Lindsay Troop 1 banner hanging on the back wall between a pair of American flags. The Scouts are seen standing at the front of the room. Lindsay's Troop 1 was the first Boy Scout troop to be established in the Tulare County area. (CSUF.)

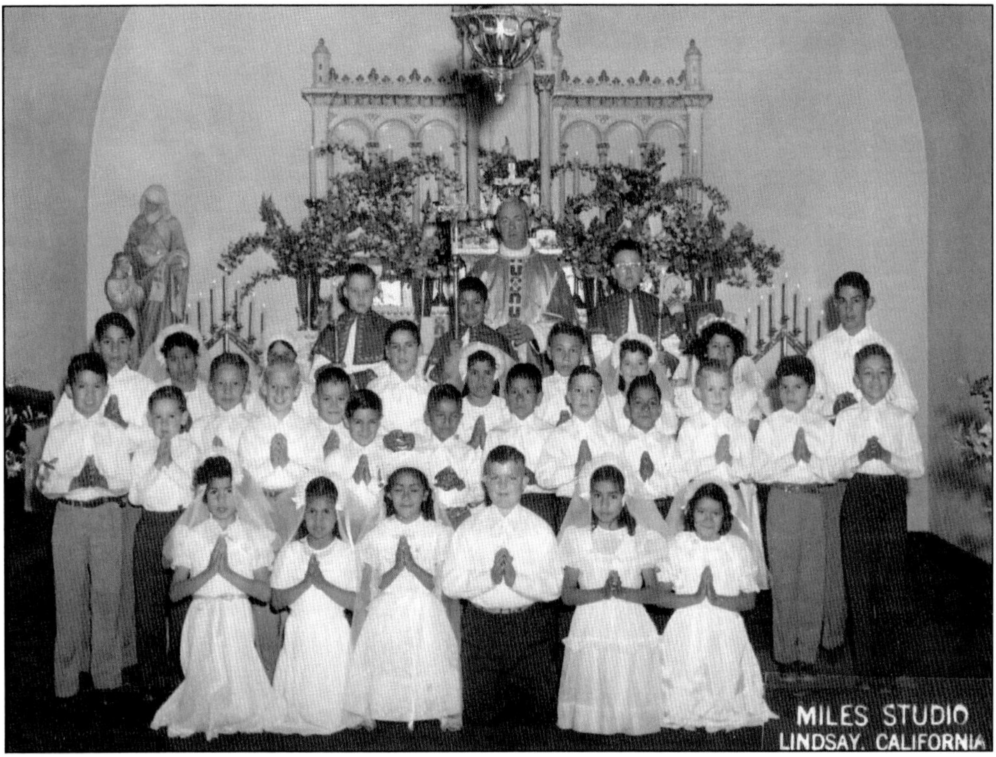

The Catholic Women's Club originated in 1914 for the purpose of raising funds to build Sacred Heart Church, which broke ground in 1925. The *Lindsay Gazette* described this structure as "a combination of colonial and rural English architecture." Landscaping supplies were donated by the Ingoldsby family. Here, young parishioners stand with Fr. Cornelius M. Casey after receiving their First Communion. (LSHRCC.)

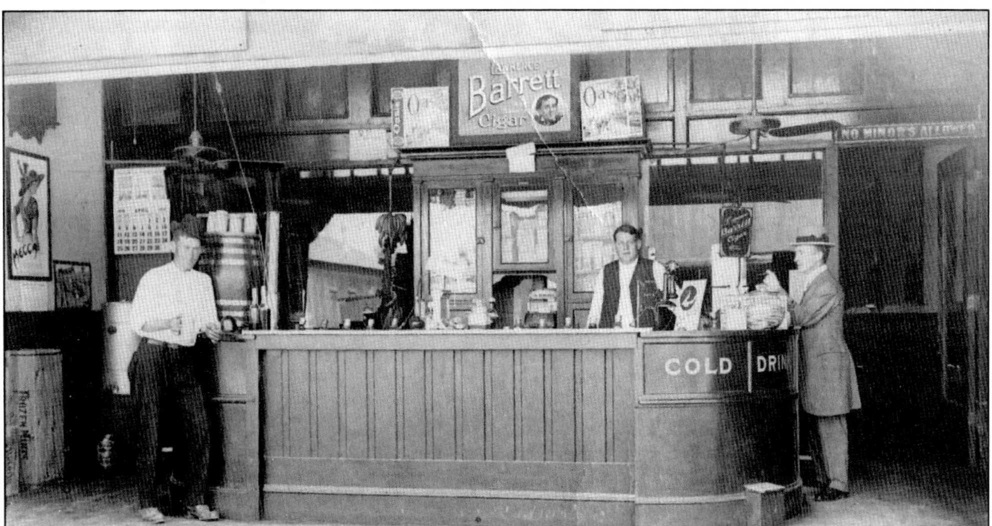

Another postcard image features the inside of a bar with a billiards room behind it. Note the April 1915 calendar at left. On the back of this postcard is the following message: "Lindsay, Cal, June 23rd. This is where I work. How old is Vermont? Your old friend, Doun." (CSUF.)

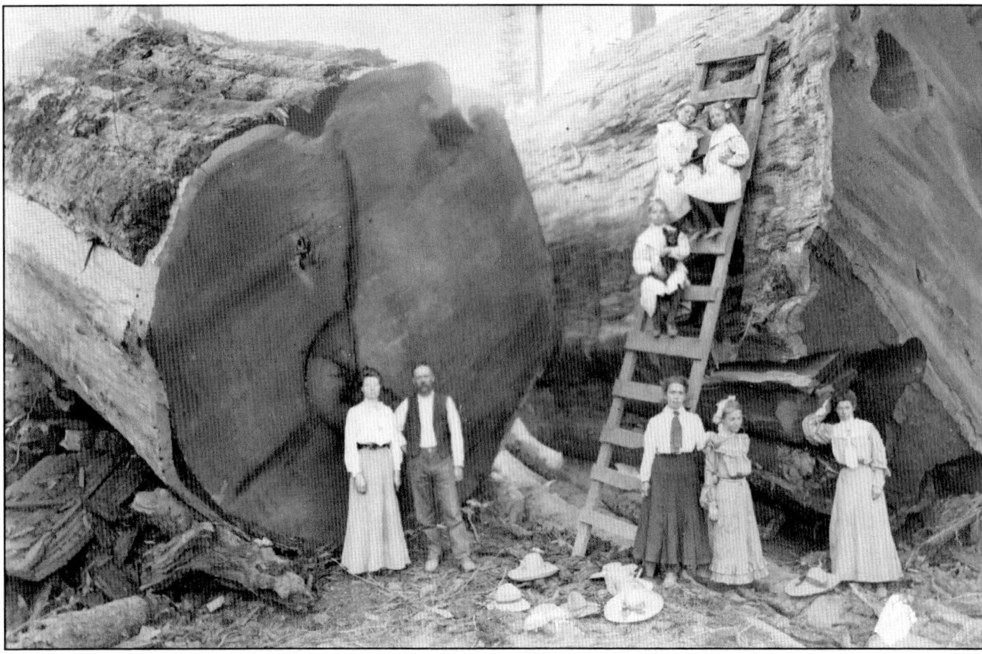

Many of Lindsay's early inhabitants traveled north to the giant redwood trees of the Sequoia National Forest to escape the oppressive heat of the summer months. Here, the Landers family, including the family dog, stops for a portrait taken by H.E. Roberts. (LMG.)

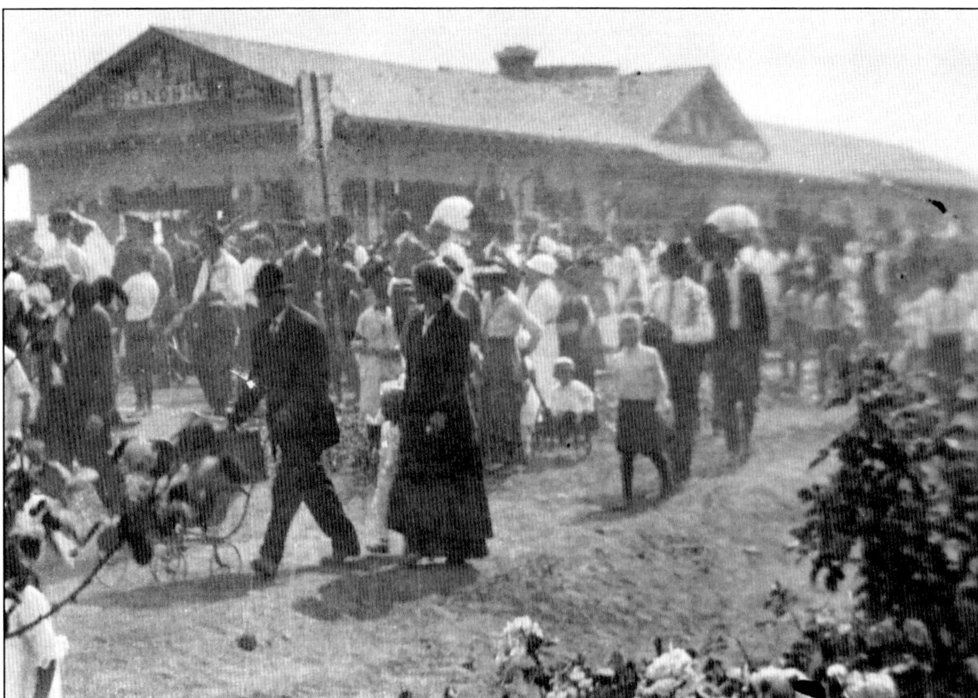

The train depot bustles with dozens of people in October 1915. Some are busy travelers on their way somewhere, while others are friends and family saying tearful good-byes or welcoming those setting foot in Lindsay for the very first time, with their baggage and dreams in hand. (CSUF.)

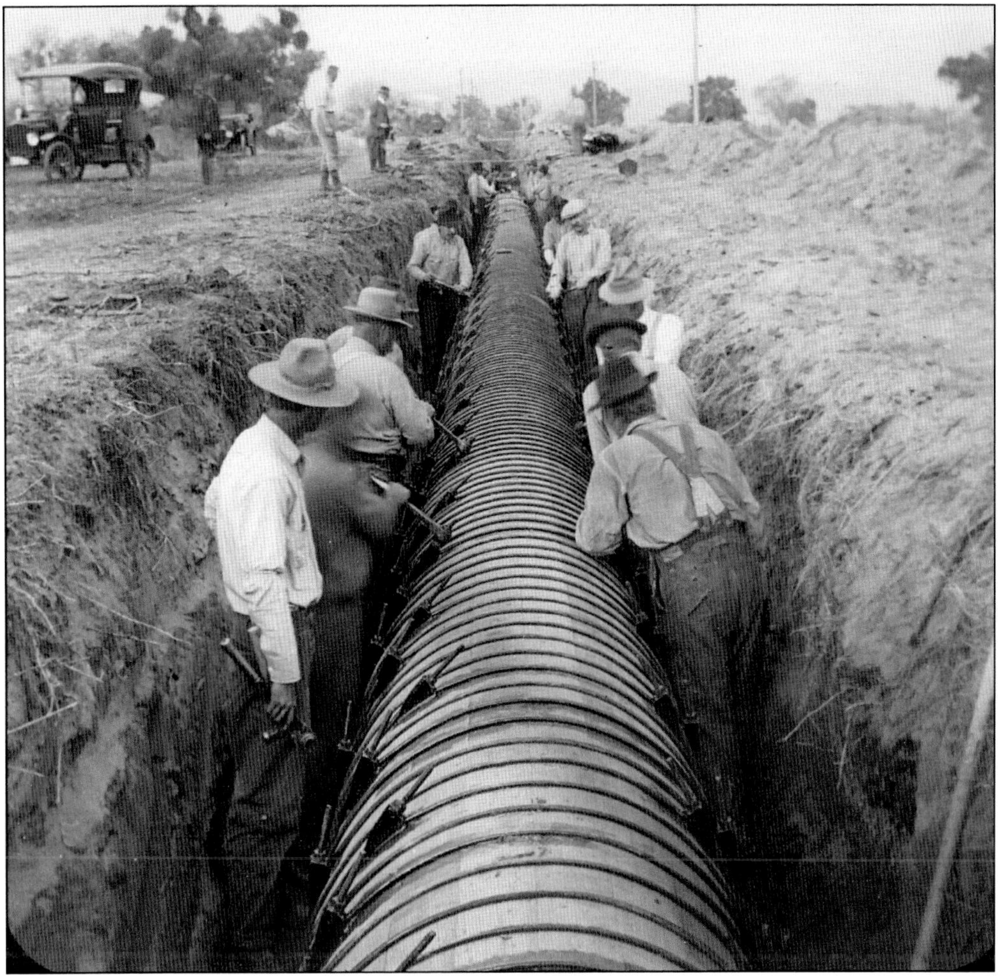

In the beginning, Lindsay's water supply seemed inexhaustible. By 1910, however, the growing need to irrigate the many thousands of acres of agriculture had become a concern. Engineer Stephen Keiffer came up with the idea of constructing a redwood pipeline to siphon water from the Kaweah Delta to Lindsay. In 1915, the Lindsay-Strathmore Irrigation District was formed as a result. It was backed by a $1,200 bond issue. From here, Lindsay acquired a well field of 1,100 acres and proceeded to drill 40 wells to begin the irrigation process. Numerous financial burdens caused various setbacks, along with a labor struggle that involved the Industrial Workers of the World. As if these issues were not enough, a huge blow was to come in 1916 in the form of a historic legal battle that would last some 15 years. (LMG.)

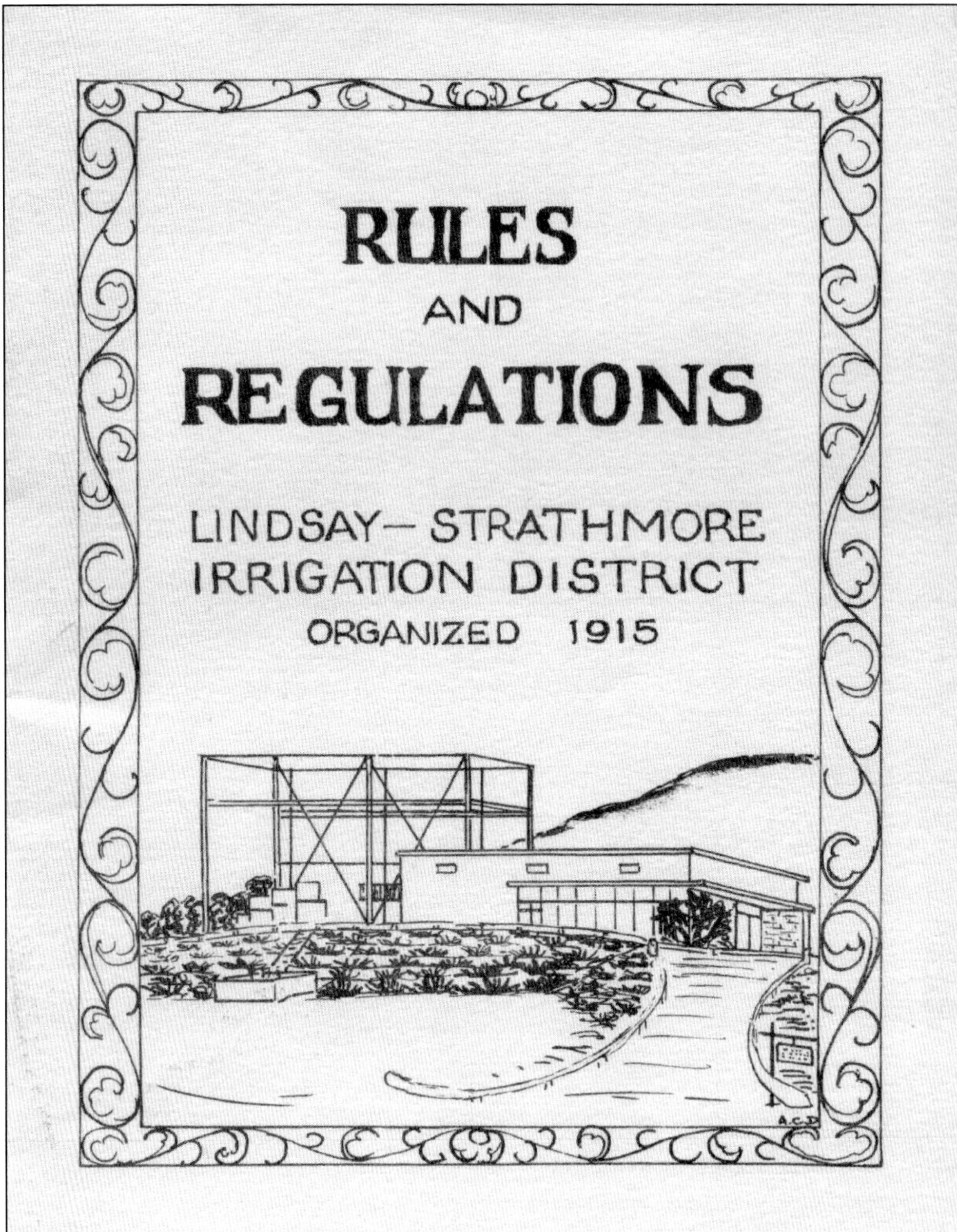

In 1916, the Tulare Irrigation District and its various allies with an interest at stake took legal action against the Lindsay-Strathmore Irrigation District for taking water from the river delta. These next years were fraught with conflict and drama, including involvement from spies, the employ of security guards, and many years of battles fought in and out of the courtroom. Finally, in 1931, a compromise was reached wherein the Central Valley Project was created solely for the purpose of bringing water to Lindsay via the Friant-Kern Canal. A.L. Evans, Starr Warson, and Walter S. Cairns performed much of the work to represent Lindsay. When this long, complicated battle for water finally came to an end, chamber president Ford Chatters welcomed members of the California State Supreme Court who visited Lindsay to mark the resolution with a celebration. (CSUF.)

A couple of adventurous Lindsay girls climb aboard a Southern Pacific Railroad water car to pose for this picture. (LMG.)

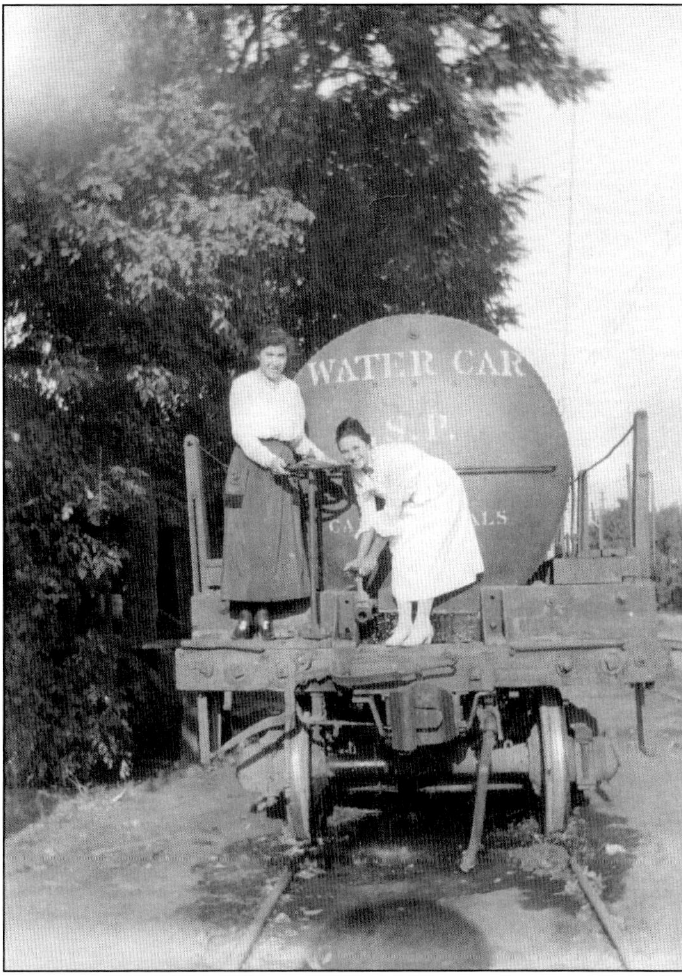

Members of the Lindsay High School girls' and boys' basketball teams picnic together in the surrounding foothills in 1916. Both hiking and picnicking were popular pastimes of the era. (LMG.)

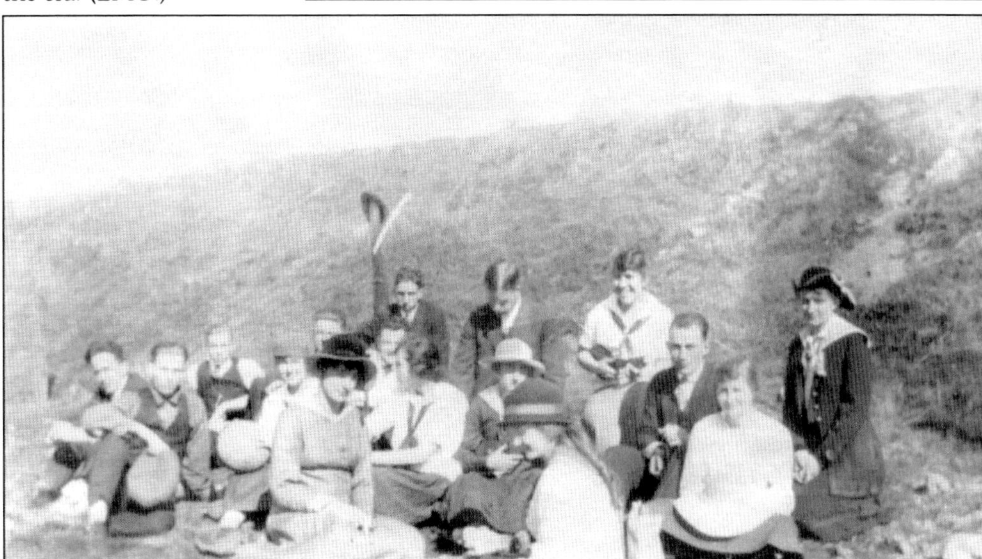

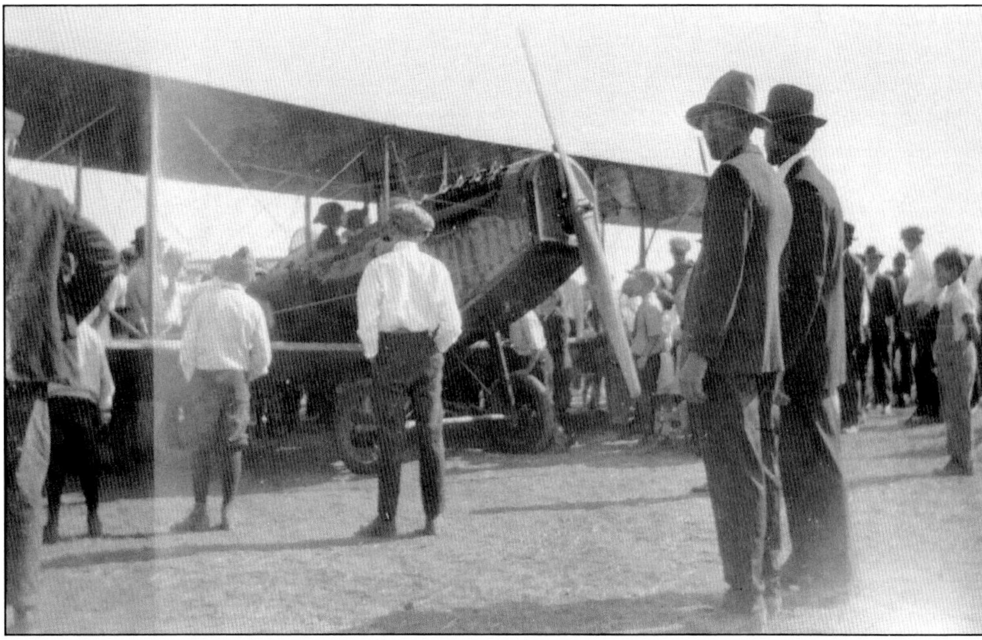

There was much excitement on the day an aviator landed in Lindsay and offered rides to anyone who wanted one. Back then, most residents never would have had the opportunity to ride in an airplane before. One can only imagine the excitement and exhilaration of flying for the first time. In this photograph, the lucky passengers are Lillian Wright and Alberta Jordan. (LMG.)

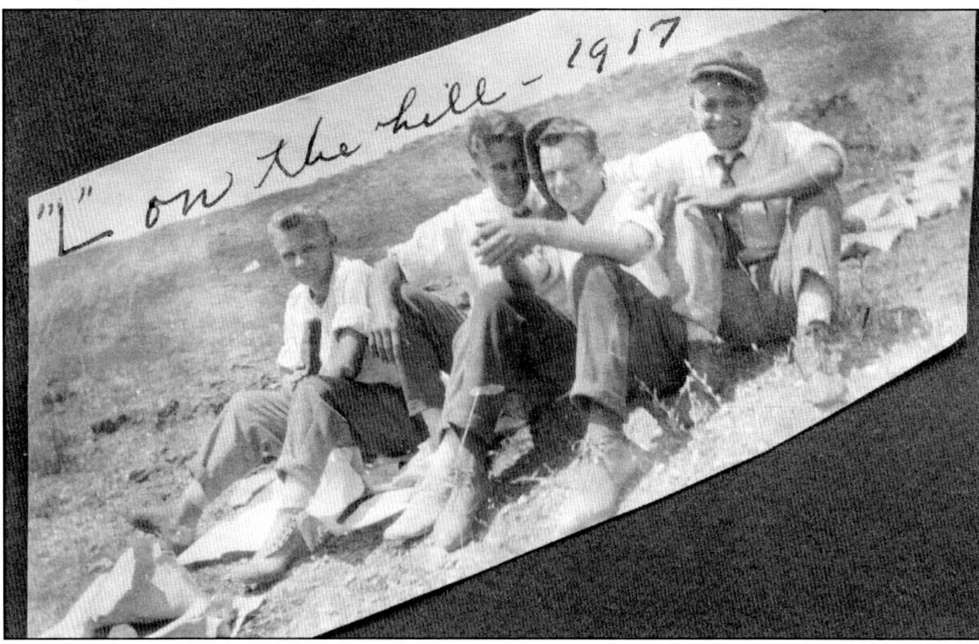

In 1917, a group of Lindsay High School boys assembled the iconic "L" for Lindsay on the hill overlooking the town. These hillside letters are a common sight across the American West. Symbolic of school pride, they were typically erected and maintained by high school students. The first hillside letter appeared on Charter Hill overlooking University of California, Berkeley in 1905. Other schools in California rapidly followed suit. (LMG.)

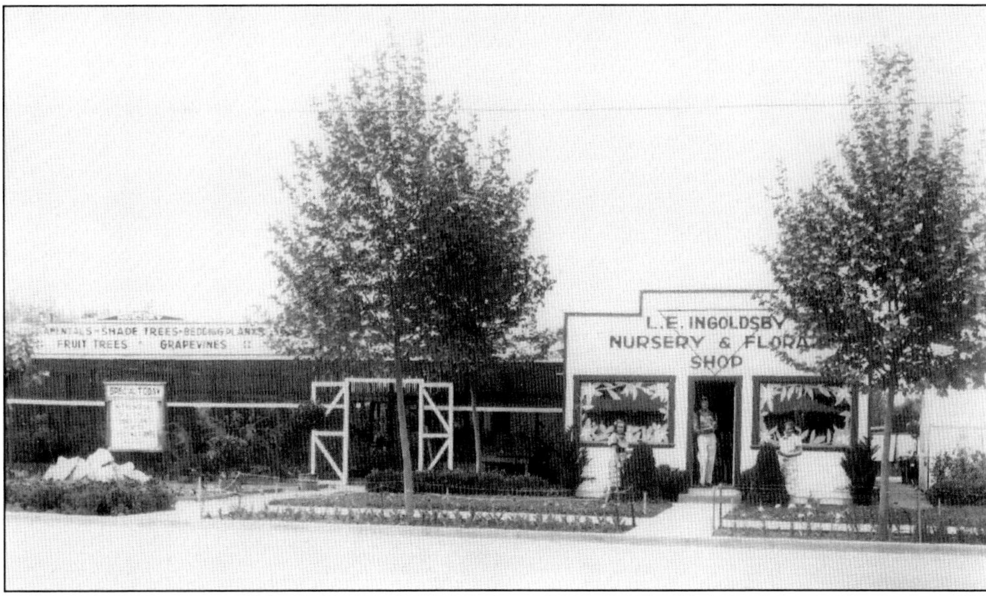

Laurence Eugene Ingoldsby began his nursery business while still in high school, growing and selling plants from his family home on Tulare Road. By the age of 19, he had opened his first store, Canary Cottage, where he sold sheet music and ran the nursery. His brother Harold hired Carol Brady, who became adept at floral arranging. Laurence and Carol married in 1923. Inglodsby's Flowers served the community for almost 90 years. (PK.)

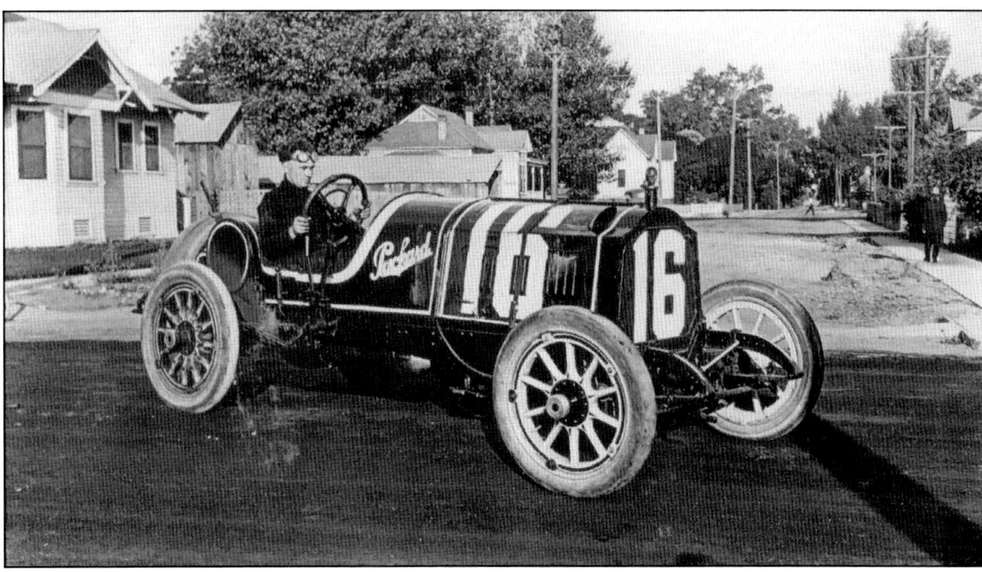

Fourth of July automobile races were a favorite pastime of Tulare County residents from about 1909 to the early 1920s. The races were more about endurance than speed, and racers could win a considerable amount of money with first prizes often being set at $1,000. Here, Clare Brady competes in a Fourth of July race in 1916. (PK.)

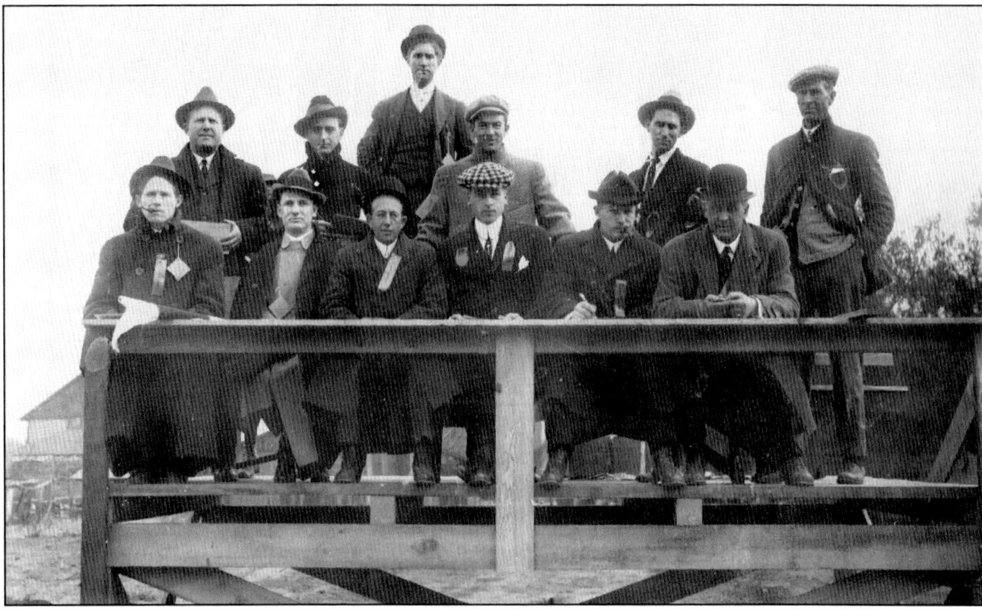

A group of Lindsay men watches an auto race from a set of bleachers. They are all wearing a ribbon that says, "I Paid 25 cents. Lindsay Automobile Races." Lindsay hosted its fair share of races. The Lawton brothers, who owned a garage in town, had quite the reputation for being racing favorites around Tulare County. (JMB.)

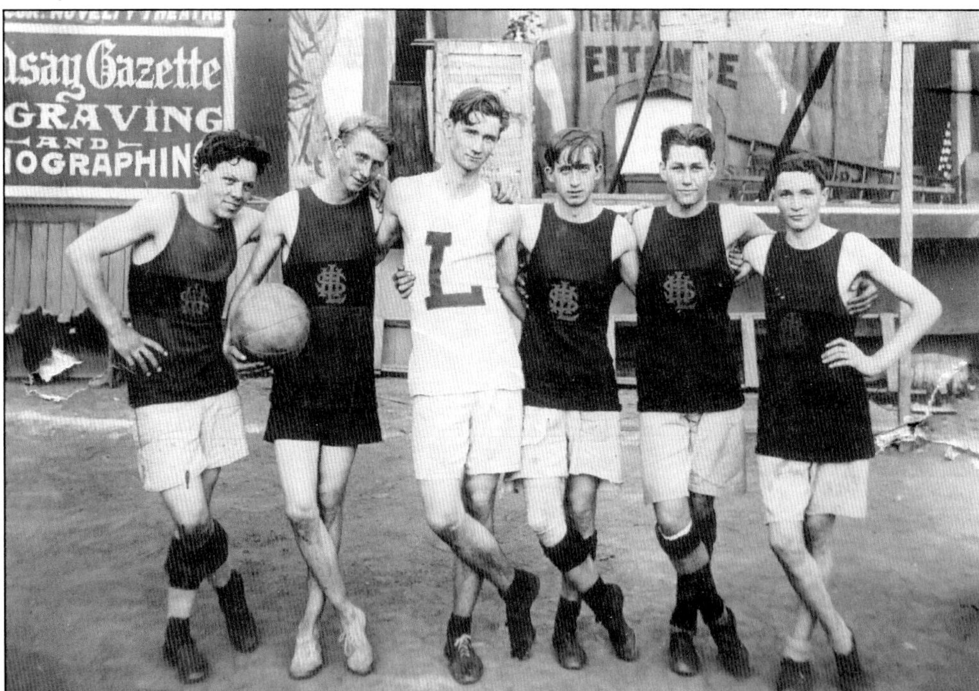

The Lindsay High School boys' basketball team of 1915 poses for their yearbook photograph in front of what appears to be a theater. The class of 1915 had a total of 13 seniors graduate on Friday the 13th, so some feared bad luck. Everyone wore a pin with the class mascot: an owl. (LMG.)

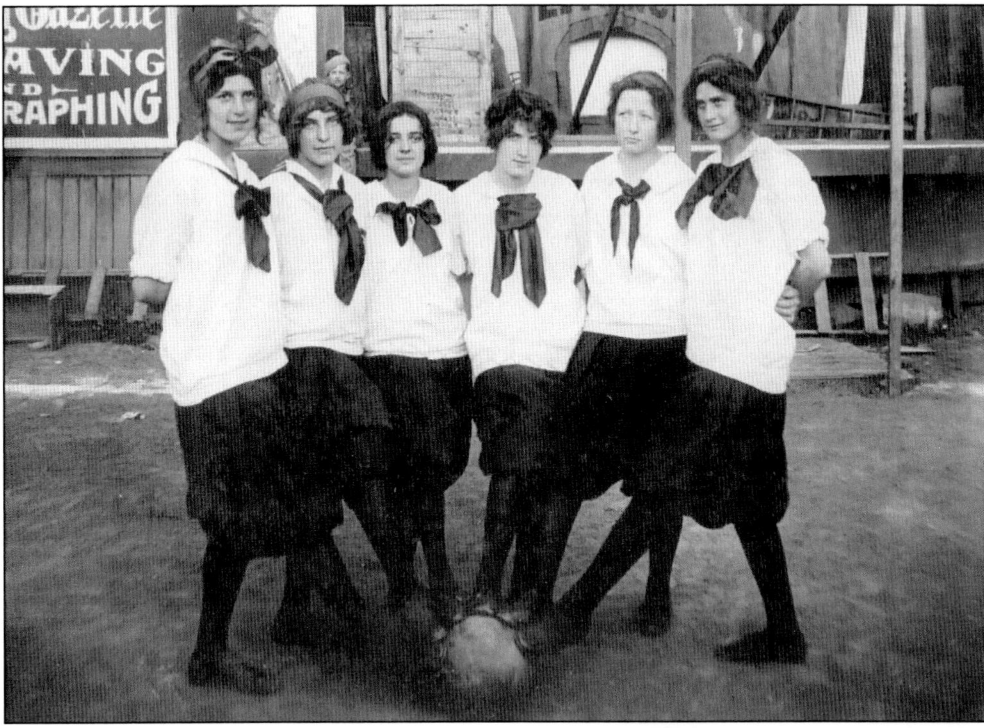

The Lindsay High School girls' basketball team of 1916 gathers for a portrait. At the time, there were only nine members of the faculty who were responsible for teaching a variety of subjects. In addition to participating in some kind of athletics, all students were very fond of creating secret clubs whose names were also kept a secret from nonmembers. (LMG.)

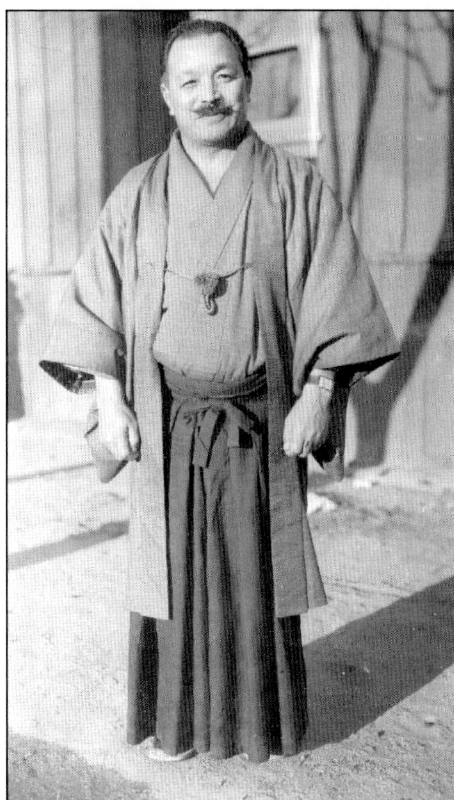

A Mr. Nakamura taught kendo, a martial art that reinforces self-discipline, at the Japanese school in Lindsay. Young students attended classes on weekends, learning languages and cultural arts. Such cultural schools were and still are common, primarily in cities where culturally diverse populations reside. Similar schools are available for German, Korean, and Jewish students. (LMG.)

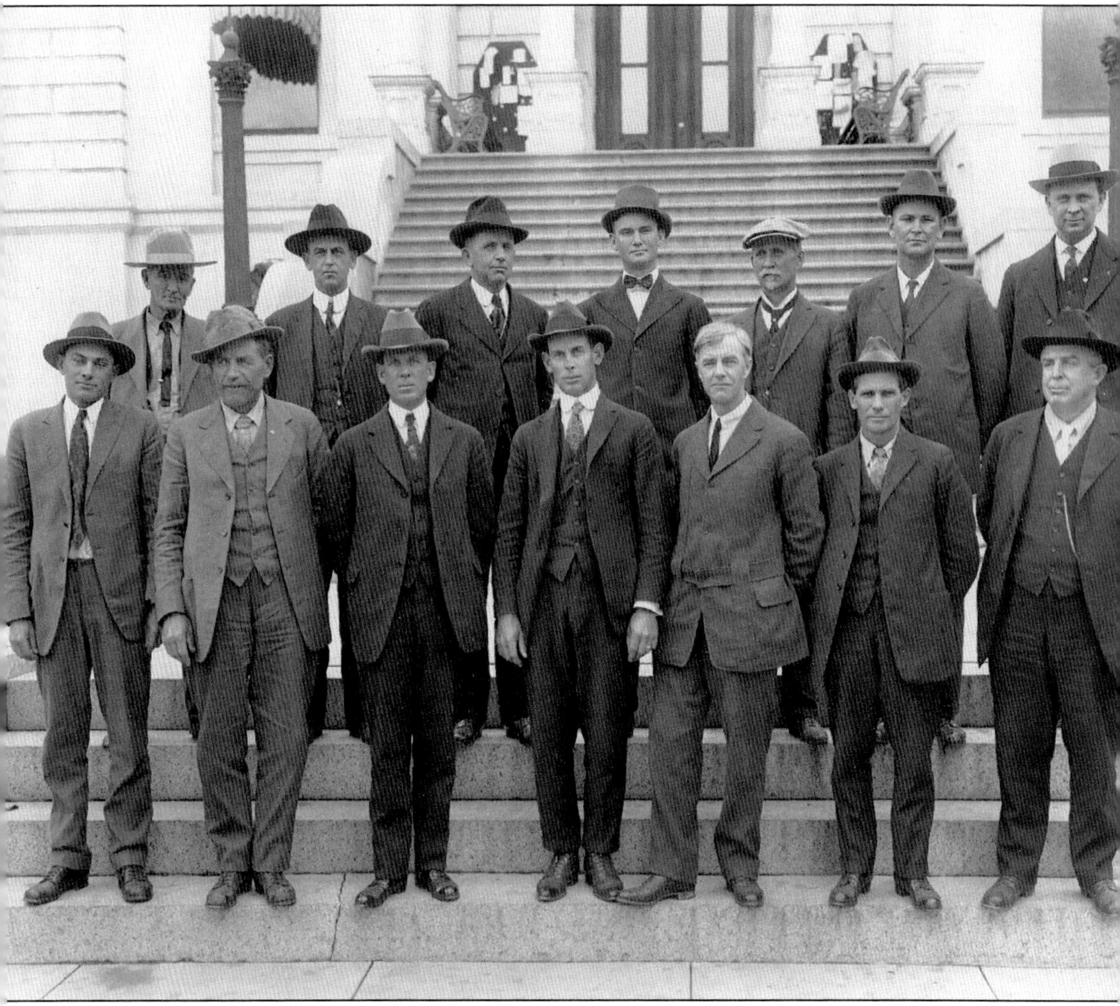

In 1917, William Hubert Brooks, husband of Annie Zalud, a member of one of Porterville's wealthiest families, was shot dead in a Porterville hotel lobby. Brooks had been spreading lies about the promiscuous nature of a business associate's wife, Julia Howe, after she had rebuked his advances. According to Howe, the rumors had broken up her marriage. Howe entered Porterville's Pioneer Hotel lobby and saw Brooks sitting there speaking with other men. Approaching Brooks, Howe took a gun out of her handbag and shot him four times. When the police arrived, Howe's only remark was "A good job done." This jury, which included Lindsay pioneer Basil Prior (first row, third from right), found Howe not guilty, as they deemed the murder a "justifiable homicide," concluding Brooks had provoked his own death. The chair, complete with a bullet hole, is on display as part of the Zalud House Museum's permanent collection. (CSUF.)

In contrast to the well-heeled socialites of Lindsay's Tuesday Club, with their tea parties and fashion shows, the Neighborhood Club, established in 1916, was definitely a thinking woman's club. As stated in their bylaws, the objective of their meetings was intended to be intellectual and cultural in nature. (LMG.)

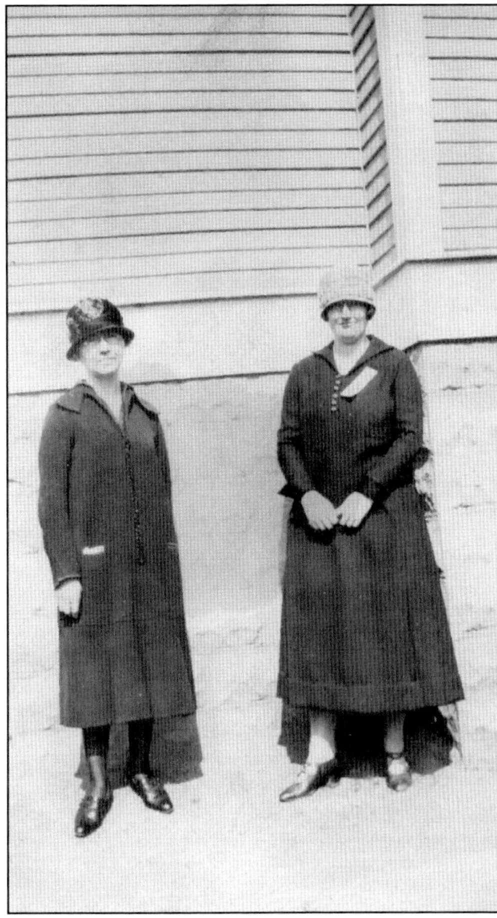

The Alta View Sanitarium was a hospital for tuberculosis patients in Lindsay prior to the Springville sanitarium opening in 1918. In the early 20th century, one out of every seven Americans died from the disease. Approximately one-third of California's population was comprised of sick and dying people seeking to be cured by the state's good weather. (GM.)

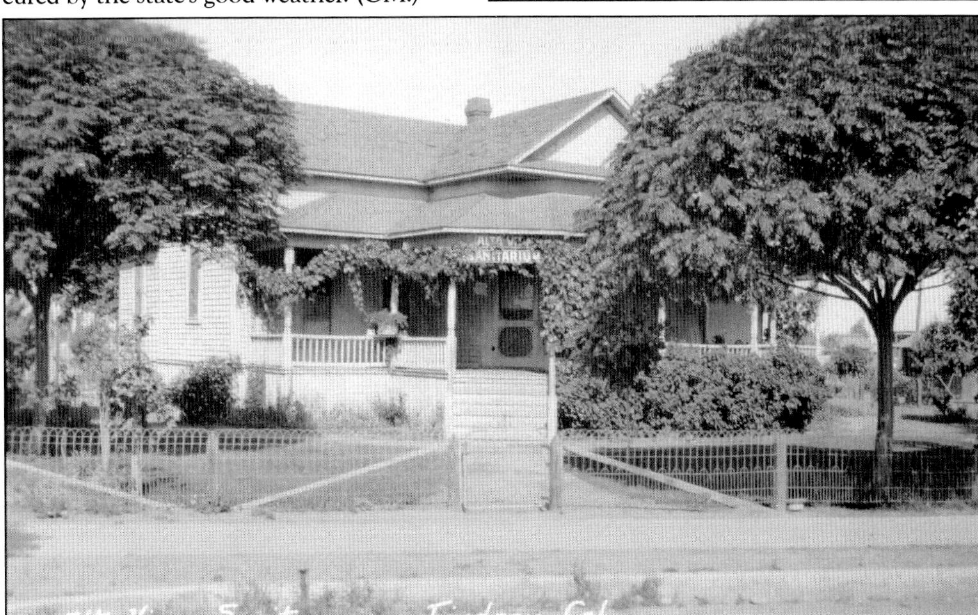

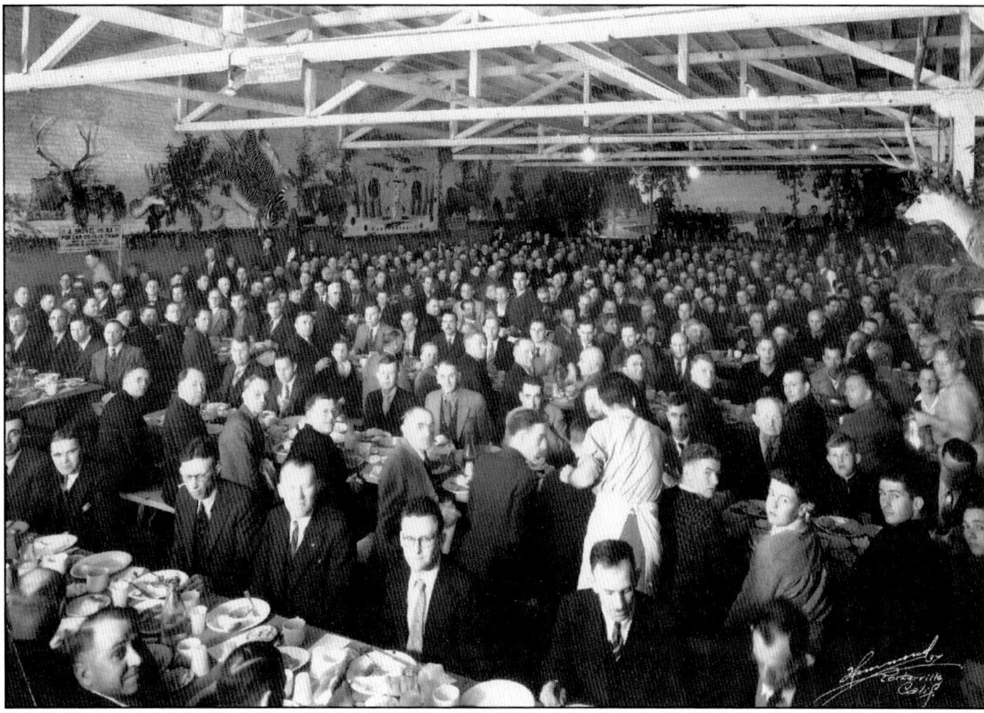

The Lindsay Fish and Game Protective Association was founded in 1919. This dinner was held in 1937 in the Ford Garage, which must have also served as the clubhouse of the Lindsay Rifle and Pistol Club. Note all the taxidermy on display, including deer head mounts and a tiger skin. According to the dinner program, everything was cooked by the association members. (CSUF.)

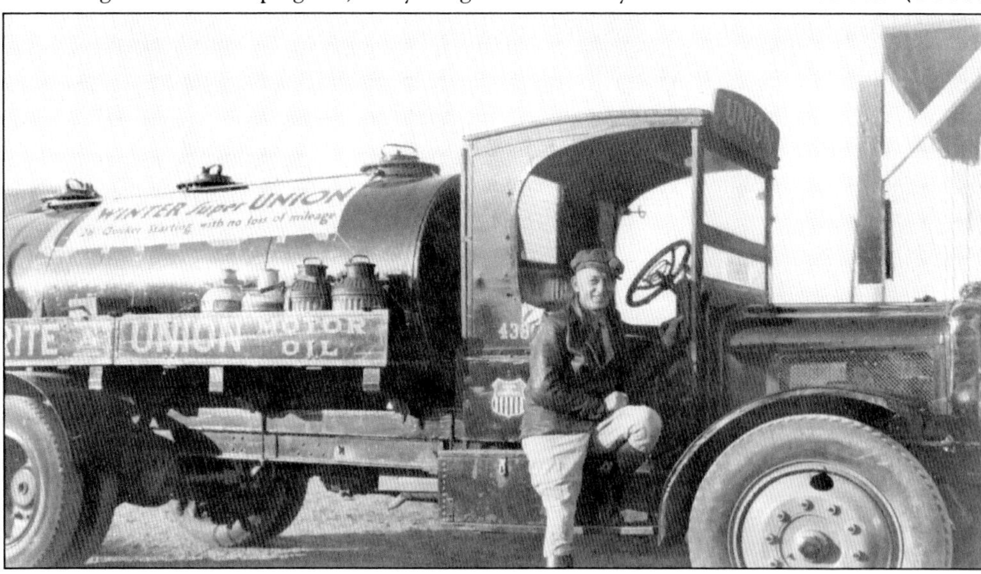

In 1920, the hunt for oil got under way when Givan Oil Lease Syndicate put down an oil derrick in Round Valley, where John Tuohy once farmed with 25 mules that were used in the Mexican-American War. Many believed oil would be tapped and Lindsay residents would become millionaires as a result. Although Lindsay was not the next big oil town, it did have short-lived success with Union Oil. (IF.)

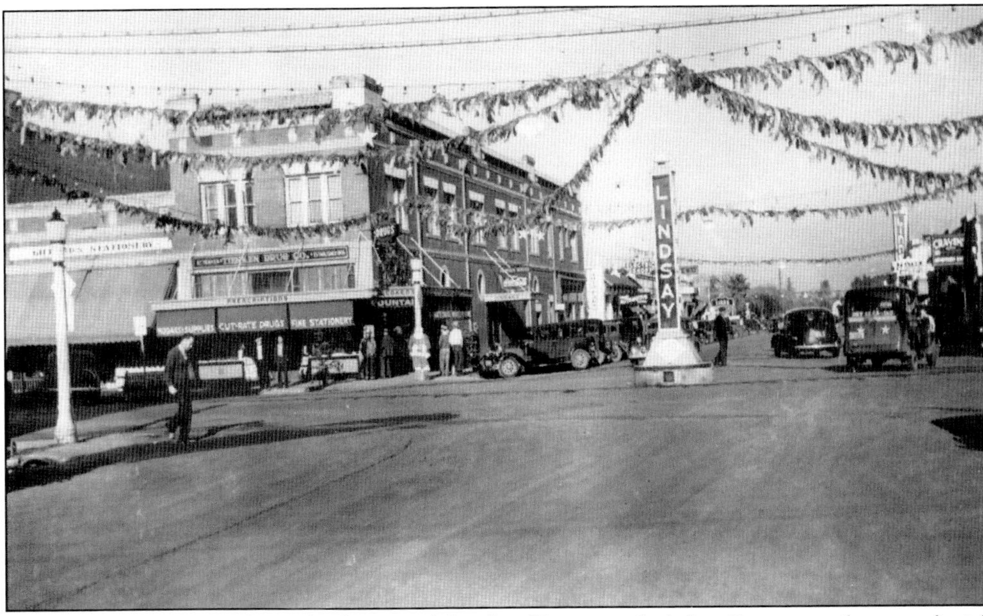

The center of town is festively decorated for the Christmas holiday. Streamers festooned with stars stretch across the streets. The center of town is marked with a pillar bearing the name of Lindsay as day-to-day community life bustles around it. A small group stands outside Tienken Drug Company and cars line the streets during this busy season around 1920. (CSUF.)

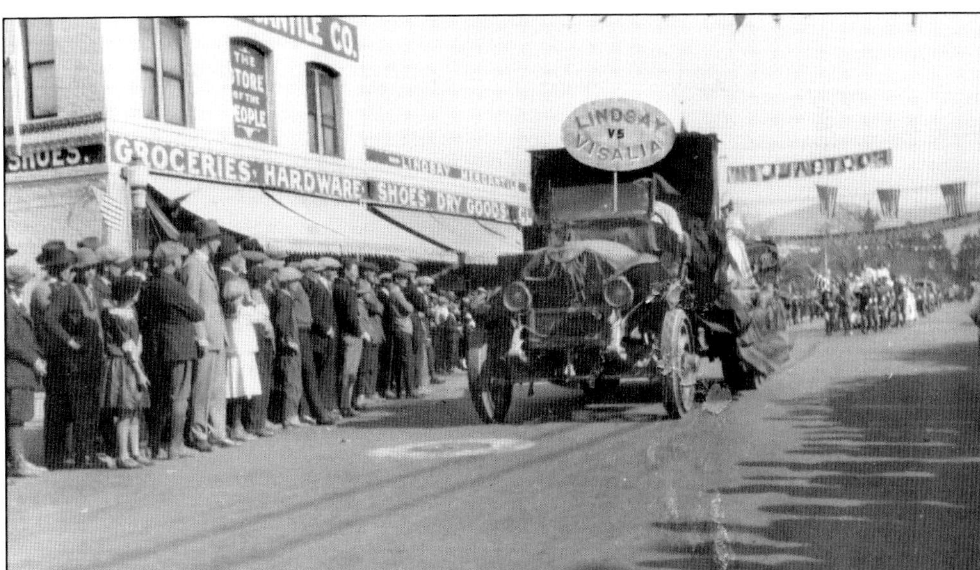

Well-dressed citizens of Tulare County come out in droves for an Armistice Day parade hosted by Lindsay in 1920. The parade car in front advertises a baseball game of Lindsay vs. Visalia to take place later that day. (LMG.)

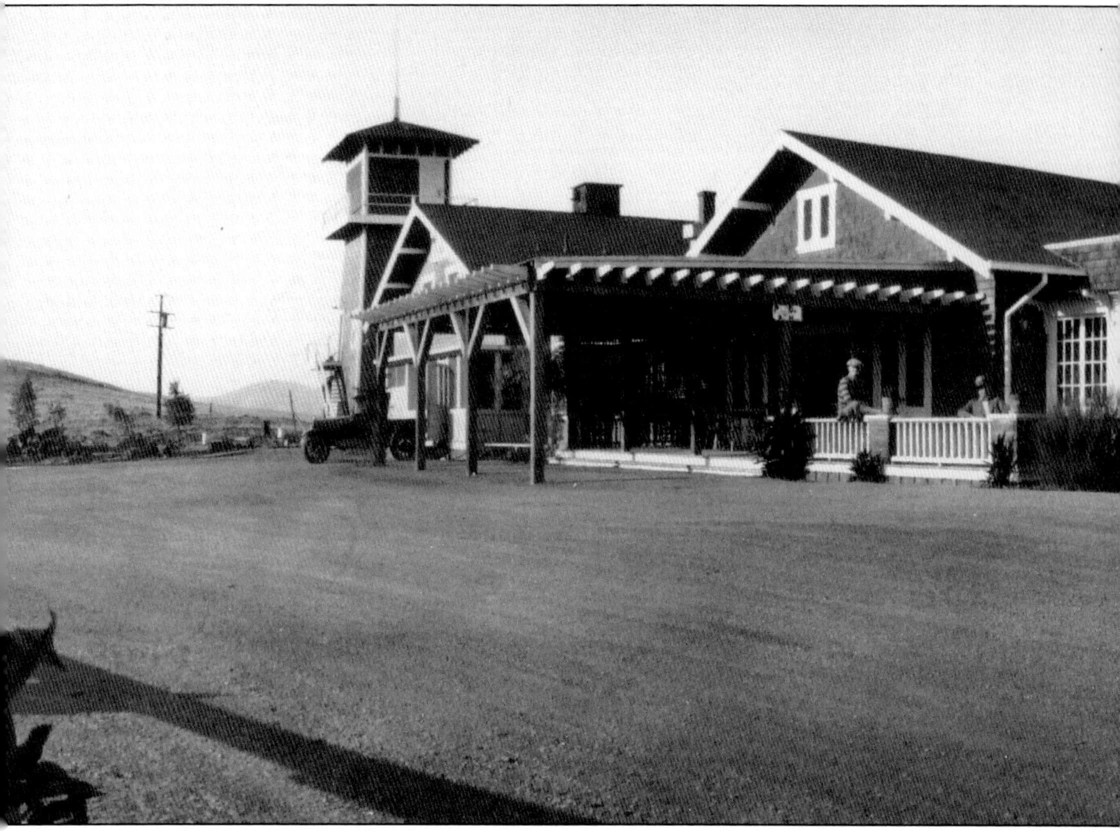

The Tulare County Golf and Country Club was incorporated in 1919, primarily by Lindsay residents. An initial membership fee of $100 was charged with an additional fee of $5 for monthly dues. The club opened on October 15, 1921, with 700 guests in attendance. Following afternoon tea was an evening dinner and dance in the ballroom, which was decorated with grapes, autumn leaves, and apples. The club featured a golf course and dining room for members, as well as living

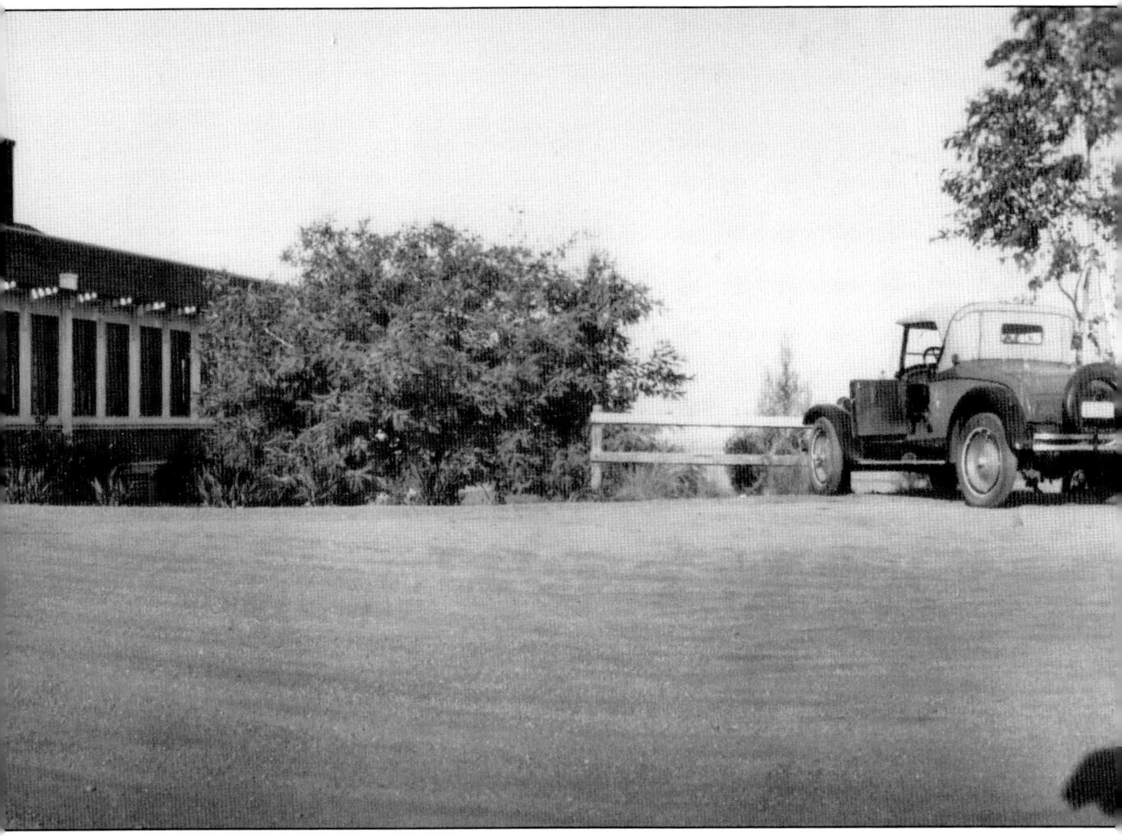

quarters for employees. Many rumors and legends are attached to the club, including high-stakes poker games, a speakeasy during Prohibition, and hidden pirate treasure on the premises. The club finally burned to the ground in 1935, when some say the local women got tired of their spouses using the facility as a house of ill repute and set it on fire. (LMG.)

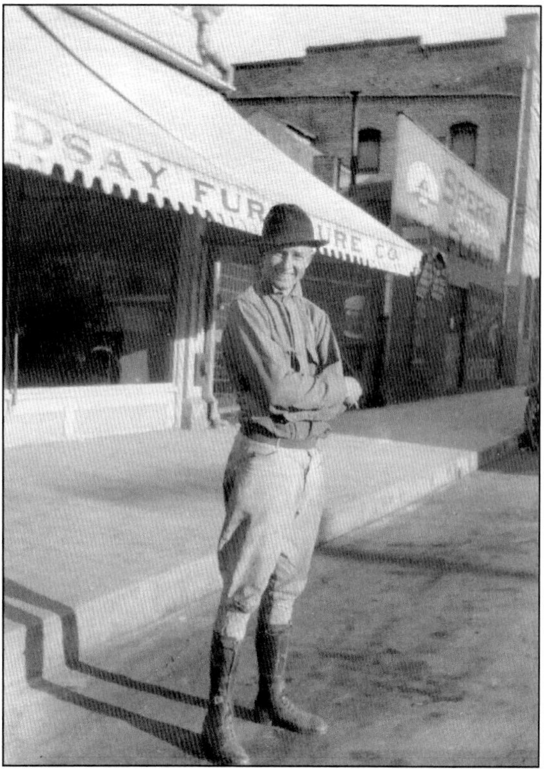

A young man stands outside the Lindsay Furniture Company in 1920. The Sperry Flour Store can be seen just down the street. Sperry Flour was based at a mill in Stockton, California. The flour brand gained a strange notoriety when it became affiliated with "Black Bart," an outlaw who committed 28 robberies of Wells Fargo stagecoaches while wearing a Sperry Flour sack over his face. (LMG.)

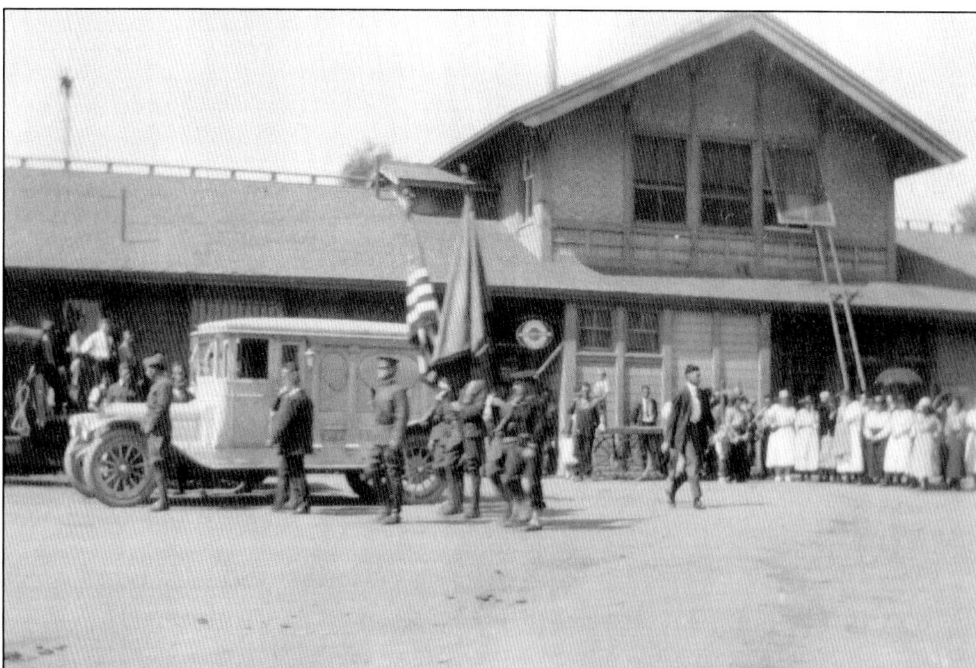

A sad scene transpires at the Lindsay train depot as people await the arrival of Lindsay's own casualties of World War I, the bodies of Julius Keeley and Arthur Sherman. Note the white hearse in the background. (LMG.)

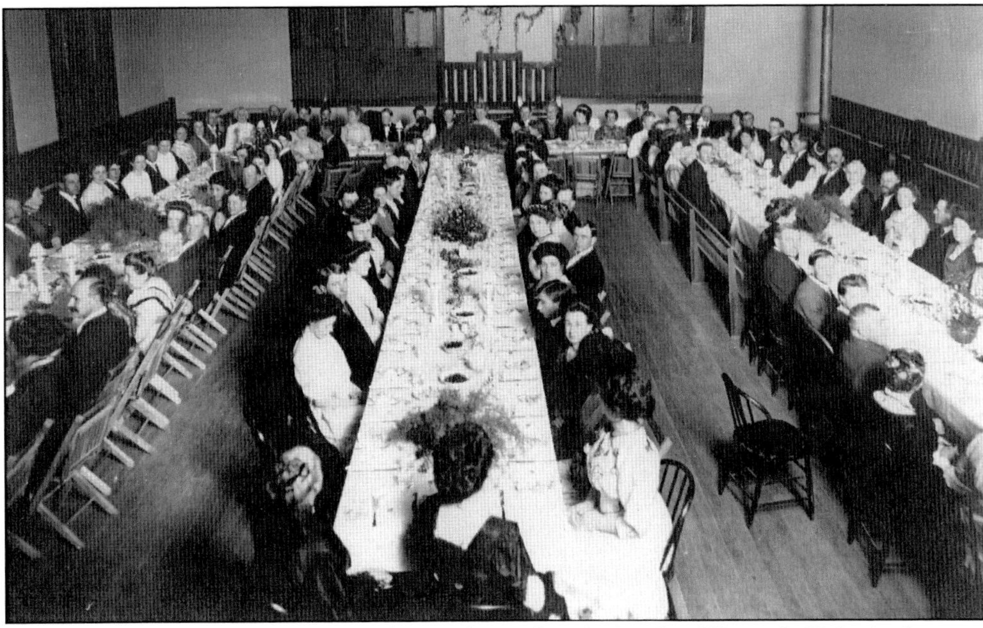

In 1925, the name of the Tuesday Club was changed to the Lindsay Women's Club. At this time, membership boasted a roster of Lindsay's most affluent and powerful society ladies. Although the club continued to support community endeavors in various ways, their focus turned to activities of leisure and entertainment, including tea parties, fashion shows, and luncheons, as well as an event known as Husbands' Night. (CSUF.)

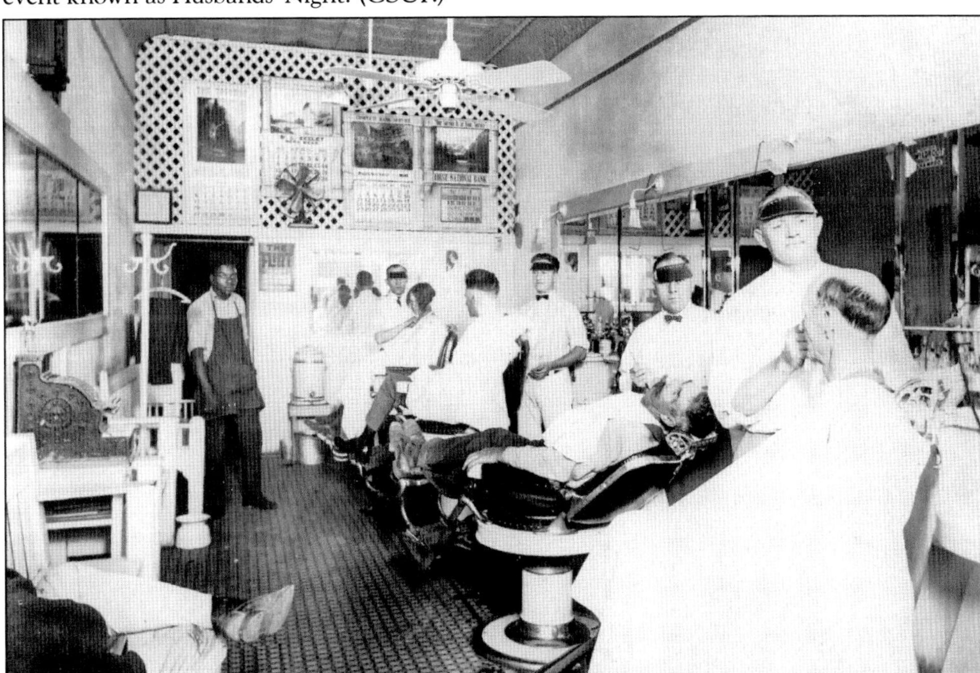

A busy barbershop is pictured in 1923. Hanging on the back wall is a poster for Harold Lloyd's film *The Flirt*, along with a row of calendars promoting many Lindsay establishments, including the Toggery, First National Bank, and W.L. Keeley Men's Wear. (PN.)

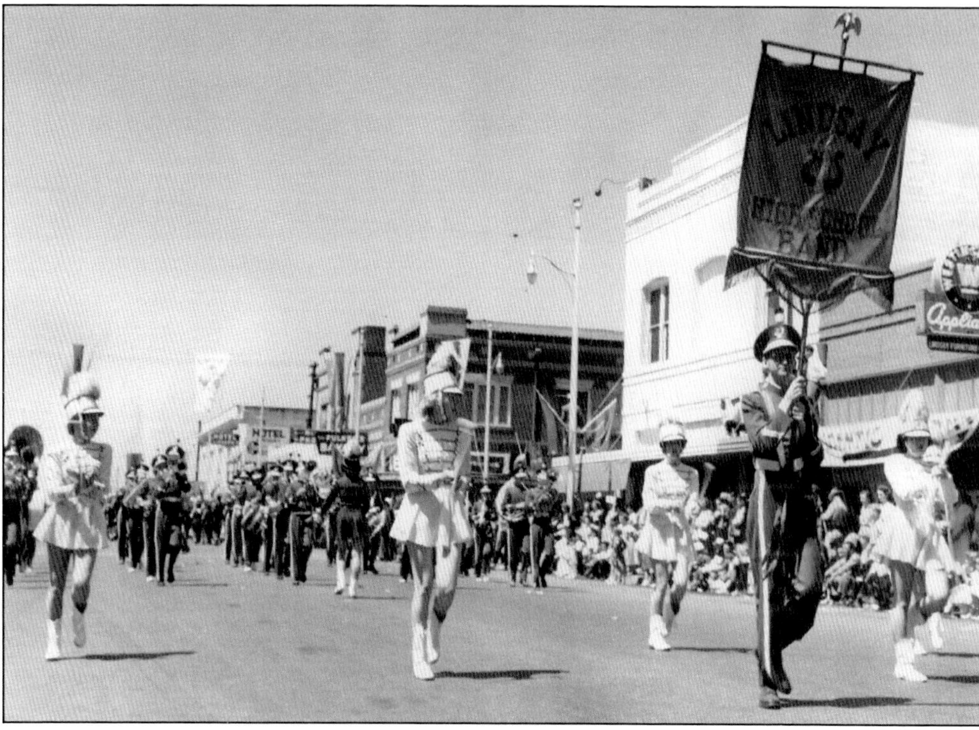

Just like the legendary musical *The Music Man*, the first music program was established by a salesman from the Conn Music Company who successfully sold instruments to the parents of Lindsay's young musicians. Conn was a successful enterprise endorsed by John Phillip Sousa. Lindsay's first music teacher was a German gentleman named Hugo Pflock who taught local students for over a decade. (LMG.)

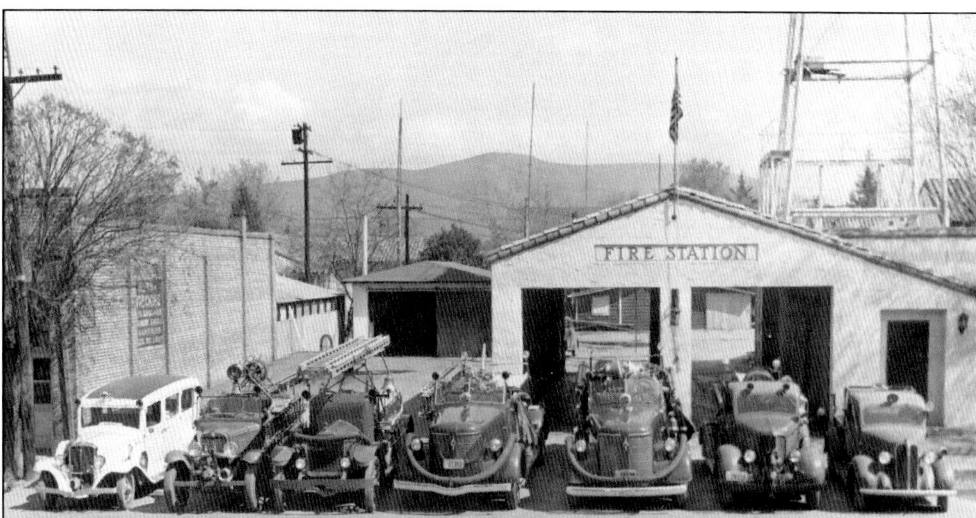

The original fire station can be seen here. At left is the location of the current fire museum, curated by Gary Meling. Three of the fire engines that appear here are now part of its collection. Two of these engines were customized to accommodate Fire Chief D.M. DeManty, who was short in stature. (CSUF.)

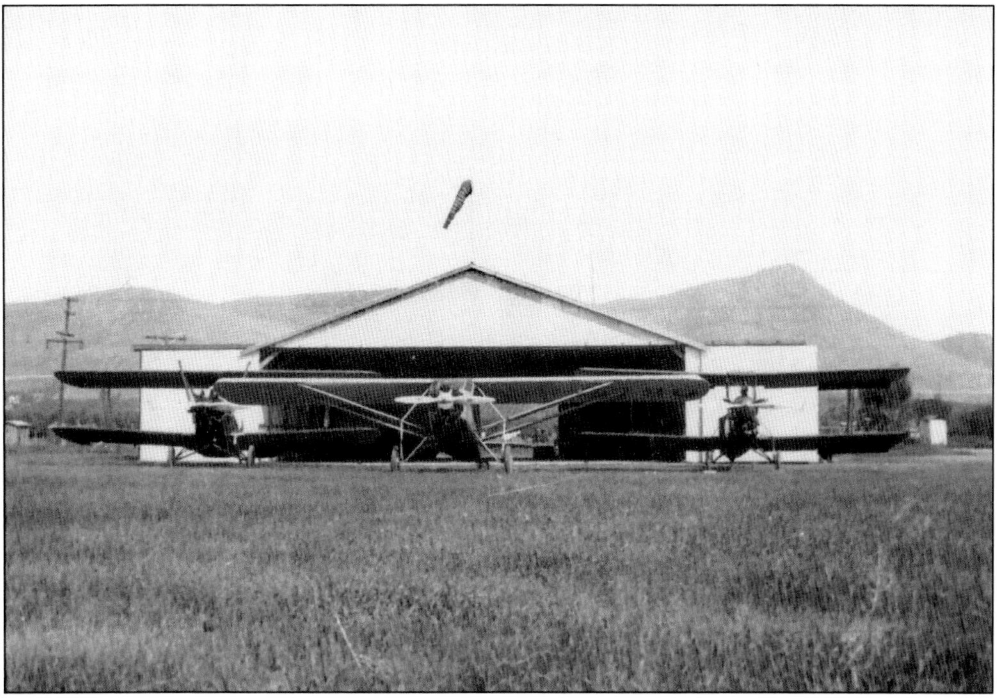

This photograph of the Lindsay Airport was probably taken in the early 1930s when it was first constructed. It later had a large sign mounted on it bearing the town's name. Lindsay resident Yosh Imoto would work at the airport "watering the planes" before classes began at Lindsay High School. He eventually learned to fly them. (CSUF.)

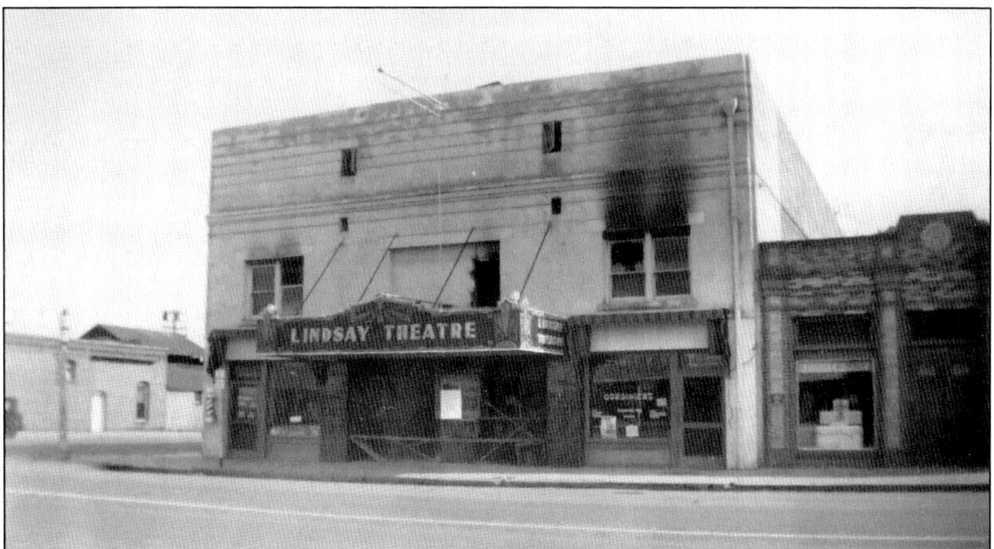

The Lindsay Community Theatre opened in 1925 as a movie palace called the Glade Theatre. At 3:30 a.m. on February 22, 1938, the theater caught fire. It was renovated in the 1960s but closed again because of poor attendance. The theater reopened in the early 1980s, and its stage has been busy ever since. In addition to its full lineup of musicals and plays, the Lindsay Community Theatre offers renowned musical acts and variety shows, which are always an attraction. (GM.)

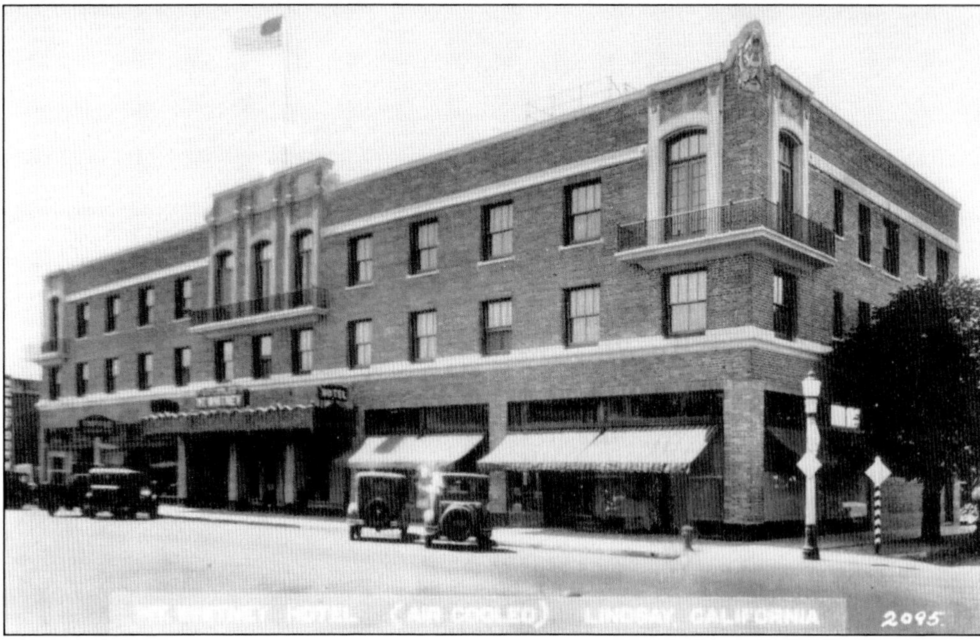

In an effort to promote Lindsay as a business and tourist center, a hotel committee was formed in 1929. The business plan was modeled after the community financing structure of Bakersfield's El Tejon Hotel. Dozens of Lindsay residents purchased stock to make the Mount Whitney Hotel become a reality in 1930. (CSUF.)

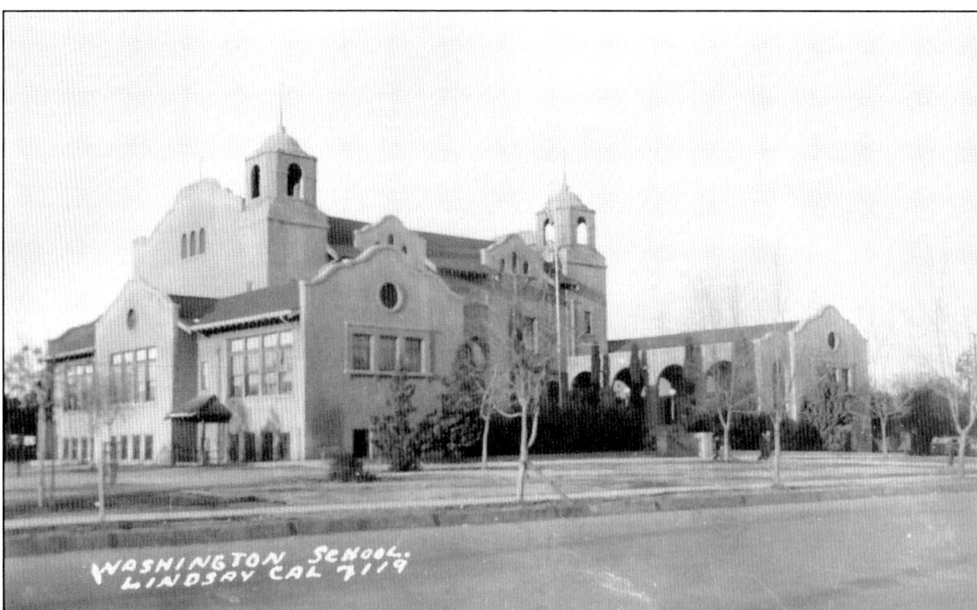

The original Washington School was constructed in 1914. Its completion kicked off what was known as the Achievement Celebration in 1915. The town's main thoroughfares had been paved, electroliers were installed in the business district, and Lindsay citrus swept the awards at the National Orange Show. This photograph of the mission-style school was taken in the 1930s. (CSUF.)

The storefront of Coday's Jewelry is pictured with owner Herve Coday standing in front. Also seen here is the Mount Whitney Lithograph building, owned and operated by Frank and Bonnie Selover. The pair worked closely with Lindsay resident historians Harold Schutt and Joe Doctor to publish the newsletter of the Tulare County Historical Society. (DC.)

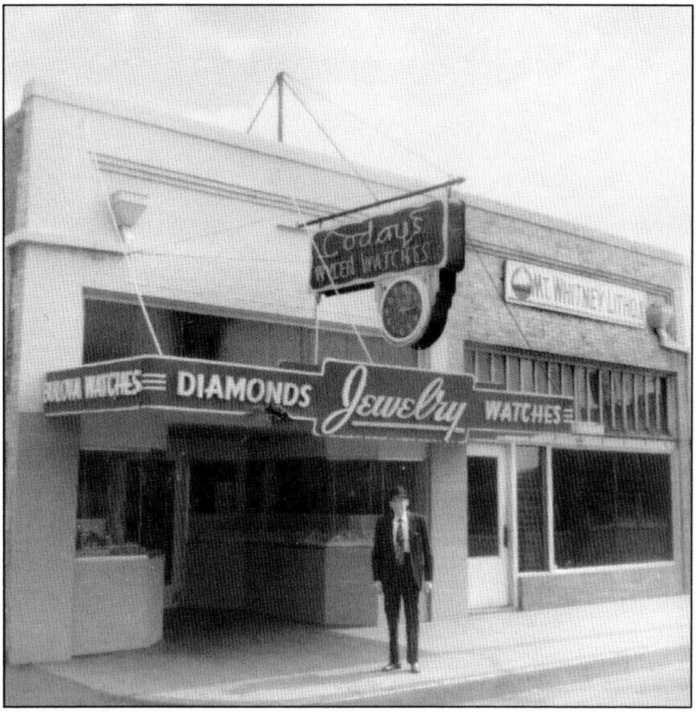

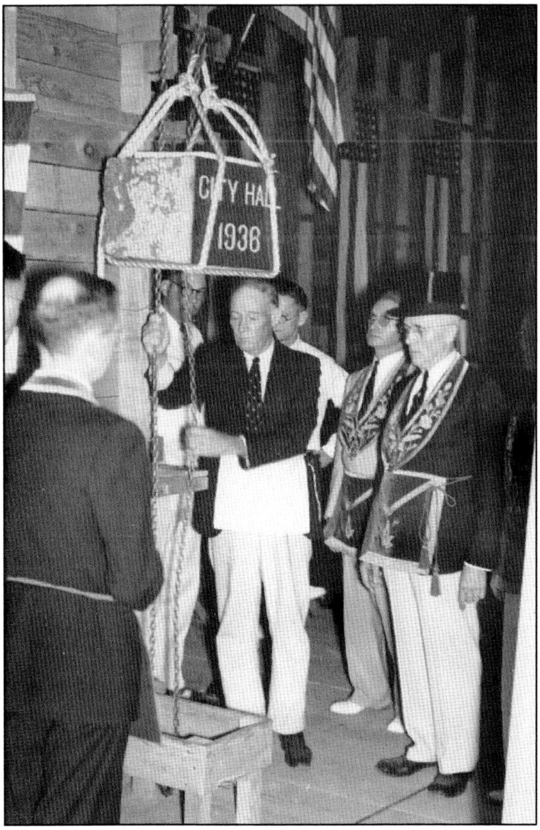

In 1936, Lindsay's Masonic Lodge was invited to lay the cornerstone of the new city hall, containing a time capsule. Dozens of documents were placed within from the town's social and civic organizations, detailing member names, their mission, and some history. Other odds and ends like business cards, wheat pennies, and commemorative brass pieces were also included. (LMG.)

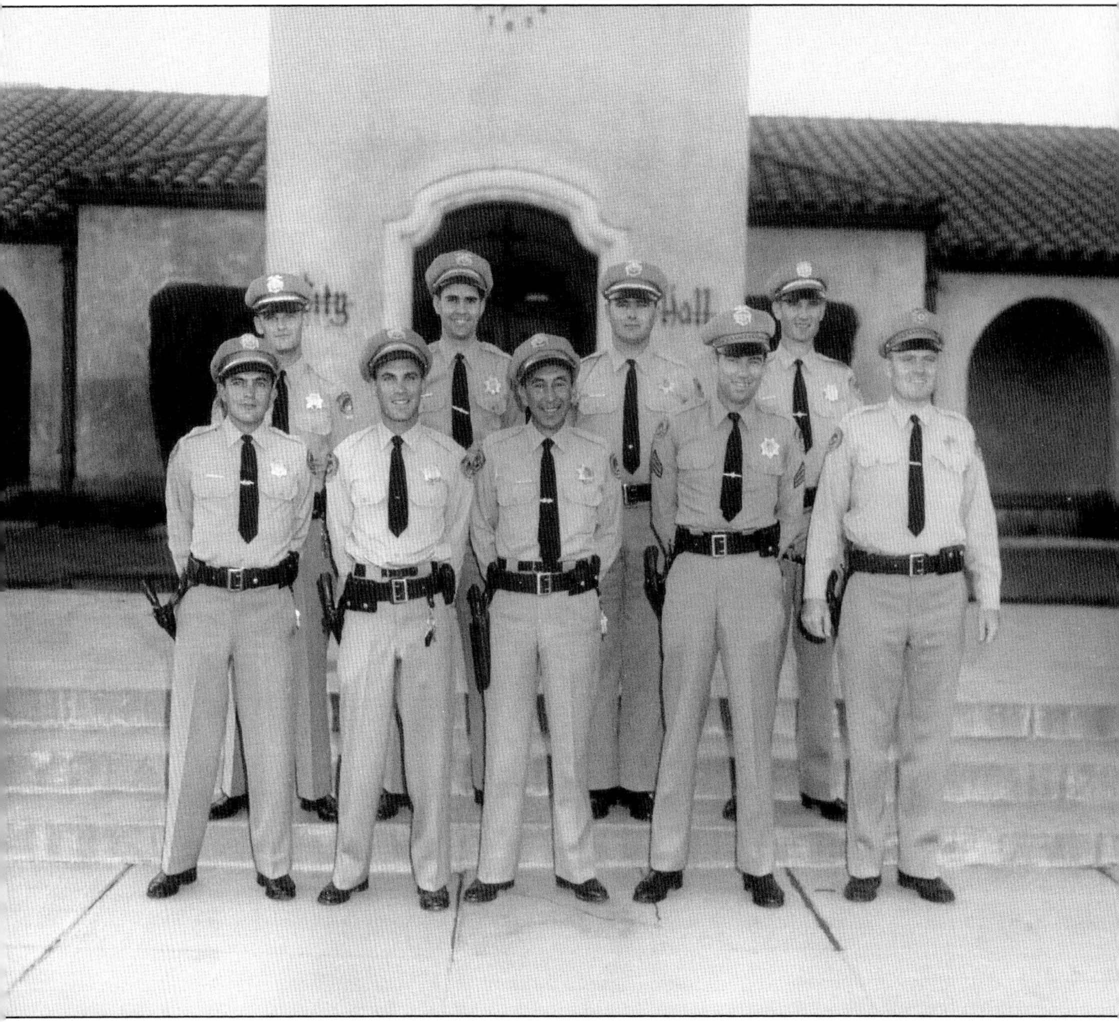

One of the most remembered officers was George Barlow, who began his service to Lindsay's police force in 1929. In 1935, Barlow responded to a call from a Mrs. Tackett, who had just escaped her husband's attempt on her life. Mrs. Tackett was able to run to safety at a neighbor's house, where they called for police assistance. When Officer Barlow arrived at the scene, the husband, Monford Tackett, was waiting outside the house, and the two men exchanged shots. Monford died at the scene. Barlow survived for 12 days in the hospital before succumbing to his wounds. Officer Barlow left behind a wife and eight children. Lindsay residents banded together and raised enough funds from all over the country to pay off the mortgage on the Barlow family home and provide financially for them as well. (LMG.)

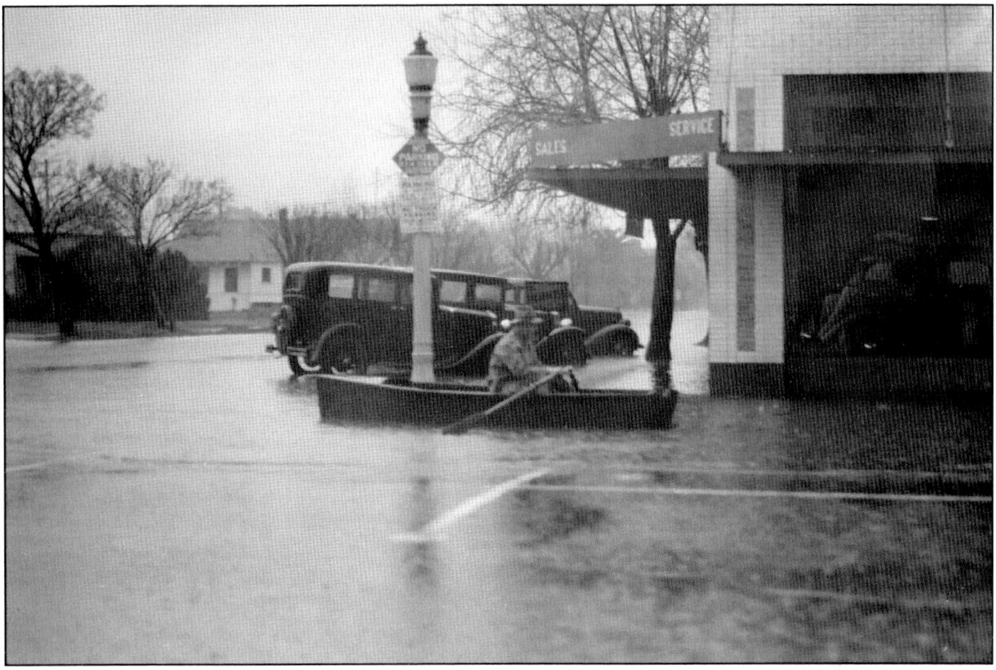

The *Lindsay Gazette* ran this photograph of R.I. Clearman paddling a boat down a Lindsay street following a flood in 1936. Such floods were not uncommon in the area. There are multiple stories of people being awoken in the night, terrified to find themselves suddenly submerged in water. (CSUF.)

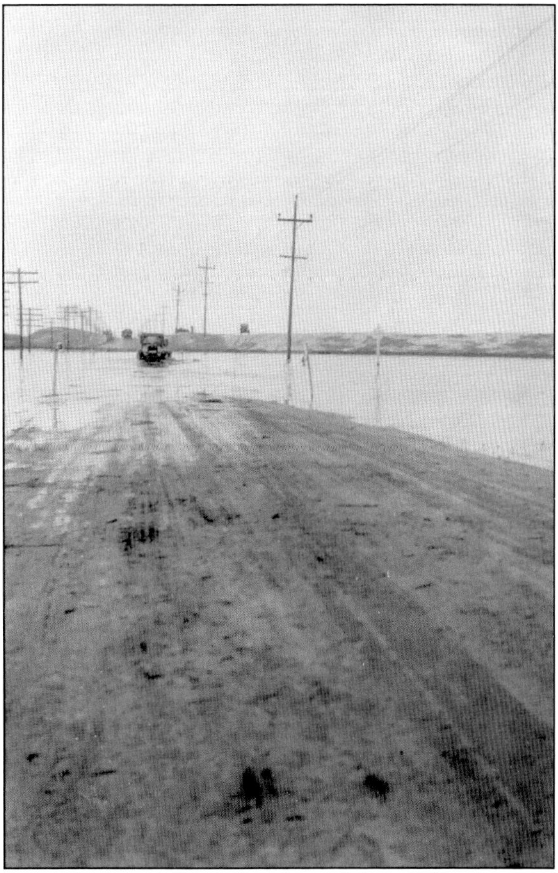

Here is another photograph of a flood in Lindsay, taken by A.C. Tienken. One particularly bad flood occurred around Thanksgiving and washed away area livestock. People reported seeing animals floating along on top of hay bales, including a turkey that was captured as it floated past a house, then cooked up for the holiday dinner. (LMG.)

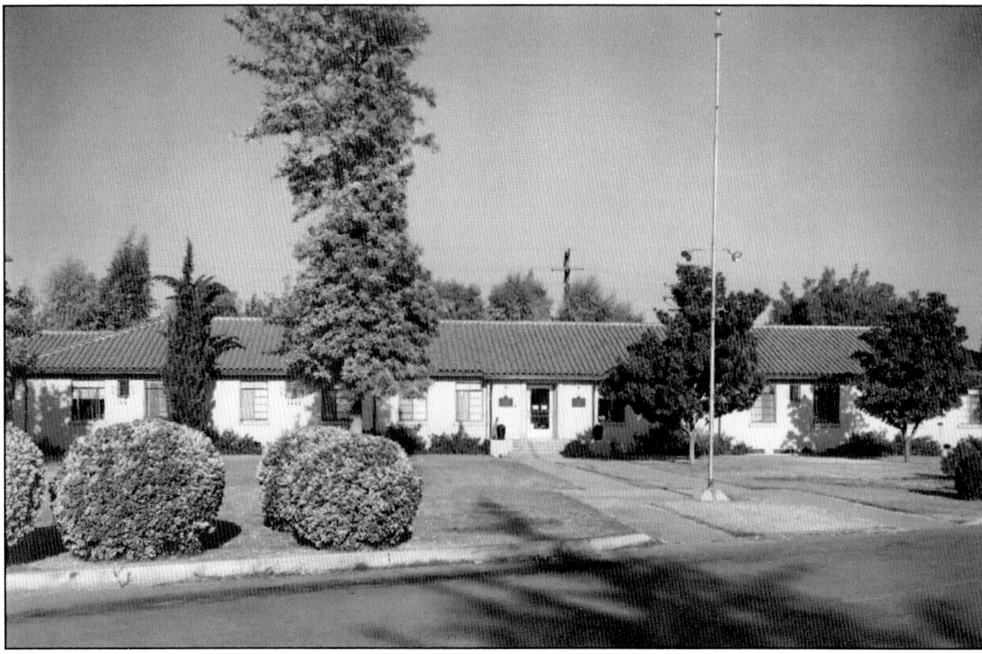

Prior to this first official hospital being established in 1941, numerous residences served this purpose. The Heard family ran one of these private clinics from their home on Gale Hill, where the current public services building now stands. In early 1936, the hospital was sold to Beulah Davis, who had been serving as the head administrator of a large hospital in Kansas. (CSUF.)

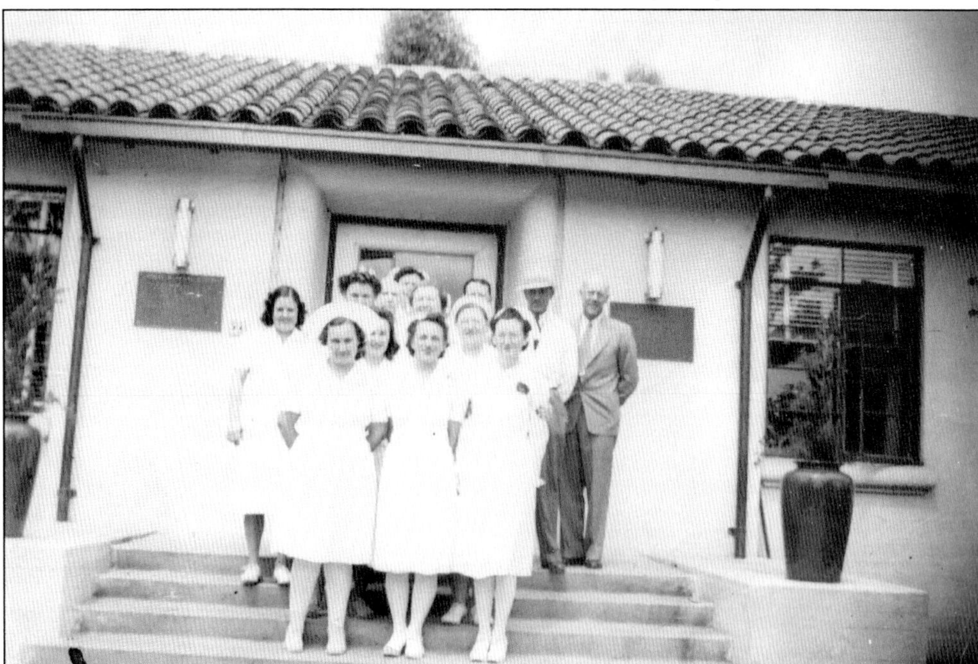

Lindsay rapidly outgrew the little residential hospital, so Beulah Davis appealed to the Works Progress Administration, which agreed to fund and build a new hospital. Davis stands among her staff, some of whom she had brought with her from Kansas, on the steps of the new hospital. (LMG.)

Fresh out of Lindsay High School in 1941, Edwin J. O'Hara enlisted in the US Merchant Marine Cadet Corps and was assigned to the Liberty ship *Stephen Hopkins*. While in the Atlantic Ocean on September 22, 1942, the *Hopkins* was attacked by Nazi surface raiders. The *Hopkins* was severely damaged, and all of her gun crew was wounded. (LMG.)

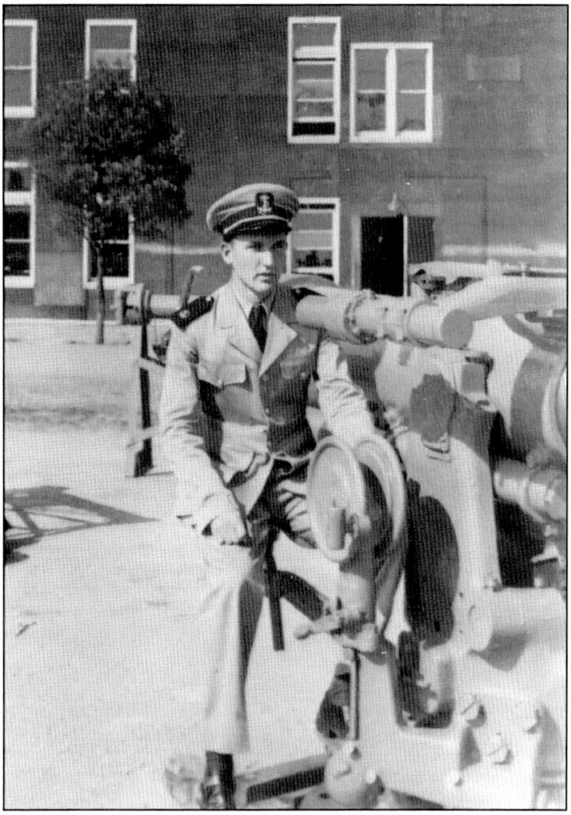

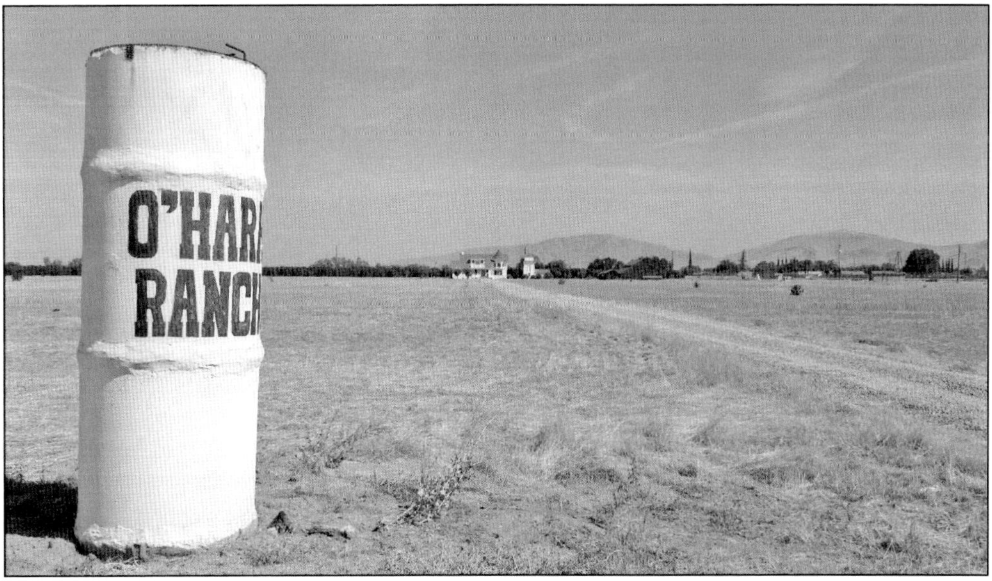

During the raid, 18-year-old O'Hara made his way to the stern's five-inch gun and fired the ship's last five shells, severely damaging the enemy ships. Sadly, O'Hara was mortally wounded on this day. He was posthumously awarded a Distinguished Service Medal, the highest honor for a Merchant Marine. At the Merchant Marine Academy in New York, a building has been named in his honor. He is considered one of Lindsay's greatest military heroes. (Photograph by DeLea Davis.)

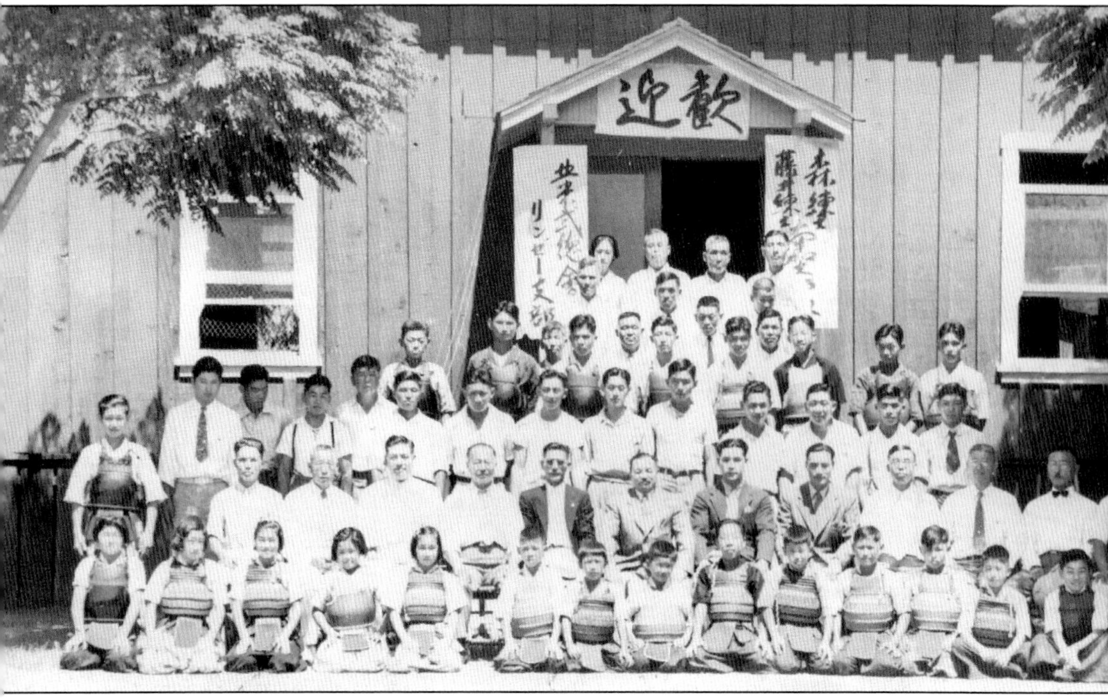

When the Japanese attacked Pearl Harbor in 1941, Pres. Franklin D. Roosevelt issued Executive Order 9066, which stripped American citizens of their civil liberties, citing reasons of national security. This set into motion one of most regrettable incidents in the nation's history by forcibly removing and imprisoning some 120,000 persons of Japanese ancestry. These Japanese American citizens, half of whom were children, were forced to leave their homes, businesses, and lives behind. Lindsay's own were sent to remote concentration camps surrounded by barbed wire and armed guards. There, they were forced to live in substandard housing and given inadequate nutrition and health care resulting in some fatalities. Although reasons of security were offered as motive, Michi Weglyn's 1976 publication *Years of Infamy: The Untold Story of America's Concentration Camps* documents otherwise: "Our government had in its possession proof that not one Japanese-American, citizen or not, had engaged in espionage, not one had committed any act of sabotage." (LMG.)

Among those Lindsay citizens unjustly imprisoned was Yosh Imoto, who was appointed unit photographer. The 442nd rescued the Lost Battalion, a company of 300 from Texas, at a sacrifice of 800 Issei and Nisei dead and wounded. They liberated the Nazi camp at Dachau, where over 32,000 were put to death. Imoto was witness to the horrors of the camps and documented it all with his camera, as this was part of his role. (Photograph by Yosh Imoto, courtesy of the Imoto family.)

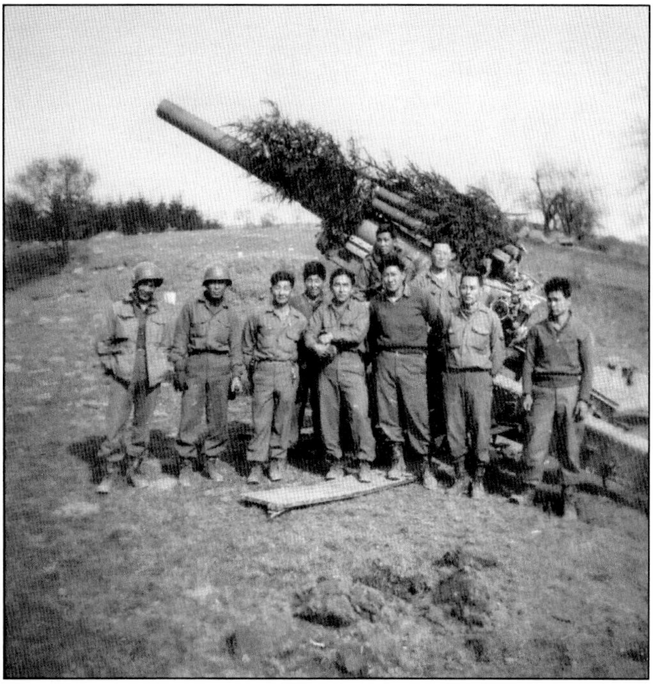

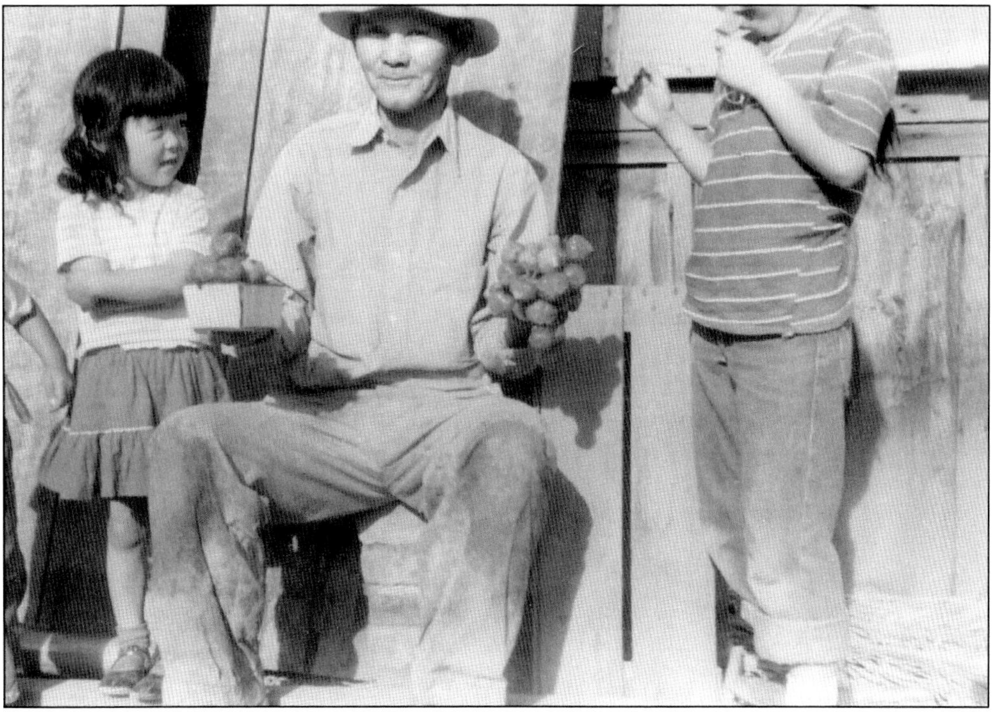

When Japanese Americans were released following the end of World War II, they faced more challenges at home. With lingering racism across the United States, many were denied housing, employment, and access to retail services. In 1988, Congress passed the Civil Liberties Act, which acknowledged that "a grave injustice was done." In this photograph is Sam Imoto, who also served in the US military. (LMG.)

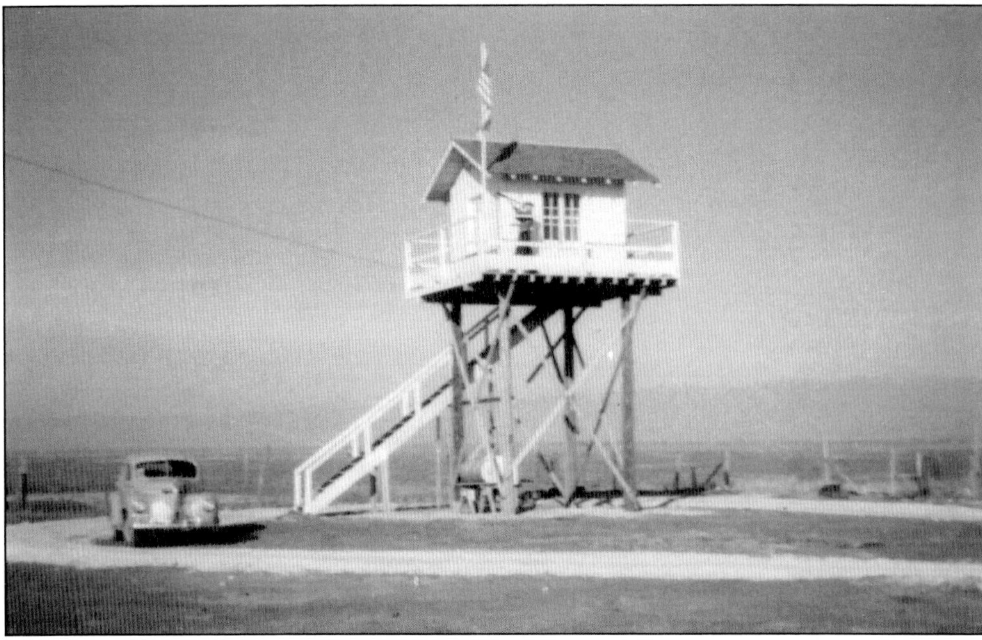

During World War II, the Army used these observation towers to gain information and protect the United States from further military attacks. Lindsay's listening and sighting tower was located near Avenue 232. The towers were manned by citizen volunteers, primarily women and members of the local Kiwanis chapter in Lindsay. (CSUF.)

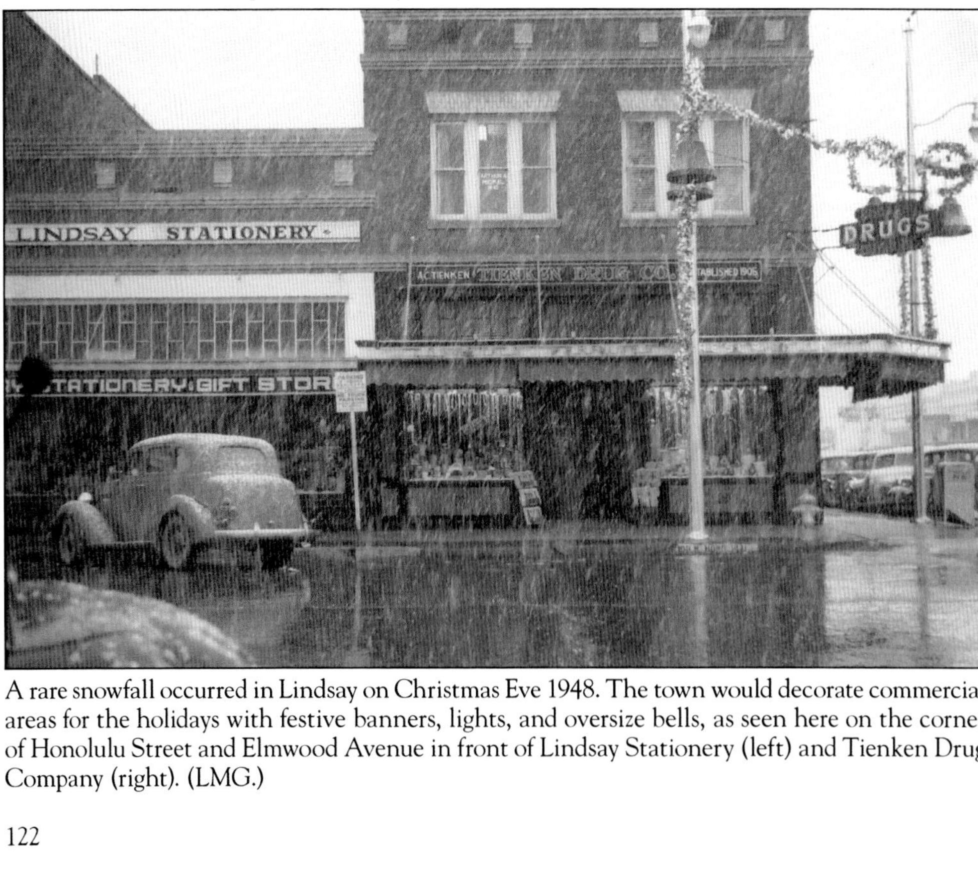

A rare snowfall occurred in Lindsay on Christmas Eve 1948. The town would decorate commercial areas for the holidays with festive banners, lights, and oversize bells, as seen here on the corner of Honolulu Street and Elmwood Avenue in front of Lindsay Stationery (left) and Tienken Drug Company (right). (LMG.)

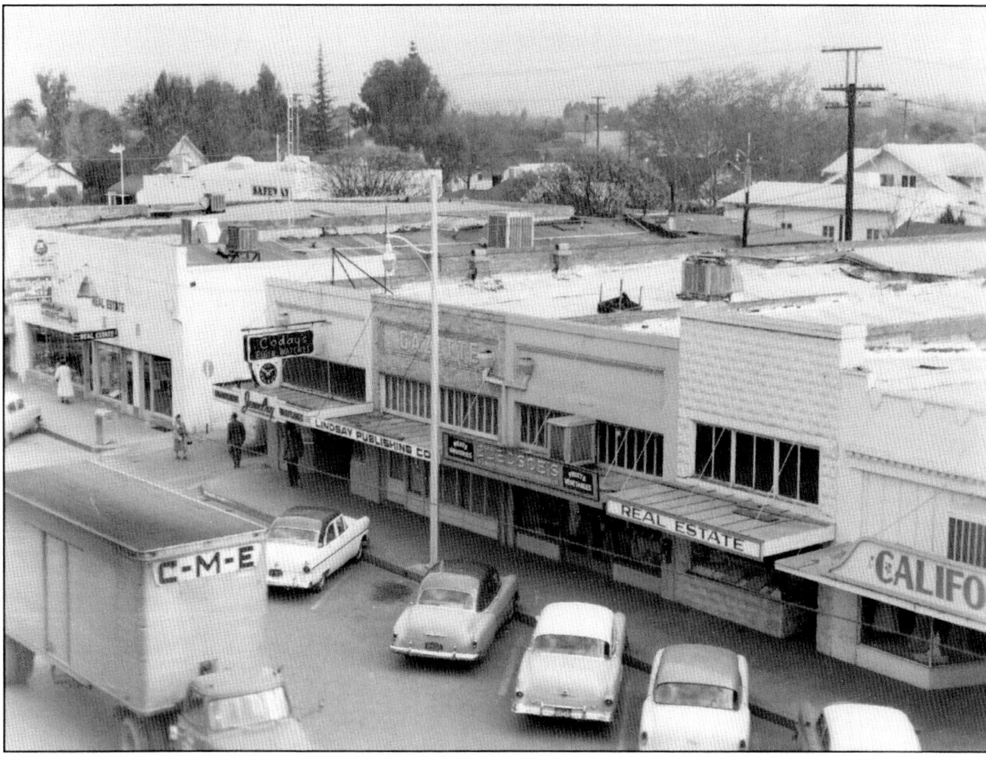

In this glimpse of Lindsay from the 1950s are many storefronts that no longer exist. From left to right are Coday's Jewelry, the *Gazette* building, Bledsoe's Grocery, and California Apparel, among others. Many of Lindsay's current residents have memories of frequenting these stores. (CSUF.)

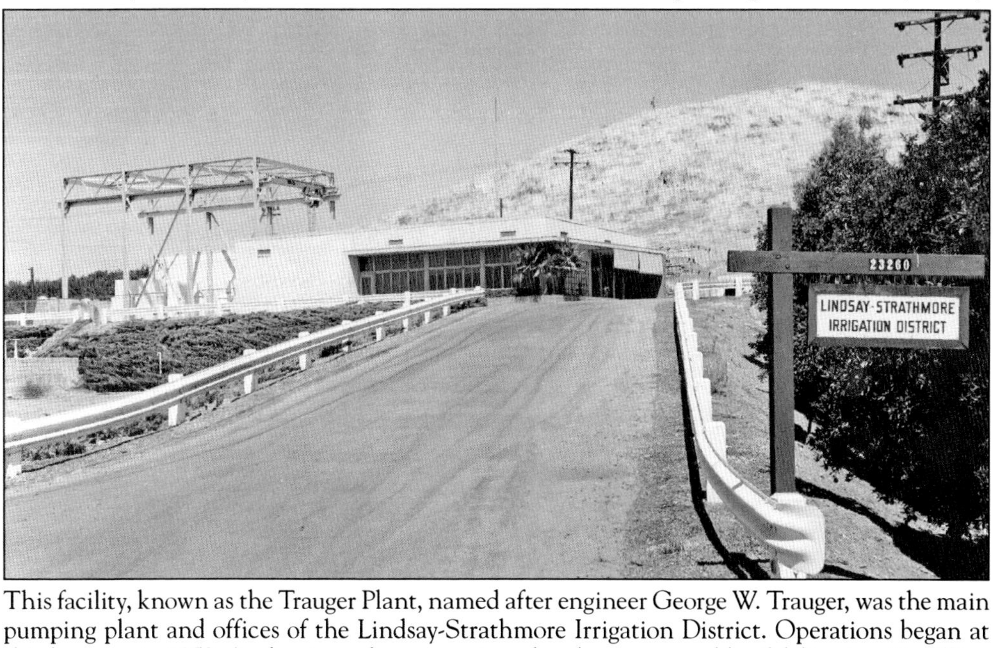

This facility, known as the Trauger Plant, named after engineer George W. Trauger, was the main pumping plant and offices of the Lindsay-Strathmore Irrigation District. Operations began at this location in 1953. At the time of construction, the plant was capable of delivering 78 million gallons of water to users per day. (CSUF.)

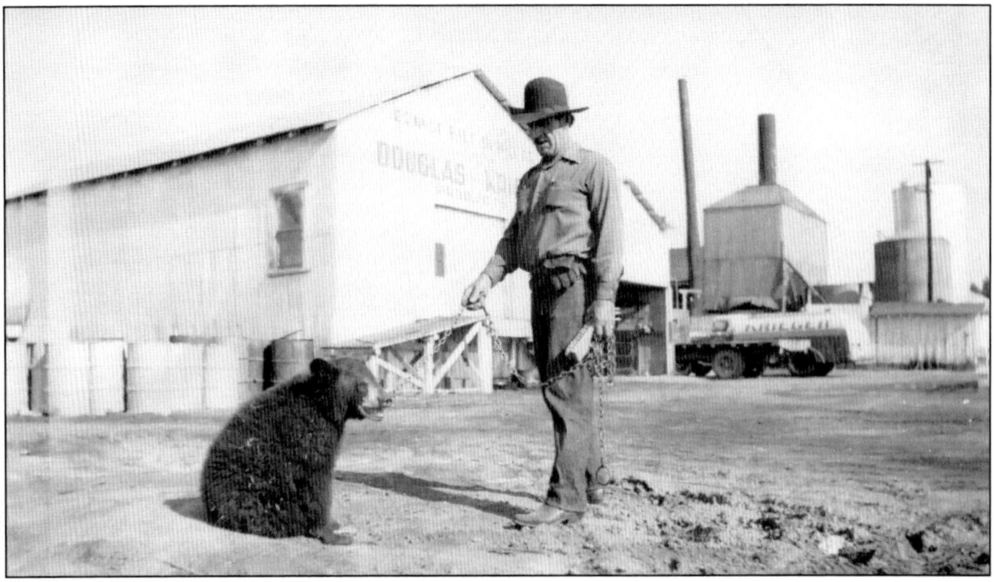

The Orange Belt Supply Company, purveyors of farm supplies such as fertilizer, had locations throughout California, including one on Bluegum Street in Lindsay. During the 1940s, it was managed by Ronald Fitton, who had managed the Union Oil plant in the 1920s. At one point, the business used a bear as their mascot, called "Little Doug." (LMG.)

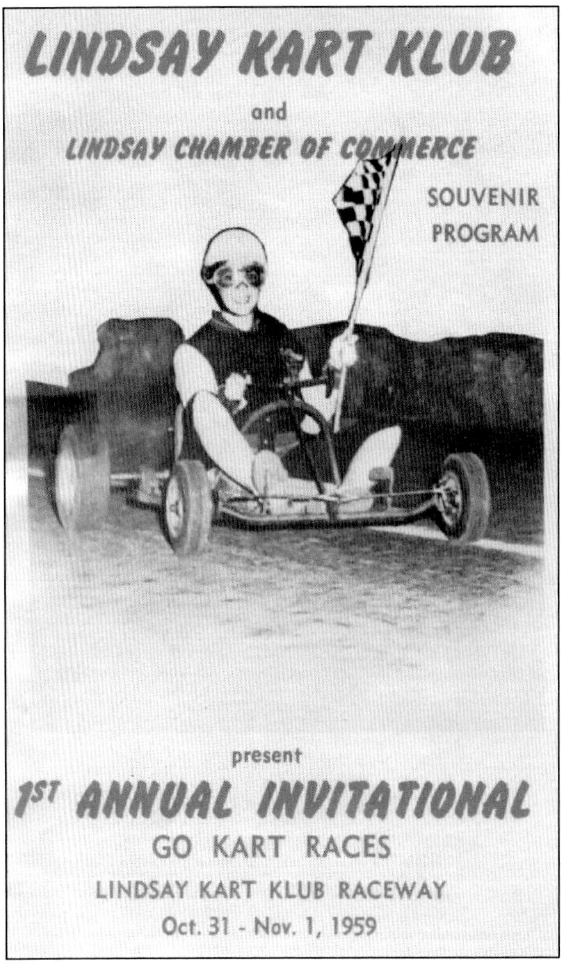

This is a souvenir program from the Lindsay Kart Klub's Go Cart Races in 1959. The Kart Klub was a local organization for residents of Lindsay and Strathmore. It proved to be so popular that a raceway track patterned after the Go Cart Raceway in Azusa was constructed in Lindsay. (LMG.)

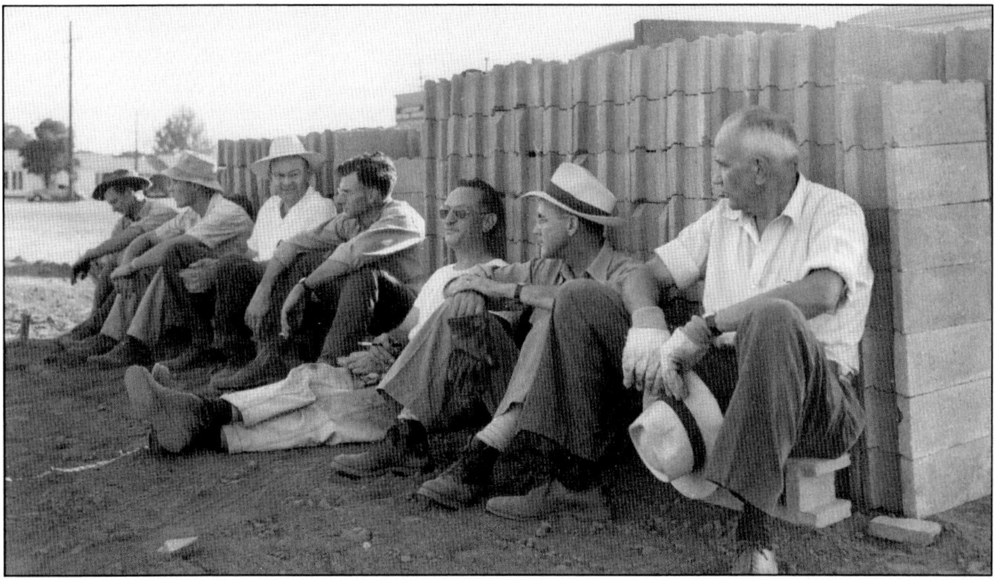

Kiwanis members rest after finishing construction on Boy Scout huts. From left to right are Len Roark, Jay Webb, Neal Barker, Fran Porter, Marx Bandy, Stary Gange, and Harold Schutt. As a leading member of the Tulare County Historical Society, Schutt passionately collected and preserved the history of Lindsay and Tulare County. His contributions to the history and social, political, and business life of the area were many. (LMG.)

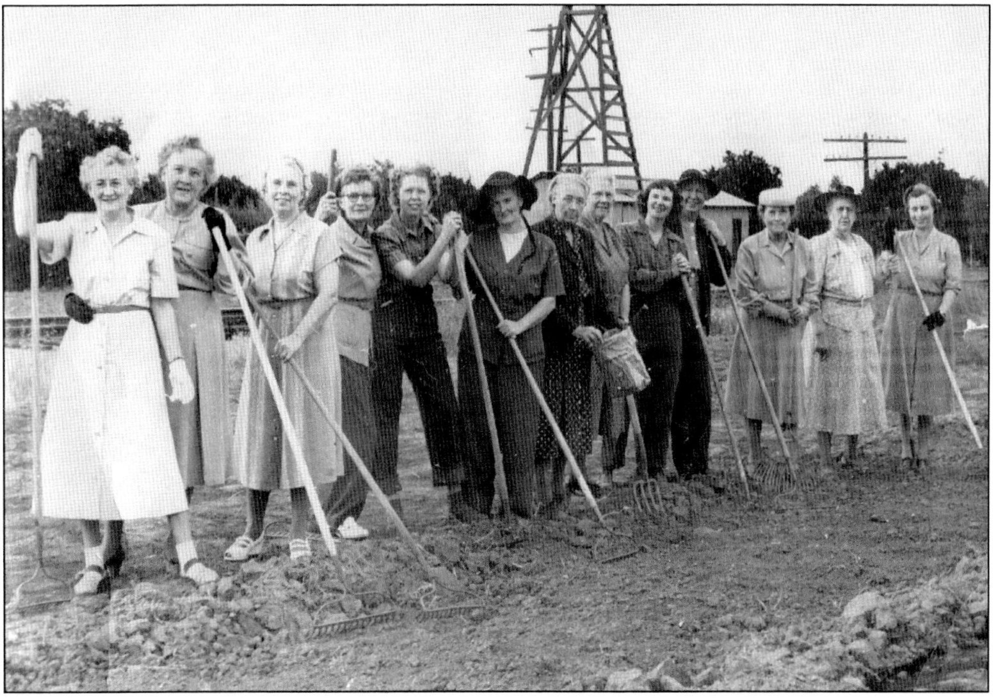

Clara Page arrived in Lindsay in 1909. She became known as "the Garden Lady" for her extensive work in establishing many garden clubs in town. Page served as president of the California State Garden Club in 1936. She was also known as a prolific artist and leading figure of the Lindsay Art Association. Here, members of a Lindsay garden club begin work on a project. (JBM.)

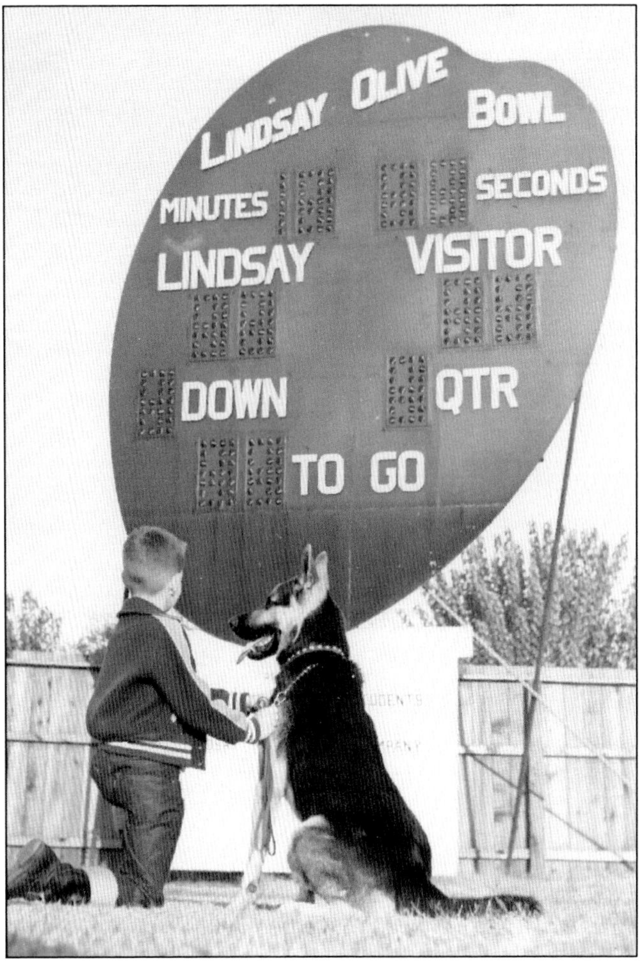

A young Bill Clark is pictured with his dog Rex in a promotional photograph for the annual Olive Bowl Junior College Championship held on Thanksgiving Day. These football games at the Olive Bowl were hosted by the Lion's Club to raise money to assist the blind and visually impaired. (BC.)

Lindsay boasts 16 fine art murals depicting the town's cultural, ethnic, and historical roots. The first mural, by Wei Luan, was painted on the side of the Lindsay Community Theatre in 2001 as part of the town's revitalization efforts following a devastating freeze and the closure of two of Lindsay's largest employers. (Photograph by DeLea Davis.)

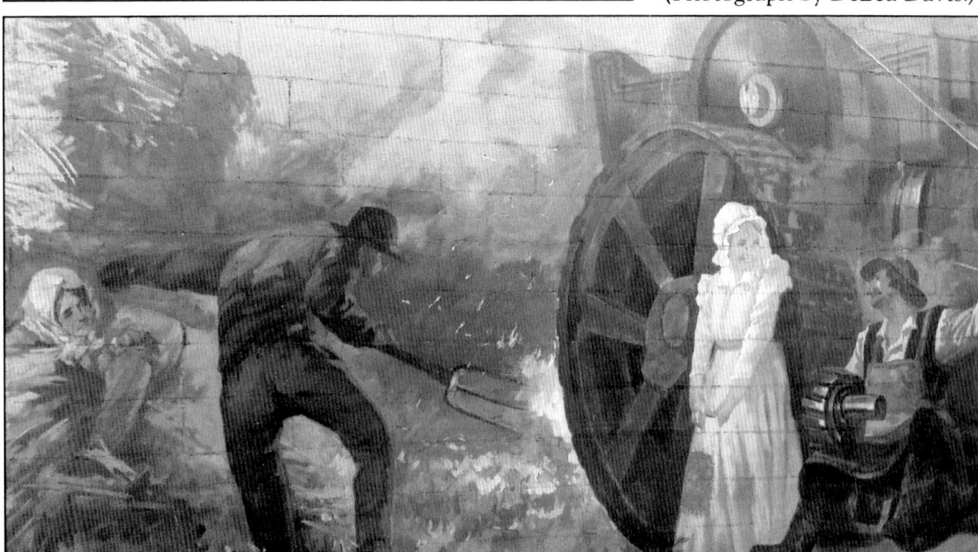

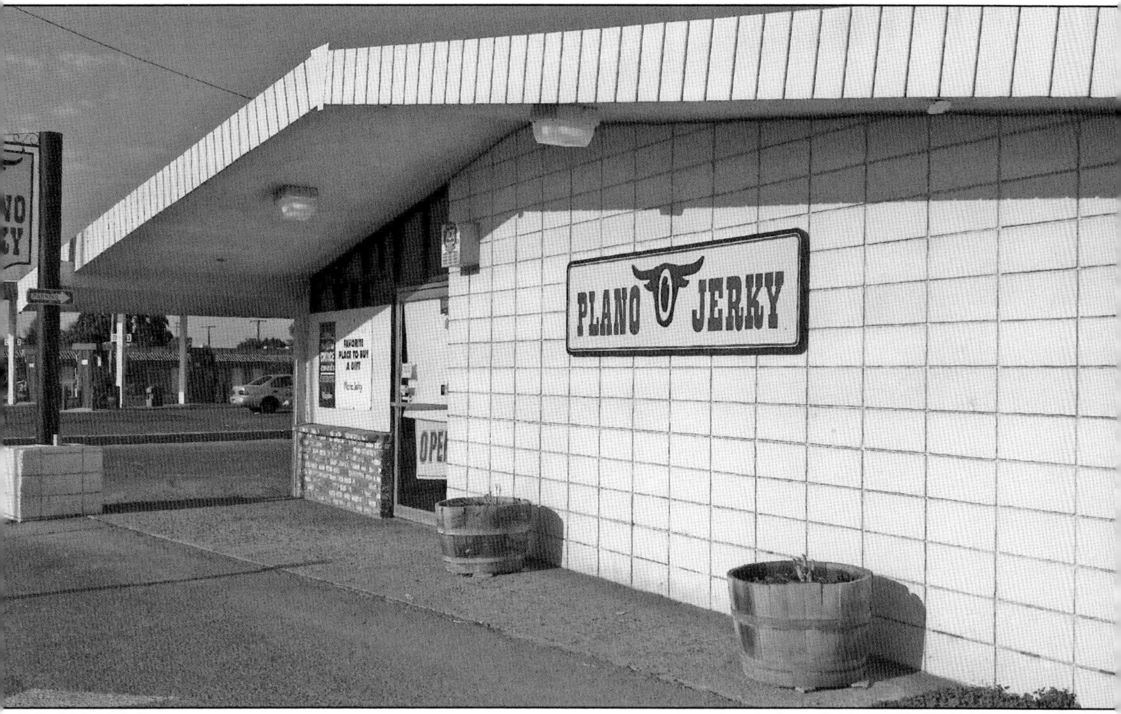

Frank Nanamura and his relatives were another pioneer family in Lindsay, arriving in the small but bustling town in the early 1900s. By 1930, the Nanamura family had set up a successful citrus ranch, only to be forced to leave everything during the regrettable events of Word War II. After Frank enlisted and served in the US military, the family returned home to Lindsay. Like true pioneers, they started over from scratch, but this time, they tried their hand at making beef jerky and combining it with a family recipe for teriyaki, which proved wildly successful. The Nanamuras moved to Porterville, and their store Plano Jerky is considered by many to be the best beef jerky the world over. (Photograph by DeLea Davis.)

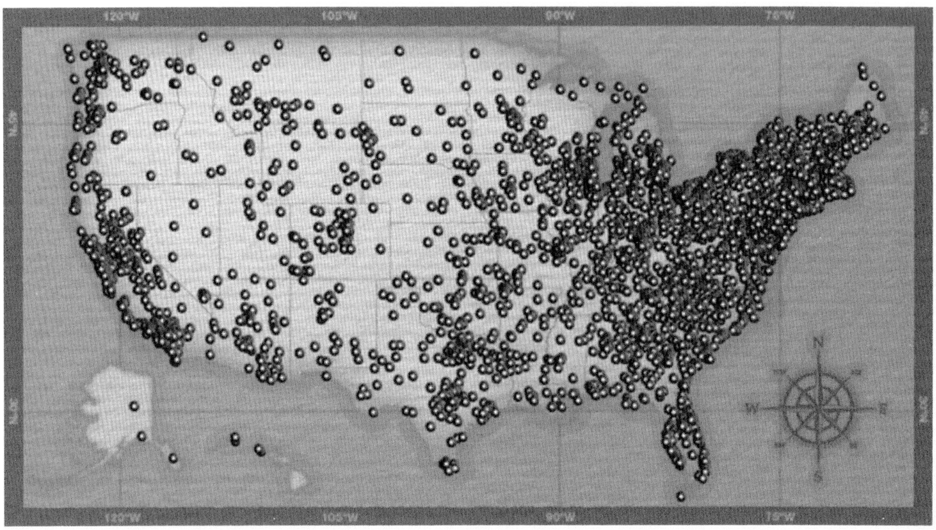

Consistent with our mission to preserve history on a local level, this book was printed in South Carolina on American-made paper and manufactured entirely in the United States. Products carrying the accredited Forest Stewardship Council (FSC) label are printed on 100 percent FSC-certified paper.

MADE IN THE USA